3

WORKBOOK
WITH ONLINE PRACTICE

Annie Cornford

CONTENTS

- Starter — page 4
- Unit 1 — page 14
- Unit 2 — page 22
- Unit 3 — page 32
- Unit 4 — page 40
- Unit 5 — page 50
- Unit 6 — page 58
- Unit 7 — page 68
- Unit 8 — page 76
- Unit 9 — page 86
- Unit 10 — page 94
- Wordlist — page 104
- Irregular verb table — page 110
- Grammar reference — page 111

Graded practice

The Grammar and Vocabulary practice in the *Talent* Workbook has been graded according to difficulty.

This is indicated where you see the following icon:

VOCABULARY: Nationalities

1. Complete the sentences with the missing words.

    0. Adem is from Turkey. He's **Turkish**.
    1. They are from China. They're ....
    2. My teacher is .... She's from Germany.
    3. He is from Chile. He's ....
    4. Maria is from Spain. She's ....

The level of difficulty is shown by the number of bands that are shaded (from 1–4). For example, an activity with this icon is more challenging than one with this icon.

STARTER A Festivals

VOCABULARY: Music genres

1. **Complete the crossword with music genres. What popular genre is missing from the puzzle?**

0 FUNK
1 B
2 C
3 E
4 H I
   E V E N T
5 J A
6 F L

The genre missing is _ _ _ .

GRAMMAR: Adverbs of frequency

2. **Choose the correct option.**

0 Mandy *always is* / *(is always)* happy.
1 I *never am* / *am never* hungry in the morning.
2 *Sometimes are you* / *Are you sometimes* late for school?
3 Helen *usually is* / *is usually* busy at the weekend.
4 *Often is he* / *Is he often* at your house?
5 Our dogs *always are* / *are always* ready for a walk.
6 There *usually are* / *are usually* lots of cool events.

3. **Put the words in the correct order.**

0 never / parents / go / my / festivals / to
   My parents never go to festivals.
1 often / doesn't / in / it / rain / June
2 on / Sundays / Ben / works / never
3 you / go / early / bed / to / do / usually / ?
4 sleeps / cat / outside / sometimes / their
5 often / listen / hip-hop / we / music / to
6 cook / always / Meiling / does / food / Chinese / ?

GRAMMAR: Present simple

4. **Write the questions with the correct form of the present simple.**

0 Wow – this T-shirt / really cost £40?
   Wow – does this T-shirt really cost £40?
1 Rosa / still live in New Zealand?
2 your grandparents / travel a lot?
3 the twins / always wear the same clothes?
4 this shop / sell computer games?
5 Dom's band / play funk and jazz?
6 you / go to school by bus?

5. **Write answers to the questions from exercise 4. Use the prompts to write.**

0 no / it / only cost £18
   No, it doesn't. It only costs £18.
1 no / she / live in Australia now
2 no / they / stay at home these days
3 no / they / usually wear different clothes
4 no / it / sell computer magazines
5 no / they / always play jazz
6 no / I / go by bike

GRAMMAR: Present continuous

6. **Complete the sentences with the present continuous.**

0 Here, take this umbrella. It **'s raining** out there. (*rain*)
1 Mum ……………… to work today because Dad's got the car. (*not / drive*)
2 Answer the phone please, I ……………… at the moment. (*cook*)
3 They ……………… some new apartments in our town. (*build*)
4 Lisa's not ready yet, she ……………… her homework. (*finish*)
5 Hurry up! I ……………… for you outside the cinema. (*wait*)
6 Joe ……………… in the garden right now. Can I take a message? (*work*)

A

7 🔊 **Complete the sentences with the present continuous of the verbs below.**

come ▪ cry ▪ dance ▪ put ▪ study ▪ write ▪ use

0　We **'re studying** grammar with our English teacher.
1　Pat .... an email to a friend from her old school.
2　We .... right now, don't go without us!
3　I think you .... that picture in the wrong place.
4　'Why .... she .... ?' 'Because the film is so sad.'
5　I couldn't find my pen so I .... yours, OK?
6　The children .... to music in their bedroom.

8 🔊 **Complete the conversation with the present continuous.**

Bill　What ⁰ **are you doing** (you / do)?
Sara　¹ .... (I / write) a letter to a DJ.
　　　　² .... (I / organise) an event.
Bill　³ .... (you / do) it alone? That's a lot of work!
Sara　It's not too bad, ⁴ .... (Sue / help) me. And ⁵ .... (we / try) to get some volunteers. Are you busy?
Bill　Well, actually, ⁶ .... (I / work) on a big assignment at the moment and ⁷ .... (I / start) to panic! I'm afraid ⁸ .... (it / progress) rather slowly.
Sara　Oh dear, and now ⁹ .... (I / waste) your time.
Bill　No problem. ¹⁰ .... (I / take) a break now anyway. How about a quick coffee?

GRAMMAR: Present simple v present continuous

9 🔊 **Cross out the incorrect time expressions.**

0　We're ~~sometimes~~ discussing our plans *now*.
1　Jared is living alone *at the moment / every day*.
2　We jog in the park *this morning / twice a week*.
3　Do you *often* stay up all night *tonight*?
4　Our relatives visit us *today / at the weekend*.
5　Are you listening to the radio *right now / at bedtime*?
6　We *never* camp under trees *at the moment*.

10 🔊 **Complete the sentences with the present simple or the present continuous.**

0　Tom often **sings** (sing) in the shower. Listen, he **'s singing** (sing) in there now!
1　I sometimes .... (get up) late on Sundays, but today I .... (get up) early.
2　Kate usually .... (leave) home before seven. She .... (leave) at six today.
3　Ned .... (play) chess with Tina at the moment but he usually .... (play) with her sister.
4　Al .... (work) at home today. He never .... (work) in the office on Fridays.
5　We often .... (cook) Mexican food at the weekend. Tonight we .... (cook) tacos.
6　The DJ .... (play) great music right now. He always .... (play) my favourite songs.

11 🔊 **Tick (✓) the right sentences. Correct the mistakes in the others.**

0　Do you want any sugar in your coffee? ✓
　　No, thanks. I'm ~~not liking~~ sweet drinks. **I don't like**
1　My brother loves reality TV shows.
2　I'm thinking this class is good fun.
3　Are you agreeing with me?
4　He's in the senior choir but he hates school concerts.
5　Are the children still believing in fairy tales?
6　Is he needing any help with those heavy boxes?

12 🔊 **Complete the conversation with the present simple or the present continuous.**

Ms Jay　⁰ **Are you looking** (you / look) for someone?
Karl　Yes, ¹ .... (I / need) to see Ms Jones.
Ms Jay　² .... (she / talk) to the director of studies right now, ³ .... (I / think). ⁴ .... (they / discuss) the timetable. Why ⁵ .... (you / want) to see her?
Karl　It's about my homework. What about Mr Fox? ⁶ .... (he / teach) at the moment?
Ms Jay　⁷ .... (I / not / know), just a minute. No, ⁸ .... (he / not / work) here today. He ⁹ .... (teach) at a different school on Wednesdays. Sorry, Karl.
Karl　Oh, ¹⁰ .... (it / not / matter). I can come back tomorrow.

Starter A

STARTER B Champions

VOCABULARY: Sport

13 Complete the sport with the missing letters: *a, e, i, o, u*. Which popular sport is not in the list?

0 CYCL_I_NG
1 R_W_NG
2 H_RS_ R_D_NG
3 B_SK_TB_LL
4 T_NN_S
5 D_V_NG
6 CL_MB_NG
7 R_NN_NG
8 SK_T_NG
9 SW_MM_NG
10 SK__NG

GRAMMAR: Past simple

14 Complete the sentences with the correct form of the past simple.

arrive • carry • plan • stop • travel • try • use

0 They ....*planned*.... to have an exciting holiday after their exams.
1 We .... hard to understand the Swiss dialect, but we couldn't.
2 He .... Pippa's heavy suitcase to the train for her.
3 I .... to the game with the team in their minibus.
4 A stranger .... my phone to make an urgent call.
5 They .... for a rest when they were tired.
6 There was so much traffic that our visitors .... late.

15 Match the verbs to their irregular past simple forms.

0 [a] do   a did
1 [ ] sit   b wrote
2 [ ] hit   c went
3 [ ] fall   d found
4 [ ] write   e sat
5 [ ] put   f felt
6 [ ] feel   g read
7 [ ] go   h hit
8 [ ] read   i fell
9 [ ] find   j sent
10 [ ] send   k put

16 Use past simple forms from exercise 15 to complete the sentences.

0 Jenny ....*felt*.... sick yesterday so she ....*went*.... home early.
1 Chris .... an angry email and .... it to the manager.
2 Someone .... my lost trainers and .... them in my locker.
3 Poor Grandma .... down the stairs last night and .... her head.
4 She .... in the sun all afternoon and .... her book.

17 Write the answers with the time expressions which are true for you.

0 When did you leave home this morning?
   I left home at half past seven.
1 When did you do your homework yesterday?
2 When did you have your English test?
3 When did your sister start school?
4 When did your parents learn to drive?
5 When did you clean your room?
6 When did you last eat?

GRAMMAR: Past continuous

18 Write questions and answers with the past continuous.

0 where / you / cycling to last night? I / go to the gym
   '**Where were you cycling to last night?**'
   '**I was going to the gym.**'
1 what / they / do at the club? they / watch the big match
2 why / he / sit in his car? he / listen to the radio
3 where / he / live at that time? he / stay with friends in Santiago
4 what / she / talk about? she / explain the rules of the game
5 why / you / laugh? our coach / tell us a funny story
6 what / she / look at? she / check for messages on her phone
7 what / you / do in my room? I / look for / a phone charger
8 why / you / shout? I / call / the children

19 🔊 **Complete the email with the correct form of the past continuous.**

Hi Jed
Must tell you about a dream I had last night.
You and I ⁰ **were skating** (skate) along a busy street.
We ¹.................... (not / talk), we ².................... (sing)! It ³.................... (rain) while we
⁴.................... (race) along, but we ⁵.................... (not / get) wet. I think you ⁶.................... (carry) an umbrella. Strange music ⁷.................... (play) and people ⁸.................... (stand) in line outside a huge stadium. Something ⁹.................... (happen) inside but I'll never know what ¹⁰.................... (go on) because then I woke up! Wasn't that weird?
Love,
Gemma

GRAMMAR: Past simple v past continuous

20 🔊 **Match the questions to the short answers.**

0 [e] Did Janek ask you for help?
1 [ ] Were the children all sleeping?
2 [ ] Was Belinda using your phone?
3 [ ] Did the Austrian skier win the race?
4 [ ] Were you both watching the game?
5 [ ] Did you see the skaters?
6 [ ] Did your parents hear the news?

a No, we didn't.
b Yes, they did.
c No, she didn't.
d No, we weren't.
e Yes, he did.
f No, they weren't.
g Yes, she was.

21 🔊 **Complete the sentences with the past simple or the past continuous.**

0 She **was driving** along the road when her car broke down. (drive)
1 Frank was talking to a friend when we .... him yesterday. (see)
2 We were walking the dog when the rain .... (start)
3 Their guests arrived while they .... the meal. (prepare)
4 We were calling for ages but nobody .... us. (hear)
5 Kate's racquet broke while she .... tennis. (play)
6 He scored the winning goal while the keeper .... (not / look)

22 🔊 **Put the words in the correct order.**

0 bath / a / her / rang / having / she / when / phone / was
She was having a bath when her phone rang.
1 raining / woke / when / up / he / it / was
2 wasn't / left / when / the / crying / baby / I
3 when / Henry / he / waiting / the / saw / was / for / her / bus
4 weren't / scored / watching / when / they / Berardi / the / goal
5 she / Maria / off-piste / her / broke / was / leg / skiing / when
6 it / horse / the / standing / ricer / her / when / kicked / by / was / her

23 🔊 **Choose the correct verb and complete the sentences with the past simple or the past continuous.**

arrive · break · carry · drop · eat ·
make · ring · see · start · ~~steal~~ ·
wait · ~~watch~~ · wear · write

0 Someone **stole** Pete's wallet while he **was watching** the match.
1 She .... her new jeans when I .... her.
2 He .... an apple when his tooth ....
3 The doorbell .... while he .... some tea.
4 When I .... at the airport my friends .... to check in.
5 Harry .... an email when the baby .... crying.
6 I .... a bowl of soup when I .... it to the table.

STARTER C — New beginnings

VOCABULARY: Transport

24 Find 13 transport words in the puzzle: look up and down, across, backwards or diagonally.

```
E L I H D D N X Z C
K O O X B I K E A P
I B S R A F P R F W
B O U R R T L I K P
R E T S I Y A A D I
O F E R R Y N K T H
T V G M M R E Y S
O A I S A T A O B Z
M N F E O M V N A W
```

25 Rewrite the sentences so that they mean the same. Use the word given.

0 I sometimes cycle to school. I go ...**by bike**... . (*bike*)
1 We got a lift with our neighbour. We went .... (*car*)
2 She flew from Auckland to Dunedin. She travelled .... (*plane*)
3 Kate and Joe walked to the shops. They went .... (*foot*)
4 I'd like to sail to the Bahamas. I'd like to .... (*ship*)
5 The bus left from the main bus station. We .... (*caught*)
6 Our teacher prefers to go by bus, tram or train. Our teacher .... (*public transport*)

GRAMMAR: Past simple

26 Write questions and answers in the past simple. Then underline the time expressions.

0 how / you / get home last night? we / take / taxi
   'How did you get home last night?' 'We took a taxi.'
1 when / you / get that great bike? I / buy it / a month ago
2 you / fly / to London Gatwick / last time? No / we / fly to Heathrow
3 where / you / have your holiday / in 2016? we / go to Thailand
4 you / hear about / train accident? Yes / I / read about it / yesterday
5 Ms Alan / teach English / at your school? Yes, but / she / leave / two years ago
6 when / you / find time to make this cake? I / make it / early this morning

GRAMMAR: Present perfect

27 Complete the sentences with the present perfect.

0 She ...**'s taken**... her driving test three times. (*take*)
1 We .... miles today. Let's have a rest. (*walk*)
2 Our neighbours .... to a bigger apartment. (*move*)
3 I .... everywhere for my keys but I can't find them. (*look*)
4 You .... a new fashion with those shoes! (*start*)
5 He .... a window because it was so hot. (*open*)
6 I .... a really good time, thank you. (*have*)

28 Complete with the irregular verbs.

0 break	**broke**	**broken**
1	bought	....
2	....	drunk
3 make	....	....
4	wore	....
5	....	had
6 think	....	....
7	ate	....
8	....	run
9 cut	....	....
10	won	....

29 Write questions and short answers in the present perfect.

0 They haven't had a hot meal.
   'Have they had a hot meal?'
   'No, they haven't.'
   She's made them tomato soup.
   'Has she made them tomato soup?'
   'Yes, she has.'
1 He's cut his finger badly.
2 They've thought about a holiday.
3 My parents haven't run a marathon this year.
4 She's bought a new pair of jeans.
5 The cat hasn't drunk all its milk.
6 He hasn't worn the shirt Kay gave him.

C

30 🔊 **Choose the correct option.**

0 I've (been) / gone to the library for you. Here are your books.
1 John's been / gone to the shops but he'll be back soon.
2 'Are your parents in?' 'No, sorry, they've been / gone out.'
3 Amy has been / gone to China twice.
4 I've been / gone on holiday. I flew home yesterday.
5 Where's the dog been / gone? He smells terrible.
6 'Have you ever been / gone on a gondola?' 'No, but I'd love to!'

GRAMMAR: Present perfect continuous

31 🔊 **Complete the sentences with the present perfect continuous.**

0 Your alarm **'s been ringing** for ages. Turn it off! (ring)
1 We .... for Kim too long, let's go without her. (wait)
2 My aunt .... with us for weeks. (stay)
3 He .... in Ben's room while he's at college. (sleep)
4 What .... you .... ? Your face is all dirty. (do)
5 How long .... he .... Polish? (study)
6 They .... tennis all morning and they're exhausted. (play)

32 🔊 **Match the beginnings and ends of the sentences.**

0 [f] Lydia hasn't written
1 [ ] Have you seen
2 [ ] She's already eaten
3 [ ] We've been travelling
4 [ ] I've just heard
5 [ ] He's never been
6 [ ] Has she ever taken

a to visit his friend before.
b the news on the radio.
c an exam in English?
d all her lunch.
e round Europe since May.
f to her uncle for ages.
g my cool new bike yet?

33 🔊 **Choose the correct option to complete the sentences.**

0 How are you, Len? I .... you for ages.
 A didn't see
 (B) haven't seen
 C haven't been seeing
1 Nina looks sad. Do you think she .... ?
 A cried   B 's cried   C 's been crying
2 You .... that computer for years. Time for a new one.
 A had   B 've had   C 've been having
3 My uncle .... a Porsche when he was younger.
 A drove   B has driven   C has been driving
4 .... your mobile yet?
 A Did you find
 B Have you found
 C Have you been finding
5 My parents .... in Bristol in 2001.
 A met
 B have met
 C have been meeting
6 You and Paul are great friends. How long .... him?
 A did you know
 B have you known
 C have you been knowing

34 🔊 **Complete the conversation.**

Elsie Sorry, I'm late.
Jade No problem. 0 **I haven't been waiting**. (I / not / wait) long.
Elsie 1 .... (you / buy) the tickets yet?
Jade Yes, 2 .... (I / book) them online yesterday. So, what 3 .... (you / do) today?
Elsie 4 .... (I / be) with Mr Borland. 5 .... (he / help) me with my algebra all term.
Jade Really? 6 .... (I / not / know) that. 7 .... (you / always find) maths hard?
Elsie Well, 8 .... (I / never enjoy) algebra, that's for sure! Last year 9 .... (I / not / get) a good grade in my GCSE. But forget all that, it's time to relax.
Jade Right. 10 .... (I / look forward to) this all day!

Starter C   9

STARTER D: My future

VOCABULARY: Jobs

35 Reorder the letters to make ten jobs.

0 t r o a c — actor
1 l d i e r u b — ....
2 o k c o — ....
3 r c d o o t — ....
4 w r y a e l — ....
5 g n s e i r — ....
6 o e r d l s i — ....
7 c r e e a t h — ....
8 a t i e r w — ....
9 t i r w r e — ....

36 Decide if the sentences are true (T) or false (F). Correct the false ones.

0 A dentist looks after your teeth. [T✓] [F]
   Vets work with water and gas. [T] [F✓]
   Vets work with animals, plumbers work with water and gas.
1 An accountant helps you with your finances. [T] [F]
2 A builder is someone who designs houses. [T] [F]
3 A pilot works in a hospital. [T] [F]
4 Carpenters are people who repair cars. [T] [F]
5 An engineer is someone who helps with electrical problems. [T] [F]
6 Lecturers teach in colleges or universities. [T] [F]

GRAMMAR: Future simple

37 Complete the sentences with the verbs below.

'll ask • ~~will be~~ • 'll meet • 'll know • will watch
won't be • won't eat • ~~won't rain~~

0 The party ...will be... outside so I hope it ..won't rain...
1 Tom can't make shelves so he .... a carpenter to do it.
2 Who .... the film with me?
3 He .... meat because he's a vegetarian.
4 I hope we .... lots of interesting people.
5 They .... the results soon.
6 She .... a great teacher; she doesn't like children.

38 Complete the sentences with the future simple. Use *definitely*, *probably* or *maybe*.

0 I 'll probably leave school next year. I'm 90% sure. (*leave*)
1 .... he .... a famous singer. Who knows? (*become*)
2 He's an apprentice now, so he .... a job. It's guaranteed. (*have*)
3 I don't know about the gig tonight. I .... with you. (*come*)
4 He .... to me. He promised. (*write*)
5 .... Tim .... the army. He's only 50% sure. (*join*)
6 You .... four A levels for medical school. I'm 90% sure about that. (*need*)

GRAMMAR: First conditional

39 Complete the sentences with *when* or *if*.

0 We'll take a walk in the park ...if... it doesn't snow.
1 .... Ned doesn't apply for the job, he won't even get an interview.
2 Tanya will definitely go to university .... she leaves school.
3 We'll study the text together .... you like.
4 The doctor said she'll phone .... she gets to work.
5 .... I'm older, I'll learn to drive a lorry.
6 You'll never be a vet .... you're scared of dogs.

40 Match the beginnings and ends to make conditional sentences.

0 [e] If he fails the exam this time,
1 [ ] If we hurry now,
2 [ ] If she hasn't got a ticket,
3 [ ] If she takes more exercise,
4 [ ] If you drink too much coffee,
5 [ ] If we don't catch this bus,
6 [ ] If our team wins the match,

a she'll feel better and fitter.
b we'll take home the trophy.
c you won't sleep at night.
d I'll give her mine.
e he'll take it again in the summer.
f we won't miss our train.
g we'll get the next one.

D

41 🔊 **Choose the correct option.**

0 If the plumber (comes) / will come, he repairs / ('ll repair) the pipes.
1 If Jane asks / 'll ask her neighbour, he probably helps / 'll probably help her.
2 You get / 'll get there quicker if you take / 'll take the fast train.
3 We don't buy / won't buy you a ticket if you don't want / won't want to come.
4 When they have / 'll have more time, they do / 'll do more reading.
5 If I win / 'll win the lottery, I buy / 'll buy you something really expensive.
6 She tell / 'll tell her parents as soon as she gets / will get her results.

42 🔊 **Complete the pairs of sentences so that they mean the same.**

0 If he graduates next year, he'**ll look for a job**.
   He'll look for a job **if he graduates next year**.
1 If I ask my boss, she …
   My boss will give me some time off …
2 If we don't have a band, people …
   People won't want to come to our party …
3 If Man U loses tomorrow, Bill …
   Bill will be really upset …
4 If we go to summer school, we …
   We'll improve our English …
5 If he chooses this course, Reno …
   Reno will find the work very hard …
6 If Clara stays up all night, she …
   Clara won't be fit for school …

43 🔊 **Rewrite the sentences with *unless*.**

0 I won't be able to see if I don't wear my glasses.
   I won't be able to see unless I wear my glasses.
1 She won't be successful if she doesn't work harder.
2 We probably won't eat outside if the weather doesn't improve.
3 The car won't start if we don't find a mechanic.
4 He won't finish the job if he doesn't have enough paint.
5 She definitely won't help you if you don't ask her nicely.
6 I won't pass my driving test if I don't have enough lessons.

44 🔊 **Choose the correct option.**

0 I'll come with you (as soon as) / unless I'm ready.
1 William will miss the boat if / when he's late.
2 She won't phone you unless / as soon as she has your number.
3 We'll stay inside until / if the rain stops.
4 Bess will get her own car unless / when she's older.
5 As soon as / Until the bell goes, we can leave the class.
6 Wait at the red light until / when it changes to green.

45 🔊 **Complete the advertisement with the words below.**

> 'll get • 'll have • 'll owe • ~~'re~~ • choose • have • join • want • will be • will offer • won't regret

GO FOR IT!
Apprentice schemes

If you ⁰ **'re** 16 and over and you ¹ _____ five GCSEs, this scheme ² _____ perfect for you. You ³ _____ hands-on work experience and pay if you ⁴ _____ us at **GO FOR IT!** What if you ⁵ _____ to go to university? You ⁶ _____ fun, probably, but you ⁷ _____ a lot of money in the end. Definitely! If you really ⁸ _____ to kick-start your career, an apprenticeship with us ⁹ _____ you a better alternative.

**Interested?
So why not join us today?
You ¹⁰ _____ it!**

STARTER E Cheap clothes

VOCABULARY: Shops

46 Complete the shop words.

0 b<u>aker's</u>
1 b _ _ _ _ _ _ ' _
2 c _ _ _ _ _ _ ' _
3 d _ _ _ _ _ _ _ _ _ _
4 f _ _ _ _ _ _ ' _
5 g _ _ _ _ _ _ _ _ _ '
6 n _ _ _ _ _ _ _ _ ' _

47 Complete the sentences with the words below.

> branch · conditions · factory · hours ·
> pay · trade · wages

0 Is there a ...<u>branch</u>... of H&M in your city?
1 You .... a bit more for ethical fashion, don't you?
2 They make those cheap jeans in a .... in Bangladesh.
3 The working .... for the children are dangerous.
4 I really believe we should buy *fair* .... clothes.
5 The women work long .... for very little money.
6 .... for the workers are higher in Europe than in India.

GRAMMAR: Subject questions

48 Complete the sentences with *Which*, *What* or *Who*.

0 ...<u>Which</u>... supermarket do you prefer?
1 ....'s going to get the milk today?
2 ....'s your favourite vegetable?
3 .... is her bag, the blue or the red one?
4 .... will happen next?
5 .... rang you earlier?
6 .... chemist's is open on Sundays?

49 Write questions to match the answers.

0 'Who ..<u>came to dinner last night</u>..?'
'My best friend came to dinner last night.'
1 'What .... ?'
'White wine goes well with fish.'
2 'Which .... ?'
'The corner shop is the nearest to the apartment.'
3 'Who .... ?'
'My mum does the shopping in the family.'
4 'What .... ?'
'Something has happened, but I don't know what.'
5 'Which .... ?'
'I want those tall pink flowers in the window, please.'
6 'Who .... ?'
'Andy Murray has won the Olympic gold medal twice.'

GRAMMAR: Object questions

50 Put the words in the correct order.

0 he / talking / who / was / to / ?
Who was he talking to?
1 they / will / do / what / next / ?
2 computer / which / use / I / can / ?
3 you / waiting / for / are / what / ?
4 with / who / holiday / go / you / did / on / ?
5 they / have / films / seen / already / which / ?
6 will / who / invite / party / to / graduation / her / she / ?

51 Complete the answers.

0 'Someone rang at five this morning.'
'Oh? Who ..<u>rang</u>.. ?'
1 'He wanted to speak to someone.'
'Who .... speak to?'
2 'Something hit your car.'
'Oh no, what .... my car?'
3 'Nora was dancing all night.'
'Really? Who .... with?'
4 'I bought this top last week.'
'Cool. Which .... from?'
5 'Dave was helping a friend yesterday.'
'Who .... ?'
6 'Olivia told us something interesting.'
'What .... ?'

E

GRAMMAR: Direct and indirect questions

52 Write if the questions are direct or indirect.

0 Where is my homework? **direct**
   Do you know where my homework is? **indirect**
1 Could you tell me what the time is?
2 Was that your older brother?
3 Can you tell me when the last tram leaves?
4 Would you mind helping me with this job?
5 Were the pizzas good last night?
6 When does this shop shut?

53 Match the questions to the answers.

0 [d] What do you wear for school?
1 [ ] Where were you born?
2 [ ] When did the match begin?
3 [ ] How much was the coffee?
4 [ ] Why is she crying?
5 [ ] What course is your sister doing?
6 [ ] Which is Janina's bike?

a It's the one with the bag on the back.
b She's cutting onions.
c She's studying law.
d I usually wear jeans and a T-shirt.
e It started ten minutes ago.
f Only a few euros.
g In a little village near Lake Garda.

54 Write indirect questions using the questions in exercise 53.

0 Could you tell me ....**what you wear for school**.... ?
1 Would you mind telling me where .... ?
2 Can you tell me when .... ?
3 Do you know how much .... ?
4 Can you explain .... ?
5 Would you mind telling me .... ?
6 Do you know .... ?

55 Write direct questions.

0 Can you tell me when the film starts?
   When does the film start?
1 Would you mind telling me how much this costs?
2 Can you explain why you are so late?
3 Could you tell me where the nearest bank is?
4 Have you any idea when Bob will arrive?
5 Do you know what the biggest UK supermarket is?
6 Can you tell me how this machine works?

56 Write indirect questions with *if* or *whether*. Use one of the expressions from exercise 54 to begin your question.

0 She usually works late. Is she working late again tonight?
   Do you know whether she's working late again tonight?
1 They moved here in 2015. Are they still living here?
2 The greengrocer sold strawberries last summer. Does he sell them now?
3 The poster said the gig starts at six. Has it started yet?
4 You've been sitting there for ages. Are you waiting for someone?
5 I really must leave at six. Will you be ready by then too?
6 The cat's sleeping under the bed. Does it usually sleep there?

57 Correct the mistakes.

0 Do you know where ~~come those cheap clothes from~~?
   those cheap clothes come from
1 Some children in poor countries works long hours.
2 Do you know are the factory conditions good or bad?
3 Could you say me where I can buy clothes with a fair trade label?
4 Would you mind explain what 'fair trade' is?
5 Can you tell me where did you buy those jeans?

Starter E 13

1 Communication

GRAMMAR PRACTICE

Past simple v past continuous

Complete the rules.
The past .... and the past .... describe past events that are completed.
We can use *ago* with the past .... to fix an event in the past.
We use the past .... to describe background actions and to set the scene.

➡ See **GRAMMAR REFERENCE** page 111

1 🔊 **Complete with the irregular past simple.**

   0 bring — **brought**
   1 buy — ....
   2 leave — ....
   3 lose — ....
   4 read — ....
   5 shake — ....
   6 spread — ....
   7 strike — ....
   8 take — ....
   9 wear — ....
   10 write — ....

2 🔊 **Complete the sentences with a verb from exercise 1 in the past simple.**

   0 The news of the floods ......**spread**...... quickly online.
   1 In the past, a paper boy or girl .... the newspapers to our door.
   2 Iris .... lots of excellent photos with her smartphone.
   3 They .... everything they had in the 2004 tsunami.
   4 They were in bed when the earthquake .... central Italy.
   5 Last year I .... a good book about the changes in social media.
   6 The wind was so powerful that the whole building ....

3 🔊 **Write questions and answers using the prompts with the past simple and *when*.**

   0 the rescue operation / begin? it / yesterday
   '**When did the rescue operation begin?**'
   '**It began yesterday.**'
   1 they / come back to this region? they / a month ago
   2 you / see the news about the earthquake? we / in August 2016
   3 the survivors / have a hot meal? they / last night
   4 the journalist / make an offer of help? she / immediately
   5 you / start your blog? I / six months ago
   6 camera crew / film the accident? they / straight away

4 🔊 **Complete the sentences with the past continuous of the verbs below.**

   arrive ▪ ~~cook~~ ▪ do ▪ not / make ▪ ~~prepare~~ ▪
   sit ▪ shake ▪ not / sleep ▪ talk ▪ watch

   0 While Jim **was cooking** the pasta, Donna **was preparing** the salad.
   1 We .... the match on TV while you .... your homework.
   2 While she .... in the bus, she .... on her phone.
   3 Help .... already .... while the walls .... still ....
   4 The children .... but they .... any noise.

5 🔊 **Choose the correct option.**

   0 She *read* / *(was reading)* the news online when she *(saw)* / *was seeing* the photo.
   1 They *had* / *were having* a holiday in Thailand when the tsunami *hit* / *was hitting* the coast.
   2 It suddenly *started* / *was starting* to rain heavily while they *helped* / *were helping* the survivors.
   3 I *watched* / *was watching* out of the window when I *saw* / *was seeing* the accident.
   4 While she *checked* / *was checking* her phone, a text message *arrived* / *was arriving*.
   5 *Did you talk* / *Were you talking* on Skype when the lights *went* / *were going* out?
   6 A big hole *appeared* / *was appearing* in the road while I *drove* / *was driving* home.

Present perfect (1)

Complete the rules with the words below.

have ▪ now ▪ past ▪ present

The present perfect is the .... tense of the verb .... + a past participle. It describes .... actions or events that still affect us ....

➡ See **GRAMMAR REFERENCE** page 111

14   Unit 1

GRAMMAR PRACTICE

6 Add a sentence. Use the present perfect.

0 The survivors are all tired. they / walk miles
   They've walked miles.

1 It's warmer in here now. I / close the windows
   ....

2 She's still busy. she / not / finish her work
   ....

3 They're at the station. their train / arrive
   ....

4 We haven't got any money. we / spend it all
   ....

5 He sent her an email. she / not / reply to it
   ....

6 I'm looking for my keys. I / not / find them
   ....

Present perfect (2)

Choose the correct option.
We can use the present perfect with *just* / *ever* when we mean 'a short time ago'. The word *already* means 'sooner than we expected'. We can use *yet* / *never* at the end of a question or a negative sentence. We can use *ever* in questions and *never* when we mean *not ever* / *not yet*.

→ See **GRAMMAR REFERENCE** page 113

7 Rewrite the sentences and put the words in brackets in the correct place.

0 I'm hungry now because I haven't eaten. (*yet*)
   I'm hungry now because I haven't eaten yet.

1 Have you done your homework? (*already*)
2 My big sister's taken her driving test. (*never*)
3 They've seen some terrible pictures on TV. (*just*)
4 Have they told us the truth? (*ever*)
5 I've read a really interesting article. (*just*)
6 Has James given us his new email address? (*yet*)

Present perfect (3)

Choose the correct option.
To measure a period of time from now back to a past event, we can use the present perfect with *for* / *since* + the length of time or *for* / *since* + a fixed time.

→ See **GRAMMAR REFERENCE** page 113

8 Match the parts of the questions.

0 [e] Have you
1 [ ] Did Bella   4 [ ] Have they
2 [ ] Has the cat   5 [ ] Did the earthquake
3 [ ] Did they   6 [ ] Did the building

a had its dinner?
b happen at night?
c fall down?
d see her own report on TV?
e had that mobile for ages?
f know what to do?
g joined the rescue team?

9 Put the words in the correct order.

0 yesterday / rescue / since / team / been / the / here / has
   The rescue team has been here since yesterday.

1 in / long / haven't / this / for / town / we / lived
2 neighbours / 2015 / they've / since / been
3 read / months / haven't / a / for / newspaper / I
4 had / for / clean / they / ages / water / haven't
5 since / she's / morning / toothache / had / this
6 tablet / since / brother / a / he / my / was / wanted / nine / has

10 Complete the news article with the verbs in brackets. Use the past simple, past continuous or present perfect form.

There ⁰ **has been** (be) a powerful earthquake in New Zealand. It ¹................ (strike) South Island at 12:02 am. People ²................ (feel) hundreds of aftershocks since it ³................ (happen). So far, thousands of residents ⁴................ (lose) their homes. One survivor ⁵................ (speak) to our reporter earlier today. 'I ⁶................ (sit) in the night bus on my way home when suddenly the quake ⁷................ (start). Everything ⁸................ (shake). The bus driver ⁹................ (stop) and the other two passengers and I ¹⁰................ (get) out as fast as possible. Just in time, too, because then a massive wall ¹¹................ (fall) on the bus! I ¹²................ (never be) so scared in all my life.'

Unit 1   15

READING SKILLS

11 You are going to read some advice about online security. Where might you find this advice?

1 In a comic.
2 On a website.
3 In a text message.
4 In a novel.

12 Read the text. Choose the best title.

1 Securing your passwords
2 Stay safe online
3 How to be an internet troll

13 [3.01] Read the text again and put sentences a–e in the correct gaps 1–5. Then listen and check.

a Did you know the **source**?
b As soon as you put that image online, it stopped being yours.
c Details like your home or email addresses and your mobile number shouldn't be posted online.
d Then keep your passwords to yourself, and keep them safe.
e Avoid **befriending** or meeting up with a person you've met online.

14 Read the text again. Decide if the sentences are true (T) or false (F). Correct the false ones.

1 Your personal information includes your addresses and phone numbers. T F
2 A password with 12 or more characters is a weak password. T F
3 Deleting pictures you posted online a year ago is easy. T F
4 It is not advisable to arrange a meeting with a person you've only met online. T F
5 Websites with addresses beginning with *http://* are secure. T F

15 Find words in the text that match the definitions:

1 to prevent something from happening: ....
2 to open a computer file: ....
3 to make contact with: ....
4 to keep someone or something safe: ....
5 to remove: ....
6 worth a lot of money: ....
7 real or true: ....
8 safe or protected: ....

Protect your privacy

Your personal information is valuable, so you need to protect it. Keep your privacy settings as high as possible in your social media activities. ¹............ Think about who you have given this information to, and how others have collected it through websites and apps.

Write it down

Have you ever given anyone your passwords? Not a great idea. It's important to have strong passwords with at least 12 characters. Avoid your birthday or your pet's name – a short sentence is best. ²............ Everyone has forgotten their password at some point, so make a list and then put that in a **secure** place – not anywhere near your computer, tablet or phone.

Think before you post

Words or images that you posted last week or last year could still be out there somewhere. Did you think of that before you sent pictures or videos of yourself? ³............ Other people can access it, download it and share it. Be careful not to post anything that you would not like to share publicly – now or at some time in the future.

16 Answer these questions.

1 Did you feel comfortable or uncomfortable with the advice in the text? Give a reason for your answer.
2 How much information in the text did you already know: all of it, most of it or not much of it?
3 Explain how you access your privacy settings.
4 What further advice could you give, from your own experience?

Stranger danger

When you were younger, your parents probably taught you not to speak to strangers. Similarly, you should never reply to a message from somebody you don't know. [4]............ It is possible that people contacting you are not who they say they are. Did you know you can block numbers from unknown senders?

Connect with care

If you shop online, look for web addresses with *https://*. Addresses with *http://* without the letter 's' are insecure. Have you ever connected to a link in, for example, an online advert or social media post? Maybe it was in your email box. [5]............ Even if the link looks authentic, as if it's from a bank or a charity, don't click on it until you're sure who sent it. If you're not sure, delete it. Cybercriminals have often stolen personal information in this way and they are hard to **track down**.

GLOSSARY

source	➤ where something comes from
befriending	➤ making friends with
secure	➤ safe
track down	➤ find

Security
Identity
Cyber Crime
Spam
Password Protection
Theft

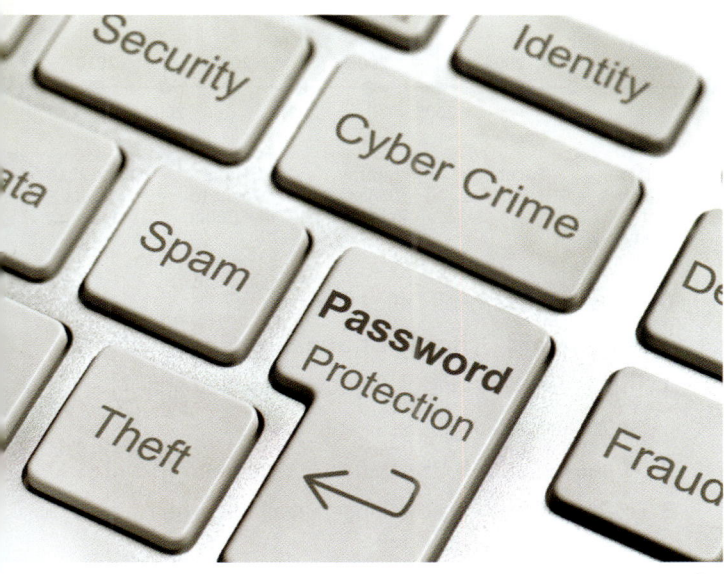

VOCABULARY

CORRESPONDENCE

17 Complete the words.

0 My brother attracted hundreds of f*ollowers*........ when he was writing his travel blog.
1 I bought my first Manga c......................... when I was 11.
2 Dickens was an English n......................... who was very popular in his own time.
3 She's made a lot of money by designing w......................... for schools and colleges.
4 In internet slang, a t......................... is someone who posts nasty messages.
5 As a young j......................... on *The Guardian* newspaper, Tim interviewed Bill Gates.
6 Annie Leibovitz has photographed famous models for fashion m......................... .

18 Add as many words as you can.

1 share *a post, a photo,* ....
2 write *a novel,* ....
3 follow ....
4 update ....
5 block ....

19 Look at the safety poster. Make a similar one with the words *STAY SAFE*.

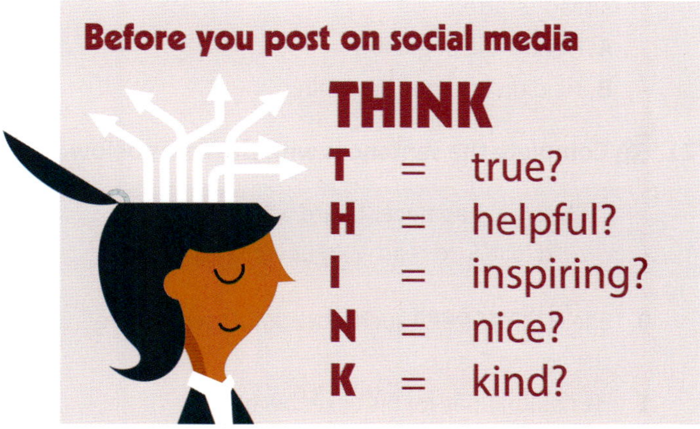

Before you post on social media
THINK
T = true?
H = helpful?
I = inspiring?
N = nice?
K = kind?

STAY
S = ...
T = ...
A = ...
Y = ...

SAFE
S = ...
A = ...
F = ...
E = ...

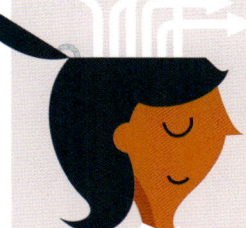

GRAMMAR PRACTICE

Past simple v past perfect

Complete the rules with the words below.

first ■ sequence ■ single ■ together

To describe a ……………… completed event we use the past simple. To show a ……………… of events, we use the past simple and the past perfect ……………… . The past perfect describes what happened ……………… .

➡ See **GRAMMAR REFERENCE** page 116

20 🔊 Read the sentences and choose the correct option.

0 I'd seen the film so I decided to read the book.
   (A) I saw the film first.
   B I read the book first.

1 The bomb had exploded when the police arrived.
   A The police arrived first.
   B The bomb exploded first.

2 The match had finished by the time we arrived.
   A We saw the match.
   B We didn't see the match.

3 They ran to the station but the train had just left.
   A They caught the train.
   B They missed the train.

4 When he turned on the TV, his programme had already started.
   A He saw the beginning.
   B He didn't see the beginning.

21 🔊 Complete the sentences with the verbs below.

'd been ■ had never heard ■ had had ■
'd lost ■ 'd read ■ 'd never seen

0 She **'d never seen** such a beautiful town before she visited Siena.

1 He couldn't pay for his ticket because he ……………… his wallet.

2 Ray knew Athens because he ……………… there many times.

3 Dad ……………… the same car for years before it broke down.

4 I went to see the film after I ……………… all the reviews.

5 My friend Jonny ……………… an opera before I took him to *Aida*.

22 🔊 Make questions with the past perfect using the verbs in brackets.

0 ……**Had**…… you ……**studied**…… (*study*) Mandarin before you moved to China?

1 ……………… you ever ……………… (*visit*) Canada before your trip in 2010?

2 ……………… Susie ……………… (*be*) in Paris long before she met Pierre?

3 How long ……………… they ……………… (*live*) in Germany before they moved?

4 ……………… the rain ……………… (*stop*) by the time you went out?

23 🔊 Complete the sentences. Use past simple, past continuous, present perfect or past perfect.

0 ……**Had**…… you ……**finished**…… (*finish*) breakfast or ……**were**…… you still ……**eating**…… (*eat*) when I ……**called**…… (*call*)?

1 He ……………… (*take*) the book back to the library after he ……………… (*read*) it.

2 Meet my neighbour Kim. I ……………… (*know*) her since she ……………… (*move*) in a year ago.

3 We ……………… (*not / hear*) from James while he ……………… (*live*) in London.

4 He ……………… (*start*) as an apprentice in 2012 and within four years he ……………… (*become*) the manager.

24 🔊 Answer the questions about the technology timeline.

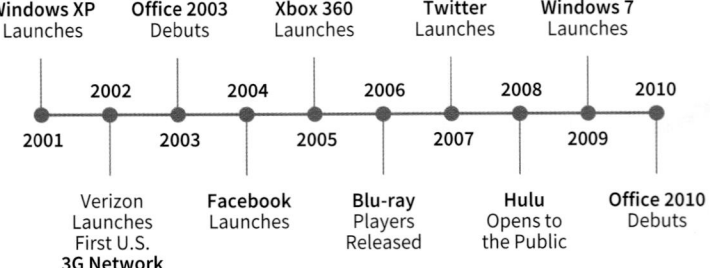

0 When did Microsoft Office first appear?
   Microsoft Office first appeared in 2003.

1 How many versions of Windows had Microsoft launched by 2009?

2 When did Xbox 360 launch its first games?

3 How long had Facebook been available when Twitter started?

Unit 1

SPEAKING SKILLS

RECOUNTING A STORY

25 Complete the dialogue with the words below.

| had an accident ▪ Really ▪ Guess what ▪ No way ▪ |
| Who's ▪ I thought you said ▪ Well |

Patricia ¹........................ ? My dad's in hospital!
Nigel ²........................ ? I didn't know he was sick.
Patricia He isn't, but he's ³........................ . He was rescuing the cat.
Nigel ⁴........................ ?! What happened to him?
Patricia ⁵........................, Alfie ran into our garden.
Nigel ⁶........................ Alfie – your cat, right?
Patricia No, he's our neighbour's dog. He's big and quite aggressive.
Nigel But ⁷........................ your dad had rescued a cat?
Patricia Yeah, Alfie the dog ran into our garden and chased our cat up a tree.
Nigel I see. What happened next?

26 Reorder the dialogue to continue Patricia's story.

Patricia Well then, the cat didn't want to come down and it was getting dark. So Dad climbed up the tree.

a ☐ Oh no. So what happened in the end?
b ☐ He did … what? Poor man!
c ☐ Hang on, how did he get up there?
d ☐ Mad man, more like. And after all that, the cat got down by itself in the end!
e ☐ He used a ladder but then the ladder fell down. So then both Dad and the cat were stuck up the tree! Dad started shouting for help but nobody was at home.
f ☐ He jumped and broke his leg.

27 We ask for clarification to check that we understand. Choose the responses that ask for clarification.

1 A massive earthquake struck our village last night.
  A No way! Really?
  B I know, it's already in the news online.
2 There was a car crash right outside the school.
  A I didn't hear about that.
  B What was that again?
3 A tiger has escaped from the zoo!
  A Did you say a tiger?
  B I hope they catch it soon.

LISTENING SKILLS

28 Look at the photo and answer the questions.

1 What meal is this family eating?
2 List the electronic devices each person is using.
3 When do you eat together with your family?
4 Is this scene typical of a meal at your home?

29 [3.02] You are going to listen to a short radio broadcast about changing habits at mealtimes. Choose the correct option.

1 Two-thirds of British families say that they:
  A meet as regularly as their grandparents did.
  B get together for a traditional Sunday lunch.
  C nearly always have their main meal together.
2 According to research, electronic devices:
  A are a cause for concern at mealtimes.
  B have changed mealtimes surprisingly little.
  C automatically stop families talking.
3 When asked, nearly half of the mothers said they:
  A allowed smartphones at the table.
  B had hidden their children's smartphones under the table.
  C had often forbidden the use of smartphones during meals.
4 The condition known as *nomophobia* describes the fear of:
  A talking on the phone.
  B not having your phone.
  C not being able to talk on the phone.

Unit 1   19

EXAM SKILLS

> **EXAM STRATEGY**
>
> **Reading and Use of English**
> **Multiple-choice cloze**
>
> With multiple-choice questions, it is important to read each option very carefully before deciding which fits the gap correctly. Never choose more than one option. Different kinds of words are tested. It is often necessary to choose between words with a similar meaning.

30 What kinds of words are they? Tick (✓) the right category (Noun, Verb or Adjective).

		Noun	Verb	Adj
0	comment	✓	✓	
1	option			
2	prevent			
3	worried			
4	detached			
5	launch			
6	sensitivity			

31 Match each of the following words to the right synonym from exercise 30.

0 [O] remark
1 [ ] separated
2 [ ] choice
3 [ ] start
4 [ ] troubled
5 [ ] compassion
6 [ ] stop

32 Below is a paragraph taken from a novel. For questions 1–6, read the text and decide which answer (A, B, C or D) best fits each gap.

0	**A** time	**B** ring	**(C)** alarm	**D** call
1	**A** catch	**B** stop	**C** lose	**D** miss
2	**A** walked	**B** skipped	**C** jumped	**D** ran
3	**A** managed	**B** succeeded	**C** resulted	**D** achieved
4	**A** strange	**B** difficult	**C** uneasy	**D** tricky
5	**A** remind	**B** recall	**C** realise	**D** repeat
6	**A** heat	**B** move	**C** shake	**D** perspire

Teresa's morning had started badly that day. She hadn't heard her ⁰............ and in fact, she was still sleeping when her mother shouted up the stairs: 'I'm off now – early meeting! You'll have to get the bus today, love, sorry. Don't ¹............ it!' The next 15 minutes had been a complete nightmare. She'd got dressed much faster than usual and had ²............ breakfast. Grabbing her school bag, Teresa raced to the bus stop and just ³............ to catch her bus. But as soon as she got on the bus, she began to feel strangely ⁴............ . She was sure there was something she'd planned to do but she couldn't ⁵............ what it was. Reaching into her pocket for her phone to check her online calendar, she realised it wasn't there. In a sudden panic, she felt around in her bag as she began to ⁶............ and sweat. Since she had been in such a rush, she'd left the phone beside her bed and now she was on her way to school! And she knew that without the support of her smartphone, her day would be a disaster.

EXAM SKILLS

> **EXAM STRATEGY**
>
> **Listening – Multiple choice**
>
> While you are listening, you may hear all the keywords, but only one option will answer the question fully. Underline the keywords in the question. This will help you focus on the important information. Then listen out for words that mean the same as the keywords.

33 Read an exam question with its choice of answers. Underline the keywords that you will listen out for.

You hear a man making a telephone call. Why has he phoned?
- A To arrange a factory visit.
- B To ask for a lift.
- C To change plans.

34 Read the transcript for the exam question in exercise 33. Is the answer A, B or C? Why were the two other options not exactly right?

> Hello! I'm calling about our trip to the factory. I've just picked up your message saying you want to change it to the Friday. That's fine with me but you know we had already planned to meet there? Well, I won't have my own transport that day, so could I possibly come with you in your car? It'd be very helpful if you could pick me up from the station.

35 Read another exam question and again underline the keywords.

You hear part of a radio programme about the media. What is the speaker reviewing?
- A A film about Bill and Melinda Gates.
- B A new Windows application.
- C A book about the creation of Windows.

36 [3.03] Now listen to the review and choose the best answer.

37 [3.04] You hear two friends talking about a school rule.

What do they agree about?
- A Their new headteacher is unfair.
- B There should be a compromise.
- C Smartphones are great educational tools.

38 [3.05] You hear a teacher talking to his class.

What does he want the class to do?
- A Write a group article for the blog.
- B To try and be original.
- C Remember the school trip.

39 [3.06] You hear part of a programme about social media books.

What is the presenter saying?
- A They don't last very long.
- B They sell very well.
- C They don't take very long to write.

40 [3.07] You hear two friends talking about their phones.

What do they both agree?
- A Phones are good for everything.
- B They couldn't live without social media.
- C Watching things on a screen is fun.

41 [3.08] You hear a photographer talking about his work.

What is important for him before taking a photo?
- A Thought.
- B Excitement.
- C Processing.

Unit 1   21

2 Advertising

GRAMMAR PRACTICE

Direct and reported speech

Complete the rules with the words below.

actual • reported • tense • verb

In .... speech, we use a reporting .... (like *said* or *told*) and then change the .... of the speaker's .... words.

→ See **GRAMMAR REFERENCE** page 117

1 🔊 **Change the sentences from direct to reported speech.**

0 'It's an effective ad.' They said (that) ...*it was an effective ad*... .

1 'I have some time now.' He said ....

2 'I want to see the movie first.' She told him ....

3 'I don't like smoky bars.' He said ....

4 'I'm trying to give up smoking.' She told me ....

5 'Jodie's bringing some friends.' Her sister said ....

6 'We're doing more research.' They told the press ....

2 🔊 **Choose the correct option.**

0 'I've booked a room with a view'. She said she (*'d booked*) / *'d been booking* a room with a view.

1 'We've been targeting you for ages.' They admitted they *'d targeted* / *'d been targeting* us for ages.

2 'I've never watched German TV.' He told us he *'d never watched* / *'d never been watching* German TV.

3 'We've heard the latest news.' They told us they *'d heard* / *'d been hearing* the latest news.

4 'These ads have been annoying me.' I told them those ads *had annoyed* / *had been annoying* me.

5 'We spoke about it earlier today.' I agreed we *'d spoken* / *'d been speaking* about it earlier that day.

6 'The results have been coming in.' The reporter said the results *had come* / *had been coming* in.

3 🔊 **Complete the sentences. Use *will*, *can*, *would* or *could*.**

0 'Bob ...*will*... come as soon as he ...*can*... .' She said Bob ...*would*... come as soon as he ...*could*... .

1 'Our holiday in the sun .... relax you.' The ad claimed their holiday in the sun would relax us.

2 'You can never believe the newspapers.' My parents told me I .... never believe the newspapers.

3 'You'll enjoy the film.' We assured her that she .... enjoy the film.

4 'You .... rely on me to help.' He promised me that I could rely on him to help.

4 🔊 ***Say* or *tell*? Choose the correct option.**

0 They (*said*) / *told* that their shop was the best.

1 Bella *said* / *told* everyone what she'd heard.

2 Did Lauren *say* / *tell* you that she wasn't coming?

3 I *said* / *told* to the waiter: 'I think you're very rude.'

4 They *say* / *tell* that there's no added salt but I'm not sure.

5 Our parents always *said* / *told* us to tell the truth.

6 Has Matti *said* / *told* that he's giving up coffee?

5 🔊 **Choose the correct option.**

0 Someone .... me that there had been an accident.
 A asked   B said   (C) told

1 Sam .... that he wouldn't be late but he was.
 A reported   B suggested   C promised

2 What did the postman say .... this morning?
 A for you   B to you   C you

3 You're wearing jeans! I .... you were going to wear a dress.
 A said   B reported   C thought

4 I .... you'd passed your driving test – well done!
 A didn't wonder   B didn't realise   C didn't tell

5 Our neighbour explained he'd been on holiday the .... week.
 A next   B previous   C last

6 Some people .... that red wine is good for your heart.
 A advise   B show   C believe

22   Unit 2

GRAMMAR PRACTICE

6 🔊 **Write the conversation from the reported sentences.**

0 Berto said he was just coming.
   Berto: **'I'm just coming.'**
1 Jill said she was waiting for him outside in the street.
   Jill: ....
2 He told her that he couldn't find the apartment keys.
   Berto: ....
3 She said she thought they were on the kitchen table.
   Jill: ....
4 He told her that he was sure she had all the keys.
   Berto: ....
5 She apologised and agreed that she did have them.
   Jill: ....
6 She said she was coming back up with the keys.
   Jill: ....

7 🔊 **Complete with the correct tense changes.**

0 'I didn't cycle, I walked to work.'
   He told me **he hadn't cycled, he'd walked to work**
1 'We began at nine.'
   They said they ....
2 'He didn't really want to complain.'
   He said that ....
3 'My mum has never eaten Japanese food.'
   She told me that ....
4 'I think it was raining all night.'
   They thought ....
5 'We've been complaining about the new menu.'
   He explained that ....
6 'I wasn't feeling well at all.'
   She admitted that ....

8 🔊 **Report the statements.**

0 'The bus left a few moments ago.'
   Someone told me the bus **had left** a few moments before.
1 'They were hoping to arrive today.'
   They said .... that day.
2 'I went to see an old friend yesterday.'
   She said .... the day before.
3 'My boss came into my office last week.'
   He told me that .... the previous week.
4 'We weren't expecting all these questions.'
   They said .... all those questions.
5 'I didn't realise that you were waiting for so long.'
   She told me ....
6 'Our teacher bought a new car a month ago.'
   They heard that .... a month before.

9 🔊 **Write the ad by putting the words into the correct order.**

NEW!
Sooper Frooty Smoothie!

0 the / smoothie / have / we / made / ultimate / fruit / !
   We have made the ultimate fruit smoothie!
1 try / smoothie / you / our / new / must / delicious
2 definitely / will / the / difference / you / taste
3 oranges / come / our / organic / from / farms
4 grow / fruit / farmers / all / fair-trade / our
5 much / other / it's / healthier / fruit / than / drinks
6 away / must / buy / you / some / right / !

10 🔊 **Now use the sentences from exercise 9 to report what the ad said.**

0 **The ad claimed that they had made the ultimate fruit smoothie.**
   ....
   ....
   ....
   ....
   ....
   ....

11 🔊 **Complete the replies.**

0 'I enjoy barbecues on the beach.'
   'Really? But I thought you said **you didn't enjoy them**.'
1 'Louis hasn't finished his essay.'
   'That's funny. He told me ....'
2 'Belinda and I are getting engaged.'
   'Are you really? But you said last week ....'
3 'Our teacher likes jazz better than folk music.'
   'I don't think so. She told ....'
4 'My parents were feeling better last night.'
   'That's good. I heard that ....'
5 'You'll love the new production of *Macbeth*.'
   'Well, my flatmate disagrees. He told ....'
6 'You must pay extra for the showers.'
   'Really? The poster in the gym said ....'

Unit 2   23

READING SKILLS

12 You are going to read about some accommodation advertised on the EasyBnB website. What does *BnB* mean and what does this usually imply?

13 [3.09] Read and listen to the text. Who do you think this apartment is most suitable for? Give your reasons.

1. A family group: parents, small child and baby.
2. An antiques dealer with his wife and their dog.
3. Four gap-year backpackers from New Zealand.
4. Two elderly couples on a mid-week city break.

14 Choose the correct option.

1. It will cost you at least .... to stay in this apartment.
   A £120 B £360 C £400
2. The apartment has recently been ....
   A sold B built C painted
3. Your arrival time is .... the time you have to leave.
   A earlier than B later than C the same as
4. You will be welcome here if you ....
   A have an animal B don't smoke
   C buy and sell antiques
5. The neighbourhood is ....
   A good for fine restaurants
   B handy for public transport
   C famous for old dealers

15 Read the text again. Decide if the sentences are true (T), false (F) or not given (NG). Explain your reasons. Then correct the false ones.

1. The apartment has four beds. T F NG
2. You can sit outside on the balcony. T F NG
3. There's a cot for babies to sleep in. T F NG
4. You can cook and eat in the dining area. T F NG
5. The apartment is connected to the internet. T F NG
6. It's a short walk to the underground station. T F NG

16 [3.10] Read and listen to three reviews from people who stayed at the apartment. Match their complaints to the information NG in exercise 15.

a ☐ The ad said ....
       but ....
b ☐ The ad said ....
       but ....
c ☐ The ad said ....
       but ....

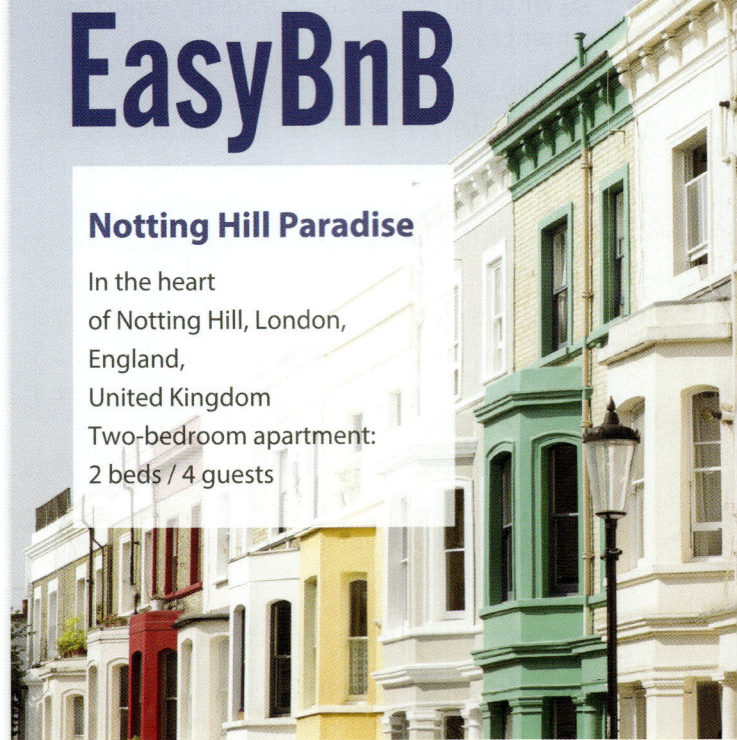

EasyBnB

Notting Hill Paradise

In the heart of Notting Hill, London, England, United Kingdom
Two-bedroom apartment:
2 beds / 4 guests

Price
£120 per night

Minimum stay
3 nights

Description
New large luxury 2-bedroom apartment in a beautiful Victorian building in fashionable Notting Hill. The apartment, which is newly decorated and well furnished, is very comfortable. There is a garden and balcony. Family friendly.
The accommodation: kitchen / dining area, bathroom and two bedrooms. Free wi-fi.

Check-in
Anytime after 1 pm

Check-out
11 am

Cleaning fee
£40

House rules
No pets or smokers allowed

Convenient central location
Ten minutes' walk to Tube station, with many buses. One minute away from the famous Portobello Road, which has the world's largest antiques market with over 1,000 dealers. You will find the most extensive selection of antiques in Britain here, as well as an amazing street food experience.

thope32
The apartment itself was great, no complaints. However, the ad said there was a balcony, but the door to it was locked. This was disappointing because it was hot sunny weather and the apartment was very warm. There was no easy access from the second floor to the shared 😣 garden.

homecooker
The flat was in a fantastic place, very trendy area. The accommodation was luxurious, as the ad claimed, but kitchen / dining area was misleading, as there was no dining table and, therefore, nowhere to sit down to eat. OK for anyone who wanted to eat out all the time.

felix354
Nice place, but the internet was a problem. The network was secured and the owner hadn't left a password, so we had to go outside to get a connection. And there was nowhere for our six-month-old baby to sleep, so … not very family friendly!

VOCABULARY

EMOTIVE WORDS

17 Choose the correct option.

0 Best holiday of our lives: we were absolutely (*delighted*) / *terrified* with everything!
1 The view of the lake and mountains was *magnificent* / *horrifying* and great for photos.
2 The toilet block was really *astonishing* / *disgusting*; dirty loos and no paper.
3 What a *wonderful* / *dreadful* setting next to the river! We loved it.
4 The five-star hotel was far *extraordinary* / *superior* to anywhere I'd ever stayed before.
5 Saying the rooms were spacious was *brilliant* / *ridiculous*. We could hardly move.
6 The ad didn't warn us about the *amazing* / *scandalous* price of food in local restaurants.
7 The kitchen was in a *disgraceful* / *appalling* state when we arrived.
8 He was unhurt after a *fantastic* / *miraculous* escape from the motorway accident.

18 Match the words that go together.

0 **g** low — **a** solution
1 ☐ home — **b** bike ride
2 ☐ perfect — **c** comforts
3 ☐ great — **d** furnished
4 ☐ newly — **e** outdoors
5 ☐ lavishly — **f** painted
6 ☐ leisurely — **g** cost

19 Complete the ad with the phrases from exercise 18.

> **0 Low cost biking holidays for all the family!** 
>
> *Tired of the usual expensive holiday options? Looking for something different that won't cost the earth? Here at the Tissington bike trail, we have the ¹ .... for you.*
>
> If you're a fan of the ² .... and love cycling in wonderful countryside, why not come to us? Our cabins are simple but cosy, with all the ³ .... you need. They are not ⁴ ...., but every room is clean and ⁵ .... at the start of every season. There are tea- and coffee-making facilities, and you are just a ⁶ .... away from the perfect English restaurant with excellent food and drink!

20 Think of the best holiday you've ever had and write your own ad for it. Use the text in exercise 19 to help you.

Unit 2 25

GRAMMAR PRACTICE

Reported speech: Questions

Choose the correct option and complete the rule.
In *direct / reported* questions, we invert the subject and verb. In *direct / reported* questions, we do not invert the subject and verb.
When we report questions, the *question words / tenses* change.
If there is no question word, we report the question with .... or ....

→ See **GRAMMAR REFERENCE** page 118

21 Underline the question words.

0 <u>How much</u> was your meal?
1 When will the sale start?
2 Where did you get that hat?
3 How good was the special offer?
4 Why didn't you read the small print?
5 Which shop has the best deals?
6 What's the new app like?

22 Make direct questions.

0 I asked (him) what time it was.
   'What's the time?'
1 She asked me how I'd heard the news.
2 He wanted to know when I'd started.
3 They asked how much we'd paid last night.
4 We asked them where we could eat.
5 She wanted to know why I was crying.
6 The man asked me when the next bus would come.

23 Report the questions.

0 'What is the postcode?' The man asked (her) **what the postcode was**.
1 'Where do you live?' He asked (me) ....
2 'Why did you want the job?' She asked (him) ....
3 'What's the matter?' I asked (them) ....
4 'How long have you been away?' He asked (me) ....
5 'When did you leave?' I asked (her) ....
6 'Which pizza will you order?' She asked (him) ....

24 Report the questions using *if* or *whether*.

0 'Can you help me with the homework?' She asked (me) **if I could help her with the homework**
1 'Is it still raining?' He wanted to know ....
2 'Does your mother need a lift?' She asked (me) ....
3 'Have you heard from Tim yet?' They asked (us) ....
4 'Were you wearing that dress last night?' He asked (her) ....
5 'Did Bill borrow my bike again?' She wondered ....
6 'Are your friends camping in the forest?' They asked (us) ....

25 Report the direct speech.

0 'Please move your car.' The policeman asked me **to move my car**
1 'Don't be late!' He told me ....
2 'Don't touch the electric fence!' They warned me ....
3 'Would you mind helping me?' She asked him ....
4 'Take a break from your computer.' We advised him ....
5 'You mustn't leave the door open.' They told us ....
6 'Come early for the best deals!' The assistant told me ....
7 'Please can you shut the window?' She asked me ....

26 Imagine you have finished school and had a job interview. Read the notes and write the questions the interviewer asked. Then write to a friend about it.

- when and where born
  When and where were you born?
- where school
- how many languages study
- when leave school
- where work first
- when leave last job
- why want this job

The interview was OK. First she asked me when and where I was born. Then ...

Unit 2

SPEAKING SKILLS

PERSUADING

27 Tick (✓) the correct column. When you say these things, are you agreeing (A), disagreeing (D) or persuading (P)?

1 Why not? A D P
2 That's a ridiculous thing to say. A D P
3 Go on, have a look. A D P
4 I really don't think … A D P
5 You win! A D P
6 Hmmm, I'm still not sure. A D P
7 So, come on, let's do it. A D P
8 I'm sorry, but … A D P
9 Well, OK, if you really want to. A D P
10 I can't believe that. A D P
11 No, they won't do that. A D P
12 Oh, OK then … A D P
13 We'll have to hurry up or we'll miss … A D P

28 Complete the conversation with phrases from exercise 27. You won't need to use all of them.

Lena Hey Paul, there's a new fitness centre in town. Look at this leaflet: 'Everything you want in a gym for less'. ¹……………… .

Paul OK, let me see it. No, ²……………… I'm not interested.

Lena ³……………… ?

Paul Because they say it's 'everything I want'. ⁴……………… . How do they know what I want?

Lena Oh really, Paul! ⁵……………… .

Paul It isn't ridiculous. Well, ⁶……………… it is. They claim it's cheap but after a month they'll increase their prices.

Lena ⁷……………… . I'm sure they won't. But ⁸……………… the offer, it's only open for one month.

Paul Hmmm, ⁹……………… . The offer's good for the first month, but then it costs twice as much! Read the small print.

Lena Oh, ¹⁰………………, Paul. ¹¹……………… ! You always were hard to persuade!

29 Answer these questions.

1 Who is persuading, Lena or Paul?
2 What is Paul doing during the conversation?
3 What does Lena do in the end?

LISTENING SKILLS

A

B

C

30 Look at the leaflets. Where might you find leaflets like these?

31 [3.11] Listen to three conversations. Which leaflets (A, B or C) are they talking about?

1 …………. Conversation 1
2 …………. Conversation 2
3 …………. Conversation 3

32 Answer these questions.

1 How many speakers are there in each conversation?
2 Two of the conversations are about food. Which ones?
3 The speakers in one of the conversations don't know each other. Which one? How do you know?

33 [3.11] Listen again and answer the questions.

1 You first hear a conversation in a furniture shop. What are the shoppers looking for?
2 Who doesn't like the leather furniture and why?
3 In conversation 2, where are the friends eating?
4 What had they not understood about the *two-for-one* deal?
5 Where is the woman calling from in conversation 3?
6 What was not clear in the leaflet from the takeaway restaurant?

Unit 2   27

ACADEMIC SKILLS

NOTE TAKING

34 Complete the advice about note taking with the words below.

> bullet points ▪ important ▪ key information ▪ more than ▪ shorter ▪ your own

0 Read the text ...**more than**... once.
1 Underline the .... points the writer is making.
2 Try and identify what is .... and what isn't.
3 Rewrite the information in .... words, using headings and .... to make the information clearer, ... and simpler.

35 Read the introduction to the article about advertising. Underline the two most important pieces of information in the paragraph.

36 Now read the article. Underline the keywords.

37 Complete the notes with key information from the text and choose the correct option.

SHOCK TACTICS and the ASA

Topics	Key information		
0 Who uses these tactics?	campaign groups, ...		
1 Who decides if ads OK?	ASA		
2 First antismoking ad	ashtray	shocking / (not too shocking)	(allowed) / banned
3 Ad with child	....	shocking / not too shocking	allowed / banned
4 Ad with hook	face	shocking / not too shocking	allowed / banned

38 Now rewrite the notes in your own words. Use what you wrote in exercise 37 to help you.

Advertising is all around us, so it is perhaps no surprise that some advertisers try to grab our attention with shocking photos or messages. These are called *shock tactics*. What is OK, and what is not? The people that decide in the UK work for an organization called the Advertising Standards Authority (the ASA).

Charities, governments and campaign groups often use shock tactics to make the public aware of a cause or to raise money. For example, advertisers have used them in the past to tell smokers to stop smoking.

5 This raises an interesting question: how far is it all right to use shock tactics? Our views might be different if they are used to advertise a good cause. One example, produced by an antismoking campaign, is a photo that didn't glamorise smoking but showed the result – a smelly dirty full ashtray. It was very direct and clear, and not too
10 shocking, so the ASA had no objection to it.
Another photo in the same campaign showed a small child wearing a protective mask full of smoke over his face. This ad was designed to make a smoker feel bad about the effects of his or her smoking on children, and was powerful and quite shocking. However, it carried
15 an important message, so the ASA had no problem with it.
An ad which the ASA did have a problem with showed how addicted or hooked a smoker can become. The photo was of a man with a fishing hook in the side of his face. The fishing line was pulling the man by his mouth. The image was very graphic, and it looked both painful and disgusting. The ASA received so many complaints about this that they had to ban it from TV and poster campaigns.

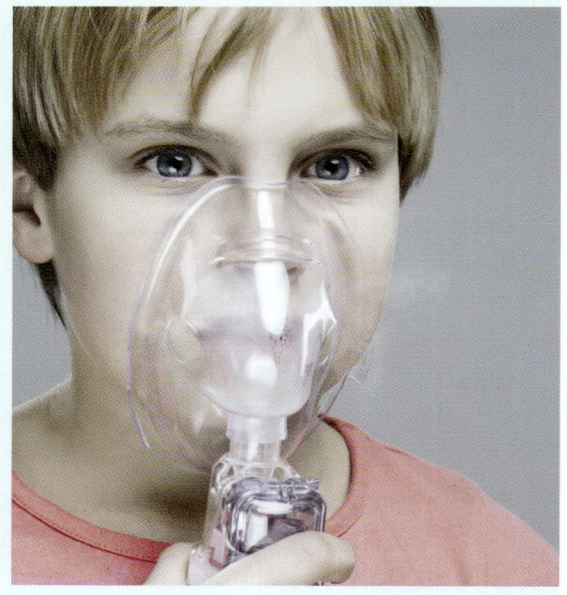

EXAM SKILLS

EXAM STRATEGY

Reading and Use of English – Open cloze

Use only one word to fill each gap. Read the words which follow the gap as well as those which come before it. Remember that if, for example, the gap is a verb, it must agree with its subject.

39 Choose the correct option.

0 My sister's tried to stop, but she still *drank / (drinks) / drinking* five cans of cola a day.
1 He wasn't interested *on / in / about* an expensive holiday in Sardinia.
2 The TV ads were so annoying *as / then / that* we switched channels.
3 She is *saving / earning / spending* up to buy a new winter coat.
4 Henry is certainly not afraid *to / of / with* saying what he thinks.
5 It was Mandy's brother *than / which / that* had helped to start her stage career.

40 Read the text below and think of the word that best fits each gap. Use only one word for each gap.

The Father of Advertising

David Ogilvy is ⁰..*thought*.. to be one of the greatest writers of advertising copy. In 1962, *Time* magazine ¹.................. him 'the most sought-after wizard in today's advertising industry'. His advice is ².................. followed by students of copywriting today. How did he ³.................. the father of advertising? ⁴.................. winning a scholarship to study history at Oxford University, Ogilvy never graduated. ⁵.................. of finishing his studies, he went to Paris to work in a hotel kitchen. Never a man to stay in one place for long, he was keen to move ⁶.................. a year. Back in England, he began a very successful career selling Aga cooking stoves. He wrote an instruction manual for Aga salespeople which became known as the finest sales manual ⁷.................. written. When this manual came to the ⁸.................. of a big advertising agency, Ogilvy was offered a job there. And the rest is history.

EXAM STRATEGY

Writing – A letter

Read the instructions carefully and underline the most important parts. Refer closely to the question to make sure you've included every part. When writing a letter or email, think about what level of formality is appropriate.

41 Read this exam question and underline the important parts.

You have bought some <u>trainers</u> and you are not satisfied with them. Write a letter to say how you bought them and mention two things you are unhappy about. Ask for a replacement or a refund. Write your letter to Mrs Branwell, the Customer Services manager.

42 Now complete the letter of complaint to Mrs Branwell, the Customer Services manager.

> acceptable ▪ Could you ▪ ~~Dear~~ ▪ disappointing ▪
> I am writing ▪ I look forward ▪
> I also would like ▪ Yours

⁰......*Dear*...... Mrs Branwell,
¹.................. to complain about the Converse trainers you supplied. I ordered them online and they took three weeks to arrive, because they were not in stock. The advertisement said they were in stock, so this was ².................. .
When I tried on the trainers, I discovered they were not the same size. The left trainer was my size (39) but the right trainer was bigger (41). This is not ³.................. .
⁴.................. please send me another pair of size 39 trainers? ⁵.................. to know how long they will take to arrive.
⁶.................. to hearing from you,
⁷.................. sincerely,

43 Read the exam question and do the task.

You have bought a pair of boots from Discount Boots Online. Write a letter to say when you bought them and mention three things you are unhappy about. Ask for your money back. Mention that you will write a negative review if you are not satisfied.
Use the letter in exercise 42 and these ideas to help you:
- not genuine designer label / fake
- not the colour you ordered
- not real leather as advertised

Write your letter to Mr Jake Renshaw in the Customer Services department.

Unit 2   29

REVISE AND ROUND UP

1 🔊 **Complete the sentences with the correct verb in the past simple.**

bring ▪ buy ▪ find ▪ hear ▪ leave ▪ lose ▪ read
shake ▪ spread ▪ strike ▪ take ▪ wear

0 Roger ....**bought**.... a cheap phone yesterday.
1 She .... her keys but I ....
  them for her.
2 I .... a book from the shelf
  and .... it to the children.
3 He .... some flowers to her house
  and .... them by the door.
4 The earthquake .... my village at ten
  and the whole house ....
5 We .... the news on the radio
  and it .... quickly online.
6 The rescue workers .... hard hats
  and bright yellow jackets.

2 🔊 **Write questions with the past simple.**

0 'Where **did you see the news** ?'
  'I saw the news on TV.'
1 'When .... ?'
  'They got to the village before dark.'
2 'Why .... ?'
  'She learnt it because her best friend was German.'
3 'How much .... ?'
  'My tablet? It cost £200.'
4 'How long .... ?'
  'The journey took four hours.'
5 'Where .... ?'
  'The aid workers came from various countries.'
6 'When .... ?'
  'He did his homework at the last minute: typical Harry!'

3 🔊 **Complete the sentences with the past simple or the past continuous.**

0 I **was walking** (walk) home yesterday when
  something really cool **happened** (happen).
1 She .... (see) her best friend
  while she .... (stand) on the platform.
2 We .... (arrive) home on New Year's Eve
  and a light snow .... (fall).
3 I .... (cook) the dinner when the lights
  .... (go) out.
4 I got your text, so I .... (know)
  you .... (not / come) to my party.

5 Nina .... (have) a lovely dream
  when her alarm .... (wake) her up.
6 .... the train .... (wait)
  when you .... (get) to the station?
7 Frances .... (work) as a waitress
  in a café, when Edward .... (meet) her.

4 🔊 **Complete with irregular past simple and the past participle.**

0	bring	**brought**	**brought**
1	buy	....	....
2	leave	....	....
3	lose	....	....
4	read	....	....
5	shake	....	....
6	spread	....	....
7	strike	....	....
8	take	....	....
9	wear	....	....
10	write	....	....

5 🔊 **Correct the wrong sentences.**

0 He's had a headache ~~for~~ last night. **since**
1 I've been waiting at the bus stop for ages.
2 We haven't seen Vikki since July.
3 Has he been working with you since a long time?
4 It's a whole year since I've been to the dentist.
5 She's been driving her mother's car for Saturday.
6 We haven't had a party since ages.
7 They haven't flown anywhere since the accident.
8 Ms Clarke has taught at this school since a long time.

6 🔊 **Complete the sentences using the correct form of say or tell.**

0 Janina .....**told**..... us yesterday
  that she couldn't come.
1 You .... you'd been on TV – is that true?
2 Has he already .... you he was leaving
  early?
3 Did they really .... that theirs
  was the best product?
4 I .... her teacher that Iris wasn't feeling
  well.
5 Someone .... that there had been
  an earthquake.
6 Caro .... she'd come but she didn't.

30 Units 1–2

7 Choose the correct option.

0 Ned still .... the book when I spoke to him yesterday.
 A didn't finish B hasn't finished
 C hadn't finished
1 The rain .... by the time we went out for a walk.
 A had stopped B hasn't stopped C did stop
2 When we reached the scene, the rescuers ....
 A was arriving B have arrived
 C had arrived
3 They wanted to say goodbye but the visitor ....
 A has already left B had already left
 C did already leave
4 She didn't want to see the film until she .... the book.
 A hadn't read B will read C had read
5 When our neighbours moved in, the flat .... empty for months.
 A had been B hadn't been C wasn't
6 After they .... the bill, they left the hotel.
 A have paid B did pay C had paid

8 Complete the sentences with the words below.

to bring · to choose · to explain · to take ·
not to drink · not to drive · not to run

0 They warned the children **not to run** round the swimming pool.
1 We advised the visitors .... a taxi from the airport.
2 She asked him .... why there was no internet connection.
3 They warned us .... water from the river.
4 He told me .... because the roads were flooded and dangerous.
5 The interviewer asked him .... a letter from his employer.
6 Rosa asked us .... which room we wanted.

9 Correct the mistakes.

0 She asked Helen what was the matter. **what the matter was**
1 Joe asked her how long she been living in Paris.
2 They wanted to know what time I arrived last night.
3 I asked him why he has decided to study Chinese.
4 She wanted to know if she can get a lift home.
5 She asked us whether we've ever been to Sicily.

CONCEPT CHECK

Read the sentences and answer the questions.

1 *She was eating breakfast when she heard a sudden explosion.*

(Answer Yes / No / Maybe)

0 Did she hear the explosion before she started breakfast? **No**
1 Did the breakfast go on longer than the explosion?
2 Did she stop eating breakfast after the explosion?

2 *My neighbour moved into the flat upstairs six weeks ago but I haven't spoken to her yet.*

(Answer Yes / No / Maybe)

0 Does the speaker know where the neighbour lives? **Yes**
1 Do we know when the neighbour moved in?
2 Has the speaker seen her neighbour?
3 Have they had a conversation yet?
4 Does the speaker expect to speak to her neighbour in the future?

3 *We ran for the train but by the time we reached the station, the train had already left.*

(Answer True / False)

0 They had to hurry to catch a train. **True**
1 They got to the station.
2 They got to the station in time.
3 They got to the station and then the train left.
4 The train left before they'd reached the station.
5 They missed the train.

4 *Gemma rang Tom at his home yesterday. He told her that he'd been on holiday the week before.*

(Answer True / False / Don't know)

0 Tom's been on holiday. **True**
1 Gemma's been on holiday.
2 Tom gave Gemma some news about himself.
3 Tom was still on holiday when he spoke to Gemma.
4 He told her about a holiday planned for next year.
5 The holiday that Tom told Gemma about was finished.

➡ See **GRAMMAR REFERENCE**
pages 111, 116–118

3 A better world

GRAMMAR PRACTICE

Revision of comparative and superlative adjectives

Complete the rules with the words below.

comparative ▪ stronger ▪ superlative ▪ weaker

We can make comparative adjectives .... with *much / a lot / far / even*, and we can make them .... with *a little / a (little) bit* too.
We can make .... adjectives stronger by putting *by far* first.
We can use *(not) so / as* + adjective *as ...* instead of the .... form.

➤ See **GRAMMAR REFERENCE** page 118

1 **Choose the best adjective and complete the sentences with the correct comparative form.**

fit ▪ happy ▪ healthy ▪ hot ▪ lucky ▪ ~~safe~~ ▪ thin

0 The world would be a ....**safer**.... place without guns.
1 She's been trying to live a .... lifestyle since her illness.
2 It's good to know you've helped someone feel ....
3 You will need a sun hat today; it's even .... than yesterday.
4 My brother won the lottery. He's always been .... than me.
5 You need to get .... if you want to walk to Santiago.
6 You look ...., Jan. Have you lost weight?

2 **Complete the sentences with the superlative form of the adjective given.**

0 I've three sisters but I'm **the youngest**. (*young*)
1 Of course I've heard of Bill Gates. He's one of .... philanthropists in the US. (*famous*)
2 Tina and Frank are .... people I've ever met. (*generous*)
3 Is Oxfam .... charity in the UK? (*successful*)
4 .... thing about that film was the ending. (*sad*)

3 **Complete the sentences with the correct forms of *good* or *bad*.**

0 His wedding day was ....**the best**.... day of his life. (*good*)
1 She's been quite ill but she's much .... now. (*good*)
2 That's .... meal I've ever eaten. (*bad*)
3 We had a very .... holiday despite the weather. (*good*)
4 Where's .... place in town to buy jeans? (*good*)
5 I'm afraid I think that's a really .... idea. (*bad*)
6 It's not a great result but it could be .... (*bad*)

4 **Underline the words that make the adjectives stronger (S) or weaker (W).**

0 ....**S**.... Jake's brother is a pop star and <u>much</u> wealthier than him.
1 .... The programme was a little disappointing in my opinion.
2 .... Was my phone much more expensive than yours?
3 .... Everyone thinks Sue's even more attractive than her sister.
4 .... Can you be a bit quieter, please? I'm thinking.
5 .... The film was a lot more exciting than the book.
6 .... The trip was far less interesting than he'd expected.

5 **Correct the mistakes.**

0 You're the ~~luckyiest~~ person I know. **luckiest**
1 The second episode was even excitinger than the first.
2 The problems of inequality are getting badder.
3 This blog is the less popular I've ever written.
4 Your ideas are by far better than mine.
5 The cost of living is more low in some countries.
6 Her story is by far the shockingest thing in the news today.

32 Unit 3

GRAMMAR PRACTICE

Comparatives and superlatives with nouns

Complete the rules with the words below.

countable • fewer • fewest •
least • less • uncountable

We can compare numbers by using (*many / a lot / far*) *more* or ……………… with countable nouns, and amounts by using (*much / a lot / far*) *more* or ……………… with uncountable nouns.
We can express superlatives with (*by far*) *the most* / ……………… + countable noun or (*by far*) *the most* / ……………… + uncountable nouns.
We can also use (*not*) *so / as* + *many / few* + ……………… noun + *as*, and (*not*) *so / as* + *much / little* + ……………… noun + *as*.

➡ See **GRAMMAR REFERENCE** page 119

6 🔊 **Put the nouns into the correct group.**

~~boats~~ • countries • ~~energy~~ • food • fun • grass •
help • ideas • meals • meat • millions •
minutes • money • music • people • photos •
problems • time • volunteers • water

Countable: **boats**   Uncountable: **energy**

7 🔊 **Complete the sentences with *fewer* or *less*.**

0 Our grandparents had a lot …**less**… money when they were teenagers.
1 He took far ……………… photos with his old phone.
2 Your cat's getting fat. You should give it ……………… meals.
3 I eat ……………… meat now although I'm not a vegetarian.
4 She couldn't manage with ……………… help than she has now.
5 We have ……………… good ideas when we're tired.

8 🔊 **Write sentences with the prompts and *as … as*.**

0 There weren't / helpers / we wanted
   There weren't as many helpers as we wanted.
1 Tessa doesn't listen to / music / she did before
2 We don't have / time / we need
3 He didn't get / good exam results / his friend
4 Does Bill prepare / meals / his sister?
5 Have you visited / countries / I have?
6 Nobody donates / money / those philanthropists

9 🔊 **Choose the correct option.**

0 He gave a ………… money to his favourite charity last year.
   A most   B far more   C less   **D** lot more
1 Julie is a ………… generous than her neighbour.
   A few more   B bit less
   C most   D more
2 This question is ………… the most difficult to answer.
   A very   B by far   C a lot   D a bit
3 We need a ………… time to complete our project.
   A lot more   B most   C fewer   D least
4 Thank you, that was ………… delicious food I've ever tasted.
   A more   B the least   C most   D the most
5 Living here is a ………… interesting than we expected.
   A little   B little bit less
   C less   D little fewest
6 Giving presents is ………… satisfying than receiving them.
   A even more   B the most   C better   D by far

10 🔊 **Look at the chart. Decide if the sentences are true (T) or false (F). Correct the false ones.**

0 Oxfam spends far ~~less~~ money on development work than on making a change. **more** T ✓
1 The charity spends less on making a change than on getting donations. T F
2 They spend as much money on getting donations as on administration costs. T F
3 The cost of emergency response is higher than development work. T F

How Oxfam Spends Every Pound You Donate

Oxfam is an international charity that works to reduce poverty around the world.

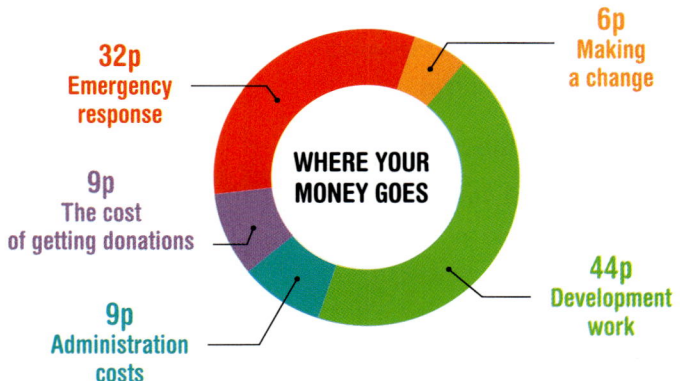

Unit 3   33

READING SKILLS

11 You are going to read an article about food miles in the UK. First look at the map. What do you think the main purpose of the article will be?

1. To describe different ways food is transported.
2. To explain how much energy food gives us.
3. To discuss the impact of transporting food for long distances.

12 [3.12] Read and listen to the text. What is the writer's point of view?

1. We should transport food fewer miles.
2. We should think more about how we transport food.
3. We should transport food more miles.

13 Complete these sentences.

1. Seasonal fruit travels large distances so that consumers can have more ....
2. Food produced in Europe sometimes goes to China where ....
3. Lorry trips are bad for the environment because they use more .... and cause more ....
4. Food produced in heated greenhouses might be less ....
5. Local food markets are popular because ....
6. Fewer food miles could have a bad effect on ....

14 Find the expressions underlined in the text with similar meanings to these expressions.

1. not the same types of weather ....
2. possibly better because of that ....
3. a surprising effect ....
4. during all the seasons ....
5. because it is clearly true ....
6. a lot more complicated ....
7. helping farmers who farm nearby ....
8. is not necessarily true ....
9. not so good for the world and its resources ....

15 Complete the summary.

More ⁰ *food miles* can damage the ¹........................, especially when ² .... are grown in one place, processed in another and ³........................ to where they are sold. However, locally produced food is not necessarily kinder to the environment, and not buying from ⁴........................ countries could be bad for them.

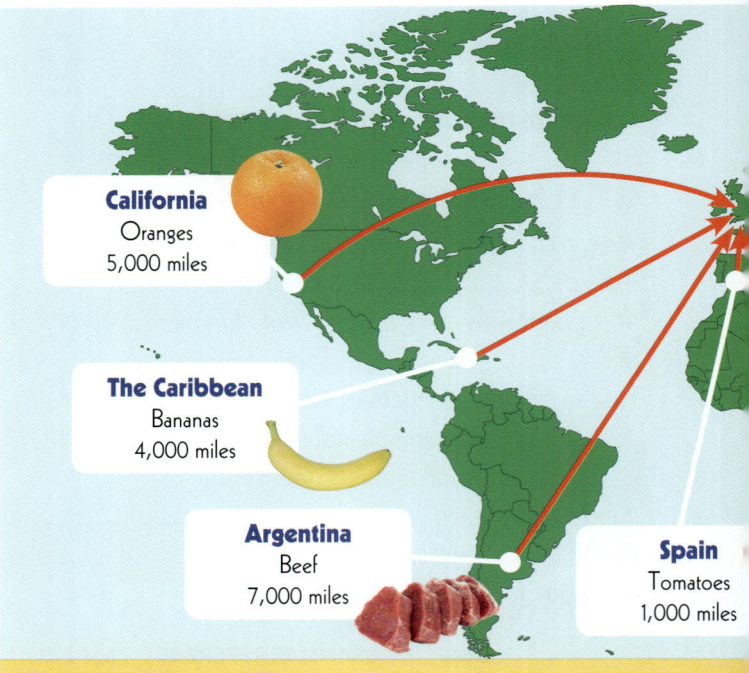

Food miles

FROM FARM GATE TO DINNER PLATE

The phrase *food miles* was first used in the 1990s as a way of describing how far food travels to reach dinner tables in the developed world. As food production becomes more globalised, it has become even easier to buy food out of season. Much of the
5 food eaten in Britain is grown in countries with <u>completely different climates</u>. For example, consumers in the UK can now choose to have seasonal fruit like strawberries <u>all year round</u>, even if it means transporting them thousands of miles. Much of the food which is produced in Europe goes by road to another
10 country for processing, before it is distributed to **retailers** and sold in supermarkets. Even worse are the products that are flown as far as China for processing before returning to Europe.

NOT SO SIMPLE?

As **awareness** of food miles increases, consumers might become even more worried about the impact on the environment, <u>and
15 with good reason</u>. Nearly one quarter of all the trips made by lorries in Britain are for food transportation. That uses a lot of fuel and causes **a great deal of** air pollution. However, the issue is <u>far more complex</u> than that. It may seem advisable to buy locally produced food, but this <u>is not always the case</u>.
20 British farmers can grow tomatoes, for instance, all through the seasons, but they do so in heated greenhouses. Therefore it could in fact be <u>less environmentally friendly</u> to have home-grown tomatoes than to transport them 1,000 miles from Spain.

VOCABULARY

WORLD RESOURCES

16 Match the words to make collocations.

0	d	fair	a	countries
1	☐	developing	b	gases
2	☐	vegetable	c	site
3	☐	farmers'	d	trade
4	☐	landfill	e	bank
5	☐	bottle	f	market
6	☐	greenhouse	g	patch

17 Complete the sentences with the correct collocation from exercise 16.

0 Katrina only buys bananas with the ......**fair trade**...... label.
1 Methane and carbon dioxide are examples of ....
2 Our local beekeeper sells his honey at the Saturday ....
3 If we use less packaging, our .... will have less rubbish.
4 Do you take all your glass to the .... for recycling?
5 My neighbour grows his own potatoes in a .... at the end of the garden.
6 It's important for farmers in .... to sell their produce to richer countries.

18 Read part of an article about recycling. Complete the missing words.

We all know that ⁰r..**ecycling**...... is important but local authorities in England are taking it a step further – now every home in England must recycle two types of ¹w........................... . Materials like food waste, paper, glass, metal and ²p........................... are easy to recycle and we must do everything we can to stop wasting these ³r........................... by sending them to ⁴l........................... waste centres. We now know that methane is a dangerous ⁵g........................... that is altering the world's climate, and ⁶r........................... that we burn at landfill sites creates more methane as well as polluting the air we breathe. It's easy to reduce waste and recycle.

New Zealand
Lamb
11,000 miles

Central Africa
Cocoa beans
3,000 miles

LOCAL ECONOMIES

Farmers' markets which sell fresh seasonal local food are more and more popular in Europe. This is a way of <u>supporting local producers</u> as well as cutting down food miles. You eat seasonal food which has not travelled far and <u>arguably tastes all the better for that</u>. However, this may have a negative impact elsewhere in the world. The local economy of developing countries may suffer badly as <u>an unexpected result</u>. The farmer in Kenya who grows green beans for export to Europe might not be able to survive if consumers in more developed countries no longer buy those beans.

GLOSSARY
retailers	➤ sellers
awareness	➤ knowledge, recognition
a great deal of	➤ a lot of

Unit 3   35

GRAMMAR PRACTICE

too many / too much, too few / too little, (not) enough + nouns

Complete the sentences with the words below.

enough ▪ little ▪ many ▪ much

Some people have too .... food, and some have too .... (food).
Too .... people waste food while others don't have ....

→ See **GRAMMAR REFERENCE** page 119

19 **Choose the correct option.**

0 Not everyone had a drink as there was too (little) / much juice left.
1 There's too much / many noise in here, please talk more quietly.
2 Too few / little people understand the problems of climate change.
3 We spent far too much / many money on electricity last year.
4 Tim couldn't park because there were too many / little other cars.

20 **Write the sentence endings using** *not enough* **and the words in brackets.**

0 She'd like to read more but she **doesn't have enough time.** (time)
1 He couldn't take a taxi because he … (money)
2 The corner shop closed down. It … (customers)
3 Can you use a cup, please? We … (glasses)
4 Your friends will have to sleep on the floor. There … (beds)
5 I can't give you the answer. I … (information)
6 They made too few sandwiches because there … (bread)

Comparative and superlative adverbs

Choose the correct option.

We can make *comparative / superlative* adverbs stronger with *much, a lot, far* or *even*, and we can make them *weaker / stronger* with *a little* or *a (little) bit*.
We can make superlative adverbs stronger by putting *by far / far* first.
We can use *(not) so* or *(not) as* + adverb + *as* instead of the *comparative / superlative* form.

→ See **GRAMMAR REFERENCE** page 119

21 **Complete the sentences with the correct adverb.**

0 Katie plays more .....**happily**..... with her friends than with her sisters. (*happy*)
1 The families can live more .... now that the fighting is over. (*safe*)
2 People are donating less .... because they don't have enough money. (*generous*)
3 My dad drives less .... than he did when he was a young man. (*dangerous*)
4 You'll have to answer more .... than that; it's best to tell the truth. (*honest*)
5 Visitors travelled less .... in the old-fashioned trains than in the new ones. (*comfortable*)
6 He shouted at me and spoke more .... than was really necessary. (*angry*)
7 The doctor was young but she advised us more .... than we expected. (*wise*)
8 Gordon did very well and graduated more .... than his teachers had predicted. (*successful*)

22 **Look at the diagram and complete the text with the words below.**

better ▪ less ▪ more ▪ most ▪ not as good as ▪ the best ▪ the least

HOW CAN WE BE MORE ENVIRONMENTALLY RESPONSIBLE?

The diagram shows different ways of treating waste. The top of the pyramid shows what ⁰....**most**.... people think is ¹.................... solution. The bottom of the pyramid shows ².................... popular option. It is clear that preventing waste is ³.................... than simply throwing away ⁴.................... rubbish. Energy recovery is ⁵.................... recycling or reuse, but it is ⁶.................... sustainable than disposal of waste, for example in landfill sites or in the ocean.

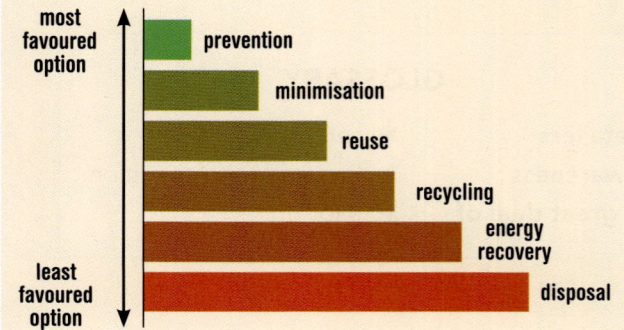

Unit 3

SPEAKING SKILLS

EXPRESSING AN OPINION

23 Write if the speakers are expressing (E) an opinion or if they are responding (R).

1 .... To be honest, I think there's too much waste.
2 .... I reckon we should donate more to that charity.
3 .... What I think is, you're never sure where your money goes.
4 .... Maybe you're right.
5 .... If you ask me, a sponsored swim would be best.
6 .... I don't think so.
7 .... In my opinion, Children in Need is a great organisation.
8 .... Well, not really.
9 .... You know what I mean.

24 Choose the two best responses to each statement.

1 You know what I mean.
   A I don't, really.   B I don't agree.
   C Yes, of course I understand.
2 In my opinion, it's a ridiculous idea.
   A Well, not really.   B I agree, it's brilliant.
   C Maybe you're right.
3 What about a fundraising swim for Water Aid?
   A Why not?   B No, I don't think so.
   C You know what I mean.
4 A sponsored silence is a bit boring if you ask me.
   A You could be right.   B I agree, walking isn't fun.
   C I disagree.
5 It's a really exciting campaign.
   A I don't think so.   B You know what I mean.
   C It's a waste of time if you ask me.

25 Put the words in the correct order.

1 interesting / opinion / had / idea / we / my / in / most / the
2 honest / I / be / really / to / don't / you / with / agree
3 I'm / maybe / sure / right / not / you're / but
4 families / sponsor / will / our / us / reckon / I
5 crazier / I / we / do / something / think / should
6 walking / boring / we / that / all / a / agree / bit / is
7 campaign / should / you / if / me / support / ask / the / we

LISTENING SKILLS

26 Look at the photo of Firooz. Can you guess what he does in his spare time? Give your reasons.

27 You're going to listen for specific information. Read the questions and underline the words that tell you what you should listen for.

1 In what year was the charity founded?
2 How many people volunteer for the charity now?
3 In what year did Istanbul&I become a registered charity?
4 How often do the Unaccompanied Minors meet?
5 How old are the boys that Firooz works with?
6 How many boys live in the centre where Firooz volunteers?
7 When did Firooz's project start?

28 [3.13] Listen to the report and answer the questions in exercise 27.

29 [3.13] Listen again and decide if the sentences are true (T) or false (F). Correct the false ones.

		T	F
1	Istanbul&I often works in collaboration with other charities	T	F
2	The charity only helps refugees.	T	F
3	The Unaccompanied Minors Project offers a range of activities.	T	F
4	All of the boys in the Unaccompanied Minors Project attend a local school.	T	F
5	The minors can stay in Istanbul after they turn 18.	T	F
6	Firooz finds he benefits more than the boys.	T	F

Unit 3   37

EXAM SKILLS

> **EXAM STRATEGY**
>
> **Reading and Use of English – Word formation**
>
> The prompt is the stem word and has other words related to it. Always read the surrounding sentence to decide which of the words best fits the gap. It could be a negative or plural form of the stem word, or there could be a suffix or prefix. The word may change completely, as in *wise / wisdom*.

30 Fill in the blanks. Then add any other related words you know.

	Adjective	Adverb	Noun
1	safe	safely	safety
2	comfortable	....	....
3	dangerous	....	....
4	generous	....	....
5	immediate	....	....
6	necessary	....	....
7	hopeful	....	....
8	successful	....	....
9	deep	....	....
10	strong	....	....
11	honest	....	....
12	angry	....	....
13	wise	....	....
14	(un)happy	....	....

31 Complete the sentences with the correct noun derived from the verbs below.

> approve ▪ collect ▪ explain ▪ perform ▪ punish ▪ refer ▪ ~~sing~~

0 Pavarotti was one of the most commercially successful ....**singers**...... of all time.
1 Violent crimes normally result in severe ...., including long prison sentences.
2 People are more likely to use Wikipedia than .... books these days.
3 The opera in Berlin was the most fabulous musical .... I've ever seen.
4 He didn't understand the teacher's .... and had to ask again.
5 The university library has a very fine .... of old manuscripts.
6 The new school regulations were unpopular and met with general ....

32 For questions 1–10, read the text below. Use the words given in capitals at the end of some of the lines to form a word that fits in the gap in the same line.

A SAD STORY

How do some people have the 0 ...**misfortune**... to end up with no home? **FORTUNE**

Norman is a 1 .... person sleeping on the streets in a city in the north of England. As a younger man he had 2 .... built up a business designing 3 .... websites for banks. However, his marriage was unhappy and his wife accused him of being 4 .... and selfish. Their 5 .... continued, leading sadly to separation and divorce.

HOME

SUCCESS
IMPRESS

RELY
ARGUE

Norman was at a big 6 .... because their flat belonged to his wife. Unfortunately for him, they did not find a fair 7 .... to this problem, and at this point, Norman's business failed too. He found himself 8 .... by his friends and was soon on the streets.

ADVANTAGE

SOLVE

ABANDON

It's an unhappy situation for Norman. He worries about his 9 .... and feels frightened a lot of the time. He can't see a way out of this terrible situation; although some people are generous towards him and he gets enough food to survive, he doesn't feel 10 .... about his future.

SAFE

HOPE

EXAM SKILLS

33 [3.14] Read the sentences and complete them as you listen to the recording.

0   Landfill waste creates ..*nearly half*.. of the UK's greenhouse gases.
1   Heated greenhouses are not as .... as you might think.
2   Shopping locally is .... the best way to buy fruit and vegetables.
3   They promised to .... of their Facebook shares.
4   Riches don't make ...., they only make him busier.
5   A group of volunteers .... a solution.
6   Supermarkets donate food that's close to its .... but is still good to eat.

34 [3.15] You will hear a classroom presentation about fundraising for charity. For questions 1–10 complete the sentences.

> **EXAM STRATEGY**
>
> **Listening – Sentence completion**
>
> Remember to read the text around the gaps so that you have an idea of what you are listening for. It may be a number, a single word or a short phrase of never more than three words. There is no need for you to rephrase because you will hear the exact words of the key information.

Tracey explained that ⁰ *Red Nose Day* is part of a larger charity called Comic Relief.
The celebrities who launched Comic Relief in 1985 were mostly ¹............................. .
Of course, they were all very funny performers. Tracey said they wanted to use laughter to raise awareness of the problems of ² .... and poverty.
The first Red Nose Day was in 1988, since when ³............................. has been raised.
Tracey's team had no doubts about where the money would be spent. They were ⁴............................. that anything they raised would go to make people's lives better.
She admitted that she and the other three members of her team could not agree about what would raise ⁵............................. . In the end, she did a sponsored run with Simon.

Not only did they raise £650 together: they also got ⁶............................., which had been their intention.
Tracey's friend Sally raised money by organising an open mic night at her ⁷............................., with the help of the owner of the bar.
They advertised the event by putting ⁸............................. all around town. Lots of friends and families went too and it was a big success.
Tracey was not at all surprised that Rashid wanted to do ⁹............................. . A sponsored silence seemed like a crazy idea because Rashid is so talkative, but he proved everybody wrong.
In the end, he was the top fundraiser, and raised a ¹⁰............................. for Comic Relief.

Unit 3   39

4 Our future

GRAMMAR PRACTICE

Future predictions: will v may / might

Complete the rules with the words below.
definitely (x2) ▪ may / might (not) ▪
probably / possibly ▪ will / won't

We use .... to express predictions when we are certain, and .... when we are uncertain. We can also use *will* .... or .... *won't* when we are certain and *will* .... when we are uncertain.

→ See GRAMMAR REFERENCE page 119

1 🔊 **Make sentences with *will* or *won't*.**

0   black-and-white photos / survive / longer
    Black-and-white photos will survive longer.
1   the weather / be / better tomorrow
2   Helena / not / take / many more photos
3   our local library / stay / open in the evening
4   that information / not / be / accessible next week
5   Gerry / study / hard for his exams
6   the teacher / be / pleased with those results

2 🔊 **Choose the correct option.**

0   'Might you study abroad one day?'
    A 'Yes, I won't.'   **(B)** 'No, probably not.'
1   'Will you ever listen to those old vinyl records?'
    A 'No, definitely.'   B 'Definitely not.'
2   'Will your visitors leave at the weekend?'
    A 'They won't possibly.'   B 'Possibly not.'
3   'Will you get a new smartphone next year?'
    A 'It's possible.'   B 'I'll might.'
4   'Will the beach be crowded this afternoon?'
    A 'It may be.'   B 'No, it will.'
5   'Won't you join the campaign to save the libraries?'
    A 'Yes, definitely.'   B 'I won't not.'
6   'Will she write a blog while she's travelling?'
    A 'No, she will.'   B 'Yes, she may.'
7   'Will Karen ever move abroad?'
    A 'She may be.'   B 'Definitely not.'

3 🔊 **Match the beginnings and ends of the sentences.**

0   [f] Younger people will always
1   [ ] I'll come
2   [ ] Sue says she'll
3   [ ] Your friends definitely
4   [ ] They'll probably
5   [ ] Those photos might
6   [ ] He may possibly regret

a   definitely save her favourite photos.
b   update their storage systems soon.
c   when I'm ready.
d   throwing away his vinyl records.
e   won't forget your birthday.
f   keep pace with technology.
g   survive best in a physical photo album.

4 🔊 **Add a sentence with *may* or *might*.**

0   I'm not sure if Ursula has returned from her holiday. she / still away   **She may still be away.**
1   Do you think the neighbours will invite us to their party? we / invitation
2   What's the weather forecast for this evening? it / …
3   Are there any vinyl shops in this town? we / …
4   It's not clear if the boys will join us. they / …
5   I can't say when the download will finish. it / …
6   I'm afraid the film will have a sad ending. you / …
7   I cannot find my phone. I / restaurant
8   Stella is still at work. she / late for dinner

Future perfect

Choose the correct option.

We use the *future simple* / *future perfect* to predict a future action or event.
We use the *future simple* / *future perfect* to say that an action or event will be finished before a time in the future.
We often use *by* + date or *in (ten years')* time with the *future simple* / *future perfect*.

→ See GRAMMAR REFERENCE page 120

GRAMMAR PRACTICE

5 Complete the table.

+	subject + **will have** + ¹.......................... Tomorrow's technology **will have** ².......................... (*forget*) today's information.
–	subject + **will not** (³..........................) **have** + past participle That way, whatever happens, you **won't have** ⁴.......................... (*lose*) them.
?	**will** + subject + ⁵.......................... + past participle In five or ten years' time, **will** our photos **have** ⁶.......................... (*disappear*)?

6 Complete with the future perfect of the verbs in brackets.

0 The boys *will have arrived* (*arrive*) by ten.
1 I .... (*become*) fluent in English in two years' time.
2 The programme .... (*not / start*) by the time we get home.
3 .... you .... (*finish*) your homework by supper time?
4 Celia's flight .... (*land*) by now.
5 .... she .... (*learn*) to drive by the time she's 18?
6 Technology .... (*not / solve*) all our problems in the next decade.
7 They .... (*finish*) building their house by the end of the summer.
8 Next month I .... (*live*) in Cambridge for two years.

7 Put the words in the correct order.

0 completed / studies / by / have / I / next / will / month / my
By next month I will have completed my studies.
1 friends / their / in / hour / they'll / met / an / have
2 test / 11 / this / have / we'll / by / o'clock / finished
3 have / two / lived / she / here / months / for / will
4 time / have / Craig / by / get / left / will / we / there / the
5 you / summer / by / started / next / have / college / will / ?
6 grandparents / together / been / June / will / 50 / in / have / for / years / my

8 Complete the email with the correct form of the verbs below.

be • eat • enjoy • feel • have • lose • ~~return~~ • see • take • write • walk

Hi Grace,
Sorry, I'm not free this weekend. My brother Max
⁰ *will* probably *return* home
on Friday, after a long walking holiday in India.
He ¹.......................... away since January.
He ².......................... a family meal because he
³.......................... (*not*) home cooking for ages.
He ⁴.......................... (*not*) his friends for months
although I expect he ⁵.......................... a blog.
He ⁶.......................... 500 kilometres by the time
he gets home, so he ⁷.......................... some weight.
He ⁸.......................... lots of photos and ⁹..........................
lots of stories to tell. ¹⁰.......................... he
.... ready to stay in one place now,
I wonder?
All the best, Josie

9 What will you have done in ten years' time? What won't you have done yet? Use the ideas in the picture or ideas of your own.

FRIENDSHIP MONEY TRAVELLING CAREER FAMILY HEALTH KIDS LOVE FITNESS HAPPINESS SUCCESS

Unit 4   41

READING SKILLS

10 In AD 45 Plutarch, a Greek historian, biographer and essayist, said this about teaching:

> *The mind is not a vessel*
> *to be filled,*
> *but a fire*
> *to be ignited.*
> Plutarch

Which of these opinions do you think is closest to what Plutarch believed?
1. Students learn best when they have acquired as much knowledge as possible.
2. The teacher's role is to stimulate in the students curiosity and love of learning.
3. The student's imagination is more important than any facts a teacher can convey.

11 Read the text. Was your answer to exercise 10 correct? Give your reasons.

12 [3.16] Read the text again. Choose the correct missing words. Now listen and check.

0	A not	(B) no	C much
1	A physically	B bodily	C there
2	A called	B so-called	C namely
3	A current	B now	C present
4	A proper	B probable	C properly
5	A accessed	B achieved	C available
6	A what	B how	C both
7	A memorise	B remember	C recall
8	A then	B after	C more
9	A clear	B truthful	C complete
10	A hardly	B harder	C hard

13 Answer these questions.
1. Who will be present in the virtual classroom of the future?
2. What will be the benefits of immediate feedback for the students?
3. Why will the role of the teacher have to change, according to the writer?
4. What does the writer think that role will be in the classroom of the future?
5. Do you think that teachers will be obsolete one day? Give your reasons.

Will teachers be obsolete one day?

In the view of many educationalists today, schools as we know them will ⁰….......... longer exist in the future. They will have been replaced by community centres open daily, 24 hours a day. Of course, computers will have become the essential element for an effective school of the future.

The *virtual classroom* will have been perfected. The subject teacher will not ¹….......... be present. Instead, there will be a technician-facilitator who **will ensure** that the technology works and that the class behaves. The expert will be a ²….......... *super-teacher*. This person will introduce and guide each lesson *via* a huge computer screen. There will be high-quality film of ³….......... events, produced professionally and updated regularly. The lessons will include relevant selections from authoritative TED Talks. There will be interactive games for students to play with other students around the world. And there will be a ⁴….......... assessment of students' work, scored and recorded online straight away.

Does this vision of a future classroom mean that teachers will one day be obsolete? So much more information will have become ⁵….......... online that the role of the teacher will have to change. Students in secondary schools today have vast amounts of data at their fingertips. This has already had an impact on ⁶….......... they acquire and share information.

For a start, it surely reduces the necessity to ⁷............ . Why commit to memory what you can access with a click of a mouse or a touch of a smartphone? The responsibility of school teachers will become less about imparting information and ⁸............ about helping students in their understanding, interpretation and application of that information.

However, it is not ⁹............ that high investment into technology improves results. Already, many governments have spent enormous sums of money on digital technologies for schools. Some countries which do not invest so much in fact perform better. A country like Singapore, renowned for its digital expertise, uses classroom technology judiciously. It is, after all, ¹⁰............ to imagine that a computer can teach dance, drama, art or even languages better than a living person.

Perhaps the answer is that we should continue to enjoy the linguistic and emotional diversity of the face-to-face classroom teacher, while at the same time **blending it** with the latest digital technology.

GLOSSARY

will ensure ➤ guarantees
blending it ➤ mixing it

VOCABULARY

TECHNOLOGY OF THE FUTURE

14 Complete the words.

0   The film *E.T.* was about a lovable a**lien**............ that landed on Earth.
1   By the year 2050, r.................... will have replaced humans in many workplaces.
2   Samantha Cristoforetti was the first female Italian a.................... to go into space.
3   Photos you post online will be out there somewhere in c.................... .
4   Astronomer Edwin Hubble proved there was more than one g.................... in outer space.
5   One day it will be possible for a d.................... to deliver your pizza.
6   The twins spoke to each other without words, by a kind of t.................... .

15 Match the words that go together.

0   *e* artificial   a   power
1   ☐   genetic   b   obsolescence
2   ☐   time   c   engineering
3   ☐   virtual   d   phone
4   ☐   solar   e   intelligence
5   ☐   smart   f   reality
6   ☐   digital   g   machine

16 Complete the sentences with the phrases from exercise 15.

0   All my friends use their **smartphones** to take and send photos.
1   Governments should encourage .... as a form of green energy.
2   The electronic *Domesday Book* is an example of ....
3   Perhaps by the next century, ... will have eradicated disease.
4   With these special .... glasses, you can imagine you're in a fantasy world.
5   If you had a ...., which year would you travel to?
6   Automated systems that use .... may be the answer to our future problems.

17 Now write your own sentences with the phrases from exercise 15.

Unit 4   43

GRAMMAR PRACTICE

Revision of future

Complete the rules.
We can use either the future simple or *be going to* to make .... We use the present continuous to talk about arrangements that are ....

➡ See **GRAMMAR REFERENCE** page 120

18 🔊 Complete with one of the verbs below in the present continuous.

> cook • come • fly • go • have • meet • run

0 We **'re meeting** our visitors at the station at 5 pm.
1 Amanda .... a party next weekend.
2 We .... in the London marathon next spring.
3 Paolo .... to my flat to watch TV later today.
4 They .... back to Prague airport on Friday.
5 He .... dinner for his family tonight.
6 My parents .... to Paris for their wedding anniversary.

19 🔊 Complete the news report with one word only.

Our local supermarket is ⁰ **going** to introduce a *walk out* system from next month. There ¹..................... be any assistants at the checkout; instead customers ²..................... use their smartphones. They ³..................... register their phones first, so the process will ⁴..................... very simple. This ⁵..................... possibly mean fewer jobs although the store manager insists that all her staff will still ⁶..................... a job, filling shelves and helping shoppers.

20 🔊 Match the beginnings and ends of the sentences.

0 [f] She is arriving
1 [ ] I feel tired
2 [ ] They're taking
3 [ ] His birthday will
4 [ ] Are you doing
5 [ ] How will they
6 [ ] She's going to

a make robots that can laugh?
b be on a Monday next year.
c so I'm going to lie down.
d anything nice at the weekend?
e visit her aunt in hospital.
f at Budapest station at ten.
g their visitors to the Space Centre.

Future continuous

Choose the correct option and complete the rule.
We use the *future simple* / *future continuous* to talk about a single action or event in the future. We use the *future simple* / *future continuous* to talk about a continuous action or event in the future.
The *future continuous* is formed like this: .... + *be* + ...

➡ See **GRAMMAR REFERENCE** page 121

21 🔊 Choose the correct option.

0 I expect the music festival .... a lot of fun.
  A it will be   B it's having   **C will be**
1 What .... for your birthday next week?
  A do you do   B will you have done
  C are you doing
2 It's soon .... possible to chat to robots.
  A going to be   B will be   C won't be
3 By this time tomorrow, we .... in the sea.
  A 'll swim   B 'll be swimming
  C have swim
4 Be careful when you lift that box. You .... your back.
  A 're hurting   B have hurt   C 'll hurt
5 They .... dinner by six.
  A won't have finished   B won't finishing
  C will finished
6 What .... in the States next year?
  A is studying Tim   B will Tim be studying
  C will Tim have study

22 🔊 Maria is writing to a friend about her fitness plan. Complete the email with the correct form of the verbs in brackets.

Hi Beatrice,
I'm planning to get fit this summer! Think of me on Monday morning when I ⁰ **'ll be running** (run) in the park. On Tuesday morning I ¹..................... (dance) but I ²..................... (not / do) anything after lunch because I ³..................... (rest). On Thursday morning I ⁴..................... (do yoga) and in the afternoon I ⁵..................... (swim). On Saturday I ⁶..................... (play tennis) before meeting you and in the afternoon we ⁷..................... (walk the dog) as usual. On Sunday morning I ⁸..................... (do yoga) again. Wednesday and Friday are my rest days – what do you think?
Love, Maria

44   Unit 4

SPEAKING SKILLS

DEBATING

23 Complete the dialogue with the words below.

> Take maths, for example ▪ No, really ▪
> When you think about it ▪ surely ▪
> Did you know ▪ Why bother

Aisha Do you think you'll be going directly to college after school, Brin?

Brin I doubt it. I'll have had enough of studying for a while. ¹........................, students who take time out of their education are more likely to find satisfying work in the end?

Aisha No, I didn't know that. But ²........................ it's better to continue studying when you're accustomed to it. ³........................ . You will have passed your prime as a mathematician by the time you're 20!

Brin I'm not planning to study maths! ⁴........................ ? Computers will soon be doing everything that mathematicians do, anyway.

Aisha I'm not sure. ⁵........................, the best years to study are when you're young. You can always travel later.

Brin ⁶........................, that's simply not true. Later on, you'll have a partner and kids. It's now or never for me!

24 Read more extracts from the dialogue in exercise 23. Write A if you think it's Aisha speaking, and B if it's Brin.

1 .... Surely, you're more likely to get a university place if you apply from school.
2 .... Universities will welcome students with more experience of the world.
3 .... You'll have more money to travel in comfort after you've been working for a while.
4 .... Why bother to wait? You'll make more friends in backpackers' hostels than in smart hotels.

25 Put the words in the correct order.

1 on / come / oh / !
2 the / not / that's / point
3 imagining / you're / it
4 do / you / say / why / that / ?
5 very / doubt / I / it / much

LISTENING SKILLS

26 [3.17] Listen to some facts about road traffic and complete the details.

1 In ...., there was serious traffic congestion on a motorway near ....
2 The queue of vehicles was .... long and drivers were stuck in it for ....
3 Even worse traffic congestion – .... of immobile vehicles – happened in ....
4 The congestion between .... and Lyon took place on ....
5 By the year ...., commercial transport will have increased by around .... compared to ....
6 Passenger traffic is predicted to have grown by ....

27 Look at the image. What is special about this car? Do you think cars like these might one day improve traffic congestion?

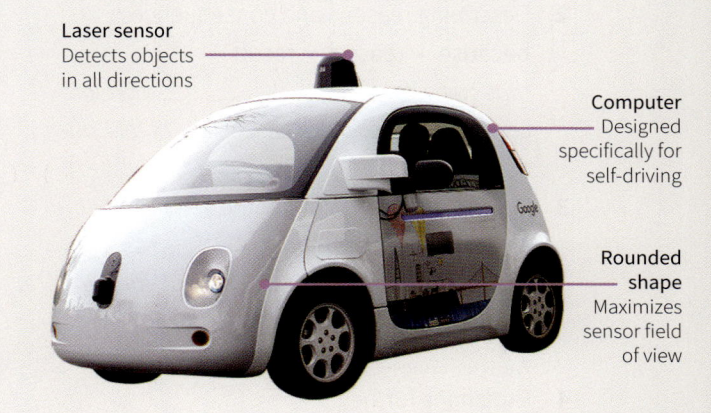

Laser sensor
Detects objects in all directions

Computer
Designed specifically for self-driving

Rounded shape
Maximizes sensor field of view

28 [3.18] Listen to a transport correspondent talking about the future of cars. Were your answers to the questions in exercise 27 correct? Why / Why not?

29 [3.18] Listen again. Complete the notes.

1 2016 estimate – car accidents killed more than ...., over .... injured.
2 With self-driving cars, car-sharing efficient – ....% fewer cars.
3 That means less ...., less .... and fewer ....
4 October 2016, Google recorded over .... miles of driverless travel using .... driverless vehicles – no accidents.

Unit 4   45

ACADEMIC SKILLS

PREPARING A SPEECH FOR A DEBATE

30 Put the advice on debating strategy in the correct order.

a ☐ End with a memorable conclusion that reflects your introduction.
b ☐ Start with a strong introduction which makes your position clear.
c ☐ Connect your points with linkers like *furthermore* or *on the other hand* to give emphasis.
d ☒ 1 Present your opinions. Remember they don't have to be your real opinions.
e ☐ Note down your points before the debate and decide which order to make them.

31 Fill in the words for each stage of the debate.

1 Beginning the presentation:
  all • statement • support
  first of ⁰ ......all........, *let me begin by saying,*
  I'd like to say I ¹ .... / *am against this* ² .... *because*

2 Describing reasons and consequences:
  because • reason • result
  that's why, for this ³ ...., *therefore, consequently, so,* ⁴ .... *of this, due to, as a* ⁵ ....

3 Making another point (on the same side):
  addition • more • only
  moreover, not ⁶ .... *that, furthermore, what's* ⁷ ...., *that's not all, in* ⁸ ....

4 Explaining further:
  example • explain • mean
  let me ⁹ .... / *give you an* ¹⁰ ...., *in other words, what I* ¹¹ .... *is this*

5 Contrasting the opposing view:
  contrary • contrast • other
  however, although, on the ¹² .... *hand, in* ¹³ ...., *whereas, on the* ¹⁴ ....

6 Emphasising:
  fact • forget
  actually, don't ¹⁵ ...., *certainly, in* ¹⁶ ...., *definitely*

7 Concluding:
  conclude • conclusion
  so, finally, as a ¹⁷ ...., *I just want to* ¹⁸ .... *by saying*

32 Look at the photo and the statement. This is the topic for debate. Add some ideas for or against.

Should babies and very small children have smartphones or tablets?

For
- Next generation will need technology more than ever
- Babies and very small children already access technology
- Entertaining and educational – interaction can be mentally stimulating

Against
- Antisocial, isolating
- Children will lose the ability to communicate by speech
- Children will learn to type not write
- Long-term effects not known

33 Write an opening paragraph, both for and against the statement. Use some expressions from exercise 31 to link your ideas.

34 Choose one of the debate topics below, or think of one of your own. Make notes for and against.

- Technology gives you information not knowledge.
- Computers will make books obsolete by 2050.
- AI will soon replace teachers and doctors.
- Mobile apps are better learning tools than books.
- Students should be allowed to have phones in school.

EXAM SKILLS

> **EXAM STRATEGY**
>
> **Reading and Use of English – Keyword transformation**
>
> For this part of the exam you need to practise paraphrasing, that is, writing sentences in another way. Make sure that the sentence you write means the same as the sentence you are given. The answer must be two, three, four or five words: not more. The keyword must remain exactly the same.

35 Underline the phrasal verbs in the sentences.

- 0 We'll <u>set up</u> a new programme for the New Year.
- 1 Never put off until tomorrow what you can do today.
- 2 He turned down her invitation as he was busy that night.
- 3 Did you ever find out the truth?
- 4 We'll go over that information after the meeting.
- 5 If I were you, I'd leave out that last paragraph.

36 Paraphrase the sentences in exercise 35. Use the verbs below.

> discover • ~~establish~~ • omit
> postpone • refused • review

- 0 We'll *establish* a new programme for the New Year.

37 Rewrite the sentences so that the second sentence means the same as the first. Use the words in brackets but you must not change them. Write between two and five words.

- 0 Paul is eager to see his Australian cousins again next month. (*looking*)
  Paul is *looking forward to seeing* his Australian cousins again next month.
- 1 There was enough food, fortunately. (*run*)
  We ...., fortunately.
- 2 We found the article on driverless cars really interesting. (*interested*)
  We .... the article on driverless cars.
- 3 I haven't seen my cousins for over a year. (*since*)
  It's over a year .... my cousins.
- 4 'I'm sorry I didn't reply to the last email,' said Janek. (*apologised*)
  Janek .... to the last email.
- 5 The girls will go ice-skating unless it snows. (*if*)
  ...., the girls will go ice-skating.

> **EXAM STRATEGY**
>
> **Writing – An essay**
>
> A successful essay will address the points made in the notes given. You will also be expected to add a point of your own, as well as a conclusion. Discuss advantages and disadvantages, give your opinion and support it with reasons and examples.

38 Look at the question and notes. Read the essay a student wrote. Find and correct 12 mistakes. The first one has been found for you.

> **In your English class you have discussed teenagers' place in society. Write an essay on this topic.**
> **Teenagers do not have an important place in society. Do you agree?**
> **Notes.** Write about:
> 1. technology
> 2. the environment
> 3. (your own ideas)
>
>   *teenagers*
> In my opinion ~~teenagers'~~ have a very important place in society. They know a lot about computers and technology because teenagers are grown up with this. I often give advices to my grandparents who don't know nothing about technology. My granny thinks her phone doesn't works but it's not charged! Also I believe teenagers are more concerning about the environment. It is there future and that is why the teenagers work hard for make better the environment. We are used to recycle our waste, for example. Teenagers know they must teach their children saving the planet.
> In conclusion, I think society needs listen to teenagers because they are tomorrow's adults.

39 You have had a class discussion about alternative types of education. You now have to write an essay using all the notes and giving your point of view.

> Which are the most important subjects to study at school and why?
> Notes. Write about:
> 1 academic subjects
> 2 artistic activities
> 3 (your own ideas)

Unit 4   47

REVISE AND ROUND UP

1 🔊 **Correct the mistakes.**

0 That was the ~~sadest~~ film I've ever seen. **saddest**
1 My best friend has three brothers but he's the older.
2 Her fifteenth birthday was the happyest day of her life.
3 The new comedian told the worse jokes we've ever heard.
4 Gemma is much more prettier than her big sister.
5 This is the less interesting part of the entire lesson.
6 Please be a bit more quicker, it's time to go.
7 His singing is by far better than mine.
8 The end of the story wasn't as shocking than I expected.

2 🔊 **Put the words in the correct order.**

0 Tanya / sister / everyone / thinks / than / little / her / cleverer / a / is
   Everyone thinks Tanya is a little cleverer than her sister.
1 less / yours / interesting / far / my / than / project / was
2 should / you / a / quicker / you / win / to / want / if / bit / be
3 we've / dangerous / more / route / the / chosen / much / is
4 the / the / they / students / class / in / are / reliable / most
5 ours / less / much / families / those / than / fortunate / are
6 had / these / most / pets / we've / are / far / dogs / by / the / energetic

3 🔊 **Write sentences using not as … as and an adjective below.**

cold ▪ complicated ▪ difficult ▪ expensive ▪ funny ▪ rich ▪ ~~sad~~

0 She's happier now than she was a year ago.
   She isn't / 's not as sad as she was a year ago.
1 My solution to this problem is simpler than yours.
2 It's warmer than it was last night.
3 His second book is more serious than his first.
4 Developing countries are poorer than developed countries.
5 Locally grown beans are cheaper than beans from Kenya.
6 This exercise is easier than the next one.

4 🔊 **Choose the correct option.**

0 We had .... fun when we lived in a big city.
   A fewer   B too less   **C much more**
1 Do modern cars really cause .... pollution?
   A a lot less   B not enough   C the less
2 There .... philanthropists in the world.
   A are too little   B aren't enough   C are most
3 The last article was .... interesting to read.
   A by far   B a little bit   C the least
4 Slow down! That's .... information.
   A much   B too much   C too many
5 The government gives .... help to the homeless.
   A too little   B many   C a little much
6 His donation was .... generous.
   A a lot better   B even the most   C by far the most

5 🔊 **Complete the sentences with the most / the least and the adverb form of the adjective in brackets.**

0 Ned and Jane don't walk fast but Hans walks **the most slowly**. (slow).
1 They all sing well except Julia: she sings .... (beautiful).
2 All the students eat their lunch fast but Jon's different. He eats .... (quick).
3 'Who visits Bella .... (regular)?'
   'Oh, her son – he goes to see her every week.'
4 Of all the boys in the class, Peter paints .... (careful). His work is a mess.
5 She knows three languages but speaks English .... (fluent) because her dad's American.
6 The last maths problem was the most difficult so we solved it .... (easy).

6 🔊 **Make sentences with the future perfect tense.**

0 tomorrow's technology / forget / today's information
   Tomorrow's technology will have forgotten today's information.
1 in five years' time / our photos / disappear
2 your train / leave / by now
3 I / not / finish my homework / by seven
4 next April / we / live here for a year
5 my colleague Peter / arrive / at the office / by 8
6 by the end of her stay / Kath / visit all the museums in London!

48   Units 3–4

7 🔊 **Choose the correct tense: future simple, *be going to* or present continuous?**

0 Please, come to the club with us; it *'ll be* / *'s being* fun.
1 I can't stop now, sorry. My train *will leave* / *is leaving*.
2 She *'s meeting* / *'s going to meet* her friend at seven.
3 When *are they flying* / *will they fly* to Dubai?
4 They *probably won't see* / *'re probably not going to see* the film.
5 That box looks heavy; Oscar *is helping* / *will help* you carry it.
6 It's snowing so I *'ll put on* / *'m going to put on* my boots.
7 *Will you* / *Are you going to* open the door, please? Someone just rang the bell.
8 *Are you doing* / *Will you do* anything after school today?

8 🔊 **Write answers to the questions using the future continuous and the words in brackets.**

0 What will you be doing, five years from now? (*run my own business*)
Five years from now I'll be running my own business.
1 How much will you be earning? (*a lot of money*)
2 Where will you and your future partner be living? (*in a luxury flat*)
3 What will you be driving? (*a powerful sports car*)
4 What will you be doing every winter? (*ski in the Alps*)
5 Who will be joining you? (*our influential friends*)
6 Will you be regretting anything? (*anything at all*)

9 🔊 **Correct the mistakes.**

0 Health is far ~~important~~ than wealth, in my opinion.
more important
1 You need to work more hard to raise money for charity.
2 That information probably is not accessible in ten years.
3 By 2050, commercial transport will double.
4 They will have remembered the meeting, so please remind them.
5 Julia will have fun with her friends on the beach by now.

CONCEPT CHECK

Read the sentences and answer the questions.

1 *Olivia is a little better at maths than her brother Berto.*

(Answer Yes / No / Maybe)
0 Does Olivia have a brother? **Yes**
1 Is Olivia very good at maths?
2 Is Berto as good at maths as his sister?
3 Is Olivia more expert at maths than her brother?
4 Is Olivia much more expert at maths than Berto?
5 Is Berto a bit less competent at maths than Olivia?

2 *Paul's meeting James outside the cinema at six.*

(Answer True / False)
0 Paul and James have arranged to meet. **True**
1 Their meeting place and time are both fixed.
2 Their meeting place is outside the cinema.
3 Their meeting time is six o'clock.
4 It isn't six o'clock yet.
5 Their arrangement is for the future.

3 *They will have forgotten these songs by the time they're 20.*

(Answer True / False / Don't know)
0 They are listening to some songs now.
Don't know
1 They are under 20 years of age.
2 They haven't forgotten the songs yet.
3 They remember the songs now.
4 Their memory of the songs will not last.
5 At some time in the future, they won't remember the songs.

4 *The band will be playing when the President arrives.*

(Answer True / False / Not sure)
0 The President is going to arrive at some point in the future. **True**
1 The President regularly comes to this place.
2 The President hasn't arrived yet.
3 The band is playing now.
4 The President will arrive before the band starts playing.
5 The band will start playing before the President's arrival.

➡ See **GRAMMAR REFERENCE** pages 118–121

5 Law and order

GRAMMAR PRACTICE

Defining relative clauses

Complete the rules with the words below.

clause ▪ object ▪ pronoun ▪ subject

A defining relative ……………… gives us information that is vital to the sentence.
If the relative ……………… (*who*, *that* or *which*) is the ……………… of a defining relative clause, we can leave it out. We can't leave it out if it's the ……………… .

➔ See **GRAMMAR REFERENCE** page 121

1 Choose the correct option.

0 They caught the prisoner *(that)* / *which* tried to escape.
1 He couldn't swim in the sea *who* / *which* was very cold.
2 The girls went to the sauna *who* / *which* opened last week.
3 He spoke to the guards *who* / *which* were very helpful.
4 They approved of the system *who* / *which* seemed highly successful.
5 Petra is a student *who* / *which* rarely fails an exam.
6 The scheme had lots of critics *that* / *which* made their voices heard.

2 Complete the sentences with *whose* or *who*.

0 She is definitely someone ……*whose*…… opinion I value.
1 At the pool, we spotted our teacher ……………… fortunately didn't see us.
2 I was happy to get a letter from a friend ……………… address I had lost.
3 They met a very interesting man ……………… sister is a famous film star.
4 Are you the people ……………… dog is missing?
5 Those are the guards ……………… make sure the gates are locked.
6 The police officers are all people ……………… have received a good education.
7 I've just read an article about a doctor ……………… stole money from old ladies.
8 Have you ever met anyone ……………… works as a private detective?

3 Underline the relative pronouns in the sentences. Write if they are necessary (N) or unnecessary (U).

0 ……U…… The woman **that** we met in the café was my aunt.
1 ………… I'll never forget the book which I read last summer.
2 ………… The reason that he's in prison is because he's a criminal.
3 ………… Do you know the boy who is talking to the headteacher?
4 ………… The people whose house we rented were not very friendly.
5 ………… Let's meet at the place where we met last time.
6 ………… This is the sweater that I bought in the sales.

4 Complete the definitions with the words below.

confidence trickster ▪ hacker ▪ kidnapper ▪ murderer ▪ pickpocket ▪ shoplifter ▪ whistle-blower

0 A ……*murderer*…… is a man or woman who has killed someone.
1 A ……………… is someone who steals something from your bag or your pocket.
2 It was a ……………… that sold me a fake Armani watch.
3 The ……………… who held the man hostage for five days went to prison today.
4 Most big stores have a detective who watches out for a potential ……………… .
5 I'm furious with the ……………… who got into my laptop and deleted all my emails.
6 The documentary about the ……………… who leaked celebrity secrets to the press was fascinating.

5 Choose the correct option.

0 The actor ………… starred in *The Great Escape* was Steve McQueen.
   A who
   B when
   C which

50 Unit 5

GRAMMAR PRACTICE

1. The afternoon .... we met down by the river was in April.
   A when B where C which
2. I'm sure I recognise the waiter .... brought us our coffee.
   A whose B when C who
3. She invited us to a Chinese restaurant .... she'd booked a table.
   A which B whose C where
4. Those are the people .... son plays in the school band.
   A who B that C whose
5. The prison goes very quiet at night .... the prisoners are sleeping.
   A where B when C who

Non-defining relative clauses

Choose the correct option.
A non-defining relative clause gives us *extra information / the most important part of the sentence*.
You could remove a non-defining relative clause and the *extra information / most important part of the sentence* would still be there.

→ See **GRAMMAR REFERENCE** page 121

6. Make one sentence with a non-defining relative clause. Join the sentences with *who* or *which*.

   0. Some of the prisoners were there for life. They are mostly under 20.
      Some of the prisoners, who are mostly under 20, were there for life.
   1. The girls over there are from a British school. They are all wearing uniforms.
   2. The winning team will play in the final. Harry supports this team.
   3. Our new flat has the most amazing views. It is on the top floor.
   4. The Tower of London was once a terrible prison. It is on the River Thames.
   5. The students visited the Police Academy Open Day. They all wanted to become police officers.
   6. The prison guard was the least popular person there. She shouted all the time.
   7. The men were arrested yesterday. They had robbed several banks.
   8. I bought a T-shirt for Judy's birthday. The T-shirt was on sale.

7. Do the quiz. Match the parts and write non-defining relative clauses.

   - Nelson Mandela
   - The Berlin Wall
   - Robin Hood
   - Mahatma Gandhi
   - Marshalsea Prison
   - The Colosseum
   - J. F. Kennedy

   - His story is legendary.
   - He died from a gunshot in Dallas, Texas, in 1963.
   - He spent 27 years in prison.
   - He was a pacifist.
   - It was built in 1961.
   - Roman gladiators fought there.
   - Charles Dickens wrote about it.

   - He was President of the United States.
   - He died when someone shot him in New Delhi, India, in 1948.
   - It came down in 1989.
   - He stole from the rich and gave to the poor.
   - It was a terrible place for prisoners in nineteenth-century London.
   - He became President of South Africa.
   - It is still a major tourist attraction today.

   Nelson Mandela, who spent 27 years in prison, became President of South Africa.

8. Complete the text with the correct words.

   Great fictional detectives
   Miss Marple is a sweet little old woman ⁰....**who**.... is also an amateur detective. Her pretty home is in a charming English village ¹............ an unusual number of murders happen. Miss Marple, ²............ is a much-loved Agatha Christie character, is perhaps not as interesting as the writer herself, ³............ life story has an unsolved mystery. Christie, ⁴............ loved to travel, made news in 1926 ⁵............ she disappeared for ten days. Real detectives never discovered ⁶............ she had been. Was this simply a publicity campaign by ⁷............ she hoped to increase her book sales? Or did she hope Mr Christie, ⁸............ was innocent of any violence, would be accused of her murder?

Unit 5 51

READING SKILLS

9 Look at the picture and read the first paragraph of the text. Do you think the story is true?

10 Put paragraphs A–D into the correct sequence of events by writing 1–4 in the boxes.

11 Read the final paragraph. Was your answer to exercise 9 correct? How do you know?

12 [3.19] Read and listen to the whole text. Then answer the questions.

1. How did the Australian authorities treat immigrants from Ireland?
2. What was remarkable about the petition signed to save Ned Kelly?
3. What were the first four crimes that they accused him of as a teenager?
4. Was he innocent or guilty of those crimes?
5. Who assaulted Ned's sister Kate?
6. How did the Kelly brothers get money to make their famous armour?
7. What crime did the gang plan in Glenrowan?
8. What was the result of the Kelly gang's last gunfight?

13 Find words in the text that have similar meanings to the following.

1. courage: ....
2. ordinary: ....
3. forgiveness: ....
4. physical attack: ....
5. stole money from: ....
6. myth: ....

14 Make your choices and complete these sentences.

1. In my opinion, it was fair / unfair that they hanged Ned Kelly because ....
   ....
   ....
   ....
2. I think Ned Kelly became a legend because ....
   ....
   ....
   ....
3. I would / wouldn't like to see or read more about him because ....
   ....
   ....
   ....

The legendary Ned Kelly, who is probably Australia's best-known gangster, has a remarkable story.

Today, his name is synonymous with valour, determination and independence.

A In June 1880, the Kelly gang were in a place called Glenrowan, where they planned to hijack a special police train. In a terrible gunfight, which lasted nearly ten hours, three of the gang members died, and Ned, badly hurt, was unable to escape. He was still only 25 years old. The police took him to Melbourne, where they sentenced him to death. On 11 November 1880, they hanged Ned Kelly, who immediately became the Australian legend he is today.

B Ned was still only 19 when he left prison, a more cynical man. It wasn't long before Ned and many of his relatives and friends were in trouble with the law again. In April 1878, when Ned was 23, a policeman came to Kellys' home, where he assaulted his young sister, Kate. In the gunfight that followed, the policeman died. The Kelly brothers went on the run, robbed two banks and used the money to make the armour which their gang became famous for.

His short and violent life has inspired hundreds of plays, songs and books as well as several films, including one in 1970, with Mick Jagger as Ned, and another in 2003, starring Heath Ledger.

VOCABULARY

CRIME AND THE JUSTICE SYSTEM

15 Complete the sentences with the words below. Then write four sentences of your own with words you didn't use.

> charge ▪ arrest ▪ witness ▪ murderer ▪ investigate ▪ suspect ▪ court ▪ release ▪ defendant ▪ ~~evidence~~

0 The crime scene investigators found ....*evidence*.... which they could use in court.
1 The police have the man in a cell and will .... him with assault soon.
2 It was when he was walking his dog that the .... saw what happened.
3 We read that the .... had tried to escape after killing the man.
4 The .... started to cry when the judge passed a life sentence.
5 The detective questioned the .... for hours before they let her leave.

16 David has visited a criminal court as part of a school project. Complete his report with the words below in the correct forms.

> accuse ▪ charge ▪ defendant ▪ guilty ▪ innocent ▪ judge ▪ jury ▪ lawyer ▪ legal ▪ offence ▪ prosecute ▪ sentence ▪ suspect ▪ swear ▪ ~~trial~~

This was my first time inside a court of law. The person on ⁰....*trial*.... was a homeless man in his forties. They ¹........................ him with vagrancy, which surprised me. I didn't know that the homeless were committing an ²........................ by sleeping on the street. They ³........................ him of stealing money, too. The police also ⁴........................ that he was a drug dealer, but for some ⁵........................ reason they were unable to ⁶........................ him for that. His ⁷........................ was a tall, serious woman who of course wanted to prove he was ⁸........................ of any crime. There was a ⁹........................, who sat at the front, but no ¹⁰........................ . The ¹¹........................, whose name was Brian, had to ¹²........................ an oath before the trial began. The judge hasn't passed ¹³........................ yet but I really hope that they will find the man not ¹⁴........................ .

C So who was Ned Kelly? Behind his famous **suit of armour**, he was a common criminal. He was a hero to Irish immigrants who were habitually discriminated against by the authorities. He had little education, but the letters he wrote were romantic and passionate. He was an outlaw with a price on his head, alive or dead. Yet when they sentenced him to death, more than 30,000 people signed a petition in which they begged for his pardon.

D In 1870, at the age of 15, Ned was in court for attacking a man, after which there was a second charge for robbery. They found him not guilty in both cases, but before long they sentenced him to six months' hard labour for **assault**. He had only been home three weeks when the police arrested Ned again, for receiving a stolen horse. This led to another prison sentence.

GLOSSARY

hijack	► take control of, often with violence
on the run	► escaping
suit of armour	► protective suit made of metal
assault	► physical attack

Unit 5   53

GRAMMAR PRACTICE

Articles: a / an, the, no article

Choose the correct option and then complete the rules.

1 We use *the / a / no article*:
- to mention something for the first time, or if we have no details.
- to talk about jobs.
- to describe something.

2 We use *the / a / no article*:
- to talk about something we've mentioned before.
- to talk about something we already know about.
- to talk about something unique, or to talk about superlatives.

3 We also use *the / a / no article*:
- in certain expressions: .... *police*, ... *theatre*, ... *twenty-first century*.
- with seas, rivers and mountain ranges and some mountains.
- with unions of countries or plurals.

4 We use *the / a / no article*:
- with the names of most mountains and lakes.
- before most countries.
- with generic expressions: *in* .... *hospital /* .... *prison / jail / court, on* .... *trial, at* .... *school / work / university*.

➡ See **GRAMMAR REFERENCE** page 121

17 🔊 Complete the sentences with *a / an* or –.

0 It was ...**an**... incredible story that Stephen told us.
1 I've just read .... very interesting book about Agatha Christie.
2 She was looking forward to having .... dinner with them.
3 The boys were at .... school when it began to snow.
4 He's .... maths teacher at my secondary school.
5 We'd love to have .... dog but my mum's allergic to animals.
6 Our new neighbours cycle to .... work on their tandem.
7 My parents would love to buy a house on .... lake in Canada.
8 Mr Grant was accused of sabotage and sent to .... court.

18 🔊 Complete the mini dialogues. Do you need *a / an, the* or – ?

0 A Tom was cycling when he was hit by ...**a**... car.
  B Really? That's terrible. Who was driving ...**the**... car?
1 A A girl I met on holiday stayed in .... B&B in .... town in .... Scotland.
  B What was .... B&B like?
  A .... girl said it was .... best she'd ever been in.
2 A The train leaves from Euston. Let's take .... taxi to .... station.
  B Shall I order .... taxi right now? What time's .... train?
3 A It's been .... miserable day. .... sky's getting dark already.
  B I think there's going to be .... storm.
  A Well, I hope it's not as bad as .... storm we had last week.
4 A I've got .... problem with my printer.
  B Call their helpline. They're .... experts.
  A Well, ... problem is .... printer's from .... States.
5 A I was in .... bed last night when I heard .... phone ringing somewhere.
  B Was it your smartphone or .... landline?
  A Neither. It was on .... TV programme! I'd forgotten to switch it off!

19 🔊 Complete the newspaper article with *a / an* or *the*.

A FOOLISH BANK ROBBER

0 ...**A**... man wanted to rob [1] .... main bank in [2] .... town where he was living. He ran into [3] .... bank and gave [4] .... note to one of [5] .... bank clerks. This poor woman read [6] .... note which said she had to give [7] .... man all [8] .... money in their safe. She did what he asked because she thought he might have [9] .... gun. [10] .... man took [11] .... money and departed in [12] .... hurry, leaving [13] .... note with [14] .... woman. However, [15] .... police caught him [16] .... very same day. [17] .... silly man had written [18] .... note on [19] .... back of [20] .... envelope. And on [21] .... other side of [22] .... envelope was his name and address.

54 Unit 5

SPEAKING SKILLS

GIVING ADVICE AND WARNINGS

20 Tick (✓) the correct column for each of the expressions.

	giving advice	responding to / asking for advice
1 What do you think I should do?	☐	☐
2 I (don't) think you should …	☐	☐
3 Do you think that's OK?	☐	☐
4 OK, I'll follow your advice.	☐	☐
5 That's what I'd do.	☐	☐
6 If I were you, I'd …	☐	☐
7 That's a good idea.	☐	☐
8 Yes, I suppose that's a good plan.	☐	☐
9 The best thing to do is …	☐	☐
10 It's a good idea to …	☐	☐
11 Do you think I should … ?	☐	☐

21 Use expressions from exercise 20 to complete the dialogue.

Andy You're looking worried, Tess. What's the problem?

Tess I'm in a dilemma. I was in a shop with my sister yesterday when I saw her shoplifting. ¹……………… ? ²……………… tell our parents or the police?

Andy ³……………… tell anyone else yet. You have no proof and she'd be in big trouble. ⁴……………… speak to her about it first.

Tess ⁵………………? Because she might get embarrassed.

Andy Of course ⁶……………… speak to her. Shoplifting is a criminal offence. And it'd be much worse for her if she gets caught. ⁷………………, anyway.

Tess OK, ⁸……………… . Thanks, Andy.

Andy ⁹……………… to talk to her quietly, in private – just a gentle warning.

Tess ¹⁰……………… . I'll do it tonight, when we're alone.

Andy ¹¹……………… . Good luck.

LISTENING SKILLS

22 Answer the questions.

Rita Hayworth and Shawshank Redemption is a novella by American writer Stephen King. It was adapted for the screen in 1992 as *The Shawshank Redemption*.
1 Do you know the story?
2 What can you guess from the title?

23 [3.20] Listen to Ben, Grace and Lisa having a conversation. What are they talking about?
1 Crimes they have read about.
2 Fictional crime.
3 Crime movies.

24 [3.20] Listen again. Decide if the sentences are true (T) or false (F). Correct the false ones.

1 Grace thinks that *The Shawshank Redemption* is a sensitive movie. ☐T ☐F
2 Ben has a low opinion of Morgan Freeman as an actor. ☐T ☐F
3 Lisa finds movies about prison escapes very credible. ☐T ☐F
4 Grace respects Lisa's knowledge of police procedural dramas. ☐T ☐F
5 Lisa prefers reading crime stories to watching them. ☐T ☐F
6 Ben finds a character called Rebus interesting because he's American. ☐T ☐F

25 [3.20] Listen again. Choose the correct option.
1 Grace was a little *surprised / amused* by her own reaction to *The Shawshank Redemption*.
2 Lisa's tone when talking about prison escape movies is *cynical / bitter*.
3 Ben's attitude to the other speakers is *supportive / sarcastic*.
4 The tone of the conversation generally is *hostile / friendly*.

26 Do you like crime novels or TV dramas about crime? Why / Why not?

Unit 5

EXAM SKILLS

27 Read the text.

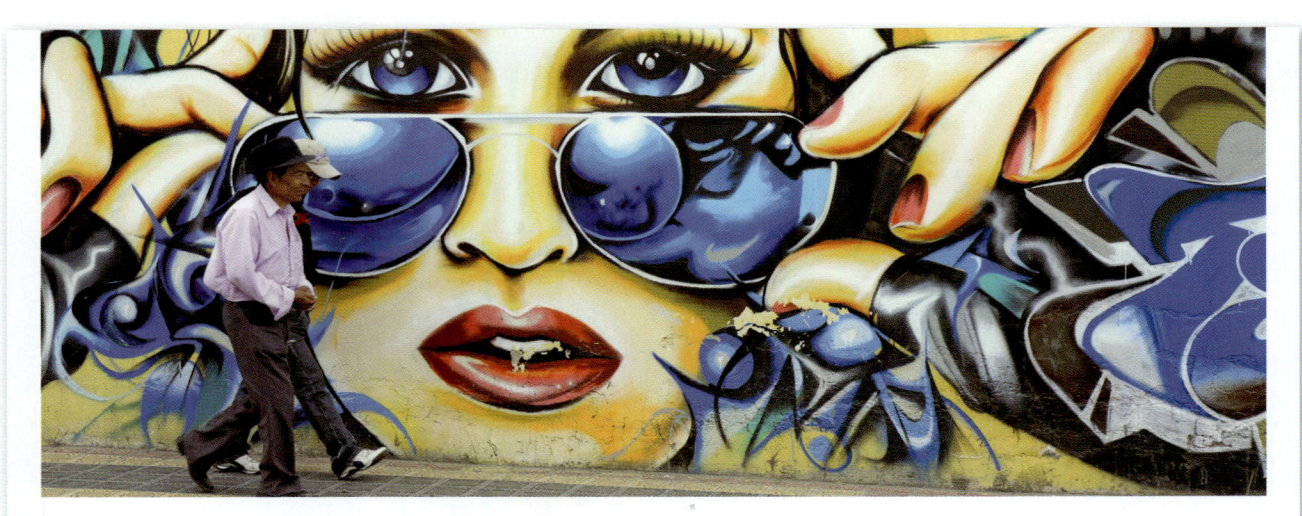

Caroline never thought, when she studied Art at college, that she would become an expert witness in criminal courts. Years of working in art galleries and museums had given her a certain fame in the art world, and her evidence in the celebrated Rothko fake case made her name in the world of prosecutors and judges too. This had led, bizarrely, to the place where Caroline now found herself. She stood for a moment in front of the tall grey fences of Wirral prison for women offenders. Her normal professional confidence had left her and she shivered in the icy wind. 'Why did I agree to come here?' she asked herself.

A severe prison guard led Caroline through a series of locked doors and finally into a small office, where the prison governor, John Westwood, greeted her with a thin smile. 'Ah yes,' he said. 'Art therapist, are you?' Caroline did not warm to the man's manner, which was facetious at best, certainly impolite. 'Not exactly,' she replied. 'I've come to see one of your prisoners whose work is world famous. Donna Bright. She's a graffiti artist.' Westwood laughed with derision. 'Artist? Vandal, more like! But she's not inside for scribbling on walls. Killed a man, you know.' 'I have an appointment to meet her,' Caroline said, determined to stay calm. 'Well, good luck with that,' said the prison governor, clearly indicating the door and the end of their conversation.

Donna Bright was smaller than Caroline had expected, and looked much younger than her 25 years. The older woman gave her a friendly smile as she took off her coat and hat. 'Nice and warm in here,' she remarked, rather nervously. 'It's very chilly outside.' 'Oh yeah?' said Donna, sarcastically. 'Oh dear, sorry … I didn't mean …' Caroline held out her hand, furious with herself for being so thoughtless. 'I'm Caroline. Pleased to meet you.' Donna's thin little hand shook hers: was this really the hand of a murderer? It was hard to believe.

At first, Caroline felt very uncomfortable. She knew that the window in the cell door was open, and that anyone could be listening. Speaking loudly, she explained that an exhibition of graffiti art in the town's main art gallery was showing some of the prisoners' work. She spoke knowledgeably and it was not long before Donna, who had been silent, started to relax and listen with interest. After a few minutes, the guard outside clearly became bored and the cell door window closed. It was then that Caroline lowered her voice and revealed the true object of her unusual visit. 'Donna,' she spoke urgently. 'The work you did on the factory wall, in the Northern Quarter, remember? You painted a man, a tall man dressed in military style? Who is he?'

EXAM STRATEGY

Reading and Use of English – Multiple choice

Read through the text before looking at the questions. The texts are often extracts from novels which focus on characters' feelings. Make sure you practise reading texts in which ideas, opinions and attitudes are expressed.

EXAM SKILLS

28 Read the questions. Choose the best answer according to the text.

0 What is the writer's main purpose in the first paragraph?
  A To give an account of Caroline's career as an art historian.
  (B) To establish that Caroline was out of her comfort zone.
  C To explain why Caroline was visiting a women's prison.
  D To suggest a link between a prisoner and a fake painting.

1 What is the prison governor's attitude to Caroline?
  A amused
  B welcoming
  C dismissive
  D suspicious

2 Why does Caroline say 'Oh dear, sorry … I didn't mean …'?
  A The temperature outside the prison wasn't really that bad.
  B She was not there to talk to Donna about the weather.
  C She realised her remark about the weather was insensitive.
  D She was angry with Donna for making her uncomfortable.

3 What do we learn about Caroline's visit in the final paragraph?
  A That she and Donna were not meeting for the first time.
  B Her role as an art therapist was to discuss Donna's work.
  C There was no reason for the guard outside to listen.
  D It had something to do with a man Donna had painted.

4 How does Caroline feel about visiting the prison?
  A confident
  B nervous
  C bored
  D curious

> **EXAM STRATEGY**
>
> **Speaking – Interview**
> You will be asked to give basic personal information about yourself in an informal conversation.
> The examiner will ask you questions about your family, your interests, holidays, school and so on.
> Don't memorise answers but be prepared to answer a range of questions in a natural way.

29 Look at the example questions. How would you answer them?

1 Who do you spend time with after school?
2 What do you like doing together?
3 Do you like reading? Or do you prefer watching movies?
4 What do you like to read / watch? Why?
5 Have you been anywhere nice recently?
6 Where would you like to go for your next holiday? Why?

30 [3.21] Listen to a student talking to an examiner. Note down the questions she was asked. How would you answer them?

1 Where … ?
2 Who … ?
3 In what way … ?
4 What … ?
5 Why … ?
6 Are there … ?

Unit 5

6 World wonders

GRAMMAR PRACTICE

The passive: be + past participle

Choose the correct option.
In *active / passive* sentences, the subject of the verb performs the action.
In *active / passive* sentences, the object becomes the subject.
In *active / passive* sentences, we don't always say who or what performed the action.
We form the *active / passive* with the appropriate tense and form of *be* + past participle.

→ See **GRAMMAR REFERENCE** page 122

1 Complete the sentences with the tense of *be* suggested in brackets.

0 Venice ......**is**...... shaken by earthquakes. (*present simple*)
1 Action .... taken to defend it. (*present continuous*)
2 It .... (not) submerged. (*future simple*)
3 Protective flood barriers .... built to support high tide. (*present continuous*)
4 Buildings .... preserved. (*present perfect*)
5 The village .... excavated. (*past continuous*)
6 It .... swallowed by the sea. (*past perfect*)

2 Are the sentences active or passive? Write A or P.

0 ...**P**... The damage was done years ago.
...**A**... The flood water did the damage.
1 .... A submerged treasure was found last century.
2 .... The bridges and pavements were old and broken.
3 .... Everyone's balconies were full of colourful flowers.
4 .... The visitors weren't invited into the museum's basement.
5 .... Children are warned not to climb on the walls.
6 .... The discoveries are being restored by art experts.

3 Rewrite the sentences to make them passive.

0 People visit London all year round.
London is visited all year round.
1 People take thousands of photos.
2 They are preserving the city.
3 We give tourists a lot of information.
4 We speak English here.
5 They are protecting the most beautiful buildings.
6 They are using modern engineering techniques.

4 Write sentences in the future passive. Use *by* and the words given.

0 this city / save / engineers
This city will be saved by engineers.
1 precious monuments / destroy / the sea
2 new buildings / construct / an Italian company
3 the air / not / pollute / car exhausts
4 roads and bridges / erode / flood water
5 sea levels / affect / climate change
6 this village / not / flood / the river

5 Match the beginnings and ends of the sentences.

0 [e] The city of Pompeii was destroyed
1 [ ] The floods in London will be stopped
2 [ ] The Taj Mahal was built in memory
3 [ ] The tomb of Tutankhamun was
4 [ ] The 2004 tsunami in Thailand was
5 [ ] The citadel of Machu Picchu was
6 [ ] The wonders of Venice will be

a discovered in Egypt in the 1920s.
b built by the Incas in the fifteenth century.
c protected against rising sea levels.
d by the Thames barrier.
e by the eruption of Mount Vesuvius.
f of a Mughal emperor's wife.
g caused by an Indian Ocean earthquake.

6 Rewrite the questions in the passive.

0 Who found the hidden treasure?
Who was the hidden treasure found by?
1 Who wrote *The Merchant of Venice*?
2 Where do they send the damaged articles for repair?
3 When will they complete the renovation of the castle?
4 Why are they closing that bridge to heavy traffic?
5 Where have they displayed the Degas collection?
6 Who built the Hanging Gardens of Babylon?

GRAMMAR PRACTICE

7 Correct the mistakes.

0 When was the Shard ~~build~~?
   When was the Shard built?
1 Her favourite crime story was written Andrea Camilleri.
2 International football plays in this stadium.
3 White dresses are usually wearing by brides.
4 Where was found the world's biggest diamond?
5 Thomas Mann's *Death in Venice* made into a film.
6 It thinks that climate change will cause great damage.

8 Choose the correct option.

0 All the plants on the balcony .... in the storm yesterday.
   A were ruined (circled)
   B ruined
   C have been ruined
1 He had to step into the road because the pavement ....
   A isn't repaired
   B was repairing
   C was being repaired
2 The work .... when we arrived at the scene.
   A was already been done
   B had already been done
   C is already being done
3 The bridges .... against the risk of high winds.
   A are being fortified
   B are been fortified
   C will fortify
4 The discussion .... by the Minister for the Environment.
   A will lead
   B will be leading
   C will be led
5 The necessary research on climate change .... yet.
   A won't be doing
   B hasn't been done
   C isn't been done
6 The reconstruction won't go ahead unless a financial agreement ....
   A will be reached
   B won't be reached
   C is reached

9 Rewrite the sentences so that they mean the same. Use the words in brackets.

0 Everyone knows who painted the *Mona Lisa*. (*by*)
   Everyone knows who the *Mona Lisa* was painted by.
1 Karl Benz produced the first German car. (*was*)
2 The stolen jewellery hasn't been found yet. (*nobody*)
3 They don't pay the archaeologists very much money. (*aren't*)
4 Someone was cleaning the café floor after the flood. (*being*)
5 Everyone agreed that the plan was a good one. (*it*)
6 The new engineering project has to be tested. (*they*)

10 Complete the article with the words below.

> carried • was done • won't be forgotten • ~~was given~~ • were hit • were left • was needed • had been made • had been picked • was reported • were ruined • had been submerged • were swallowed

In August 2005, a hurricane warning ⁰ *was given* in the US and shortly afterwards, many neighbourhoods of New Orleans ¹............ by Hurricane Katrina. It was a disaster that ²............ . By the next day, 80% of New Orleans ³............ under water, nearly 2,000 people had died and over 400,000 people ⁴............ homeless. It was clear that aid (clean water, food and shelter) ⁵............ urgently. As is often the case, people living in the poorer neighbourhoods ⁶............ the hardest. For those who survived, what damage ⁷............ ? Some homes ⁸............ structurally undamaged, but it ⁹............ that nobody in the entire city had escaped without some losses. When residents finally returned to see what they could salvage, they found that pieces of furniture ¹⁰............ up and ¹¹............ away by the water. In other words, they ¹²............ .

Unit 6 59

READING SKILLS

11 Look at the photo of a house in Amsterdam. In what ways do you think this Dutch city is similar to Venice?

12 [3.22] Read and listen to the text. Was your answer to exercise 11 correct?

13 Choose the correct option.

1. The Netherlands is a country which has always ....
   A been rich and flat
   B had rising sea levels
   C been at war with water

2. A lot of the reclaimed farmland was once ....
   A peat   B clay   C sea

3. The water was first pumped off the land using ....
   A electricity   B wind   C steam

4. Drying out the farmland made it ....
   A worse   B lower   C poorer

5. Modern Dutch buildings are constructed on poles made of ....
   A sand and clay
   B clay and cement
   C cement and metal

6. Amsterdam houses have irregular roofs because ....
   A some of them have sunk
   B they have all sunk
   C they look elegant when they sink

7. A characteristic of old Amsterdam houses is that ....
   A they are very grand
   B they have no stairs
   C they are not straight

8. The top floors of old canal houses were designed to ....
   A keep the furniture dry
   B store dry goods
   C have metal hooks

14 Underline two or three key pieces of information from each paragraph of the text. The key information in the first paragraph has been underlined for you.

15 Make notes from the key points. Use bullet points, not full sentences.

The crooked houses of Amsterdam

Arriving at Amsterdam's Schiphol airport, a visitor may well be surprised and alarmed to learn that the runways and all the buildings are four metres below sea level. The name *Netherlands* means lowlands, and this small rich country has always been flat and low. It sits on a river delta, mainly consisting of peat and clay. Much of the farmland was reclaimed from the sea, long before climate change caused rising sea levels.

The battle against water has been fought by Dutch engineers since the Middle Ages. Firstly, water was pumped off the land by windmills, many hundreds of which can still be seen. Next steam and then electricity were used to drain the water off the land, making it a very fertile peat which was good for Dutch farmers. However, this process had an unfortunate effect: it not only dried the ground but also made it sink.

So how could the famous Dutch city of Amsterdam be built on sinking land? The answer is: the houses were built on wooden poles. These poles were pushed deep into the peat, clay and water until they reached solid sand, which could be as far as 12 metres below the surface. In recent building projects, cement and steel are used.
The poles under the older elegant houses along the city's canals, however, are made of wood from the spruce tree. These wooden poles erode at different stages, so some houses sink while others don't. This gives the houses the irregular rooftops that visitors to Amsterdam find so charming.

VOCABULARY

BUILDINGS AND MATERIALS

16 Complete the words.

0   W **OO** L
1   B R _ C K
2   C _ T T _ N
3   G _ L D
4   M _ R B L _
5   L _ _ T H _ R
6   S _ L K
7   L Y C R _
8   P _ P _ R
9   C _ N C R _ T _
10 P L _ S T _ C
11 G L _ S S
12 S T _ _ L
13 R _ B B _ R
14 L _ _ D
15 W _ _ D
16 L _ N _ N
17 S _ L V _ R
18 P _ L Y _ S T _ R
19 C _ P P _ R

17 List the words for fabrics in exercise 16.

Natural: _wool,_   Synthetic: _____

18 Choose the correct option.

0   Cars are made of *concrete* / (*metal*).
1   Plastic is made from *oil* / *paper*.
2   *Wood* / *Wool* is the raw material for making paper.
3   Houses often have roofs made of *brick* / *slate*.
4   Cotton and *sand* / *silk* are fabrics for clothes.
5   Mountain paths are often made of *rocks* / *diamonds*.

19 Complete the text with the words below.

> animal ▪ clay ▪ glass ▪ plastic ▪ steel ▪ ~~stone~~
> synthetic ▪ windows ▪ wood ▪ wooden ▪ woollen

Many houses in Europe are built of ⁰ _stone_ from the ground or brick, which is made from ¹_____ . The nomadic people of Mongolia live in round tents called *yurts* made of ²_____ skins or ³_____ fabrics. These yurts don't have ⁴_____, but there is a circle of clear ⁵_____ in the roof which allows the light to get in. The doors of yurts are usually made of ⁶_____ . The inside of the yurt is constructed with ⁷_____ poles, and furnished with thick ⁸_____ carpets. People in the capital city of Ulaanbaatar, however, live in tall buildings made of ⁹_____, concrete and a lot of ¹⁰_____ .

Does this building method explain why some of these grand old merchant houses along the canals appear to lean forwards? Not really, because in fact many of them were actually built that way! The top floors were originally dry places for storing the imported cotton, spices and cocoa. These goods were brought along the water and lifted on metal hooks from the boats to the top floors. This was easier when the top of the building was leaning forward. As Amsterdam houses traditionally have very narrow stairs, this method of getting large pieces of furniture upstairs is still used today.

GLOSSARY

peat	➤ a type of soft soil
clay	➤ a thick heavy soil
drain	➤ remove water from
poles	➤ long, thin sticks of wood or metal
erode	➤ to be rubbed away slowly

GRAMMAR PRACTICE

Passive with *can* / *can't* / *could* / *couldn't*

Complete the sentences with the words below.

could be limited • can be forecast • can't be avoided

Hurricanes ……………… but disasters ……………… though damages ……………… if risk areas had impact-resistant buildings.

➡ See GRAMMAR REFERENCE page 122

20 🔊 **Make passive sentences with *can* and *can't*.**

0 this project / not / do / alone
   This project can't be done alone.
1 the earthquake / feel / in our village
2 the answer / find / at the back of the book
3 our research / not / finish / this month
4 those trees / not / save / by eco-activists
5 stones / use / to build houses
6 new techniques / explain / by experts

Passive: Verbs with two objects

Complete the sentences.

A They offered an award to her.
P ……………… was offered ……………… .
A They offered her an award.
P ……………… was offered ……………… .
A They will send ……………… .
P Pictures **will be sent** to the scientists.
A They will send ……………… .
P The scientists **will be sent** pictures.

➡ See GRAMMAR REFERENCE page 122

21 🔊 **Rewrite the sentences with the word given.**

0 An important message has been sent to her.
   They **sent her an important message**.
1 We will give them one meal a day.
   They ……………… .
2 They have awarded our class first prize.
   Our ……………… .
3 She has been sent an unusual photo.
   Someone ……………… .
4 NASA has offered my brother a job.
   My ……………… .
5 They showed us a film about an ancient city.
   We ……………… .

Passive with *say*, *believe*, *know*, *think*

Complete the rule.
We form the passive with *say*, *believe*, *know*, *think* in this way:
Impersonal passive: it + ……………… + *said, known, believed, thought* + ……………… .
Personal passive: subject + ……………… + *said, known, believed, thought* + ……………… .

➡ See GRAMMAR REFERENCE page 122

22 🔊 **Put the words in the correct order.**

0 said / declining / are / be / to / numbers
   Numbers are said to be declining.
1 that / distances / known / fly / swans / long / is / it
2 Roman / ruins / from / the / thought / be / to / times / were
3 flight / the / dangerous / be / said / very / to / was
4 information / useful / is / be / to / their / thought
5 archaeologists / highly / are / the / be / skilled / known / to

23 🔊 **Read the article and choose the correct option.**

Priceless mosaics found in Istanbul

Two precious ancient mosaics [0] *is found* / (*have been found*) under the floor of a ninth-century mosque in Istanbul. They [1] *discovered* / *were discovered* during routine work which [2] *was being done* / *was doing* by archaeologists at the site. The mosque [3] *thought* / *is thought* to date from the time when the region [4] *governed* / *was being governed* by the Roman Empire.
The priceless mosaics [5] *have now been removed* / *have not been removed* from the site for conservation. In one of the mosaics, which [6] *believes to be* / *is believed to be* unique, an ark [7] *will be seen* / *can be seen* with pairs of animals, including elephants, bears, lions and leopards. In another, stories about soldiers [8] *are showed* / *are shown*. The soldiers are trying to escape and [9] *are being eaten* / *are eating* by a giant fish.
Ancient mosaics [10] *made* / *were made* of thousands of pieces of glass or tiny coloured stones called *tesserae*. These [11] *were stuck* / *were stick* to walls or floors with a type of cement. This find is of extraordinarily good quality and [12] *is said to be* / *is said being* very well preserved.

62 Unit 6

SPEAKING SKILLS

DESCRIBING PEOPLE AND PLACES

24 Complete the sentences with the correct form of *look* or *look like*.

1 That girl .... very familiar!
2 He is said to .... his younger brother.
3 Iris .... really tired when I saw her yesterday.
4 Do you think dog owners .... their dogs?
5 We used to have a neighbour who always .... angry.
6 She moves so gracefully, she .... a ballerina.

25 Choose the correct option.

1 Their apartment looks very luxurious, *doesn't it / looks it*?
2 You're not going out wearing that dress, *are you / aren't you*?
3 My cousin and I don't look alike, *doesn't he / do we*?
4 Their house has got a balcony. *Get it / Has it*?
5 The people in the photo all look sad, *doesn't it / don't they*?
6 He's the one sitting next to you. *Is he / Does he*?

26 Complete the dialogue with the phrases below.

> Are you sure ▪ Can you say that again ▪
> Is that really ▪ Really ▪ Sorry, what was that ▪
> What did you say ▪ What do you mean

A I've just come back from an exchange trip to Scotland.
B ¹........................... ?
A I said I've been in Scotland. Look, this is where my friend's family lives.
B Wow! ²........................... where they live?
A Well, of course they only have part of it!
B ³........................... ?
A I mean, it's a castle, right? They've got an apartment in it.
B ⁴........................... ? It looks amazing.
   ⁵........................... your friend's name was?
A I didn't. It's Dougie McDougal.
B ⁶........................... ?
A Dougie McDougal.
B Dougie McDougal? ⁷........................... ? That's a very funny name.

LISTENING SKILLS

27 Look at the photo. What is the relationship between these people, in your opinion?

28 [3.23] Listen to a boy talking about his sister. Check your answer to exercise 27.

29 [3.23] Read the sentences and underline the keywords in each sentence. Think about what you might need to fill the gap: a name, a number, a date? Then listen and complete.

1 Sandy now is .... years old. At the age of .... she cycled first from Portland, Oregon, to ....
2 That journey was a distance of over .... miles.
3 Sandy then cycled through different countries: ...., ... and .... until she reached Colombia.
4 In Bogotá, Sandy met Victor, who is from ....
5 Victor was learning ....; his native language is ....
6 His language is spoken by over .... people.
7 Sandy and Victor got married and now have a ....-year-old boy called Pedro.
8 They've lived in .... for .... years but they visit Chris's family for a .... every ....

Unit 6   63

ACADEMIC SKILLS

INTERPRETING A GRAPH

30 Complete the advice on interpreting a graph with the words below.

> formal ▪ purpose ▪ relevant ▪ ~~visual~~ ▪ words

Graphs are a ⁰ **visual** way of presenting information. You need to transfer this information into ¹ .... Make sure you understand the ² .... of the graph. That is also the purpose of your text. Use clear, ³ .... language and only include ⁴ .... information. Read it again – could you draw a graph from your text?

31 Look at graph A and answer the questions.
1. What is the purpose of the graph?
2. What does the vertical axis show?
3. What are the lowest and highest numbers shown?
4. What does the horizontal axis show?
5. What are the earliest and latest years shown?

A Sea floods in Boston, MA, since 1970

[Bar chart showing Flood days: 1970s ~2, 1980s ~1, 1990s ~1.5, 2000s ~3, 2010s ~9]

32 Complete the summary of the information in graph A with the words below.

> 2000s ▪ annually ▪ bigger ▪ days ▪ decades ▪ fewer ▪ flooded ▪ ~~rise~~

Since 1970 there is thought to have been a ⁰ **rise** in the sea levels of about nine centimetres all over the world. Research into the number of days cities were ¹ .... has shown this rise. In Boston, Massachusetts, for example, there were two ² .... of floods per year during the 1970s. The next two ³ .... were better, with ⁴ .... days of flooding in the 1980s and 1990s. However, there was a rise to three days in the ⁵ ...., and a much ⁶ .... rise in the 2010s, when there were three times as many days ⁷ ....

33 Look at graph B and read the two summaries. Which is correct?

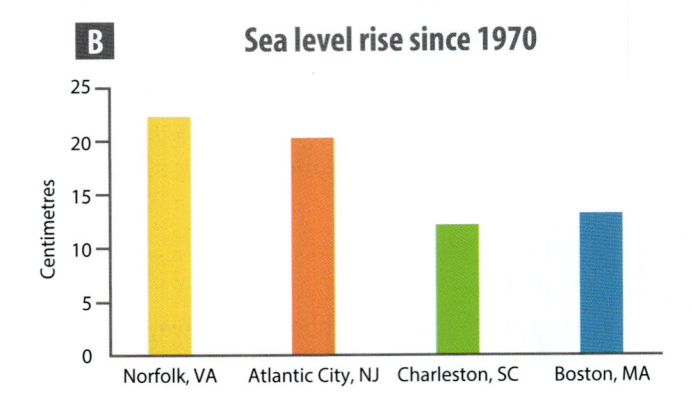

B Sea level rise since 1970

[Bar chart in Centimetres: Norfolk, VA ~22; Atlantic City, NJ ~20; Charleston, SC ~12; Boston, MA ~13]

Summary 1
The purpose of graph B is to show how much sea levels have risen since 1970 in four different cities of the United States. The vertical axis shows the number of centimetres the sea has risen. The lowest number shown is 12 centimetres for Charleston and the highest number shown is 22 centimetres for Norfolk. The horizontal axis shows the four cities where measurements were taken: Norfolk, Virginia; Atlantic City, New Jersey; Charleston, South Carolina; Boston, Massachusetts.

Summary 2
The purpose of graph B is to show how much sea levels have risen since 1970 in four different cities of the United States. The vertical axis shows the percentage of centimetres the sea has risen. The lowest number shown is 12 centimetres for Boston and the highest number shown is 25 centimetres for Norfolk. The horizontal axis shows the four cities where flooding happened: Norfolk, Virginia; Atlantic City, New Jersey; Charleston, South Carolina; Boston, Massachusetts.

34 Look at graph C and answer the questions in exercise 31.

C Sea floods in Charleston, SC, since 1970

[Bar chart showing Flood days: 1970s ~2, 1980s ~4, 1990s ~7.5, 2000s ~10, 2010s ~11]

35 Write a summary of the information in graph C, comparing the information in graph A.

EXAM SKILLS

> **EXAM STRATEGY**
>
> **Listening – Multiple matching**
>
> The focus of this exam is listening for detail, attitude or opinion of the speakers. The questions will be a different way of saying what the speakers say. Read the questions carefully so you know what you'll be listening for. If you're unsure about an answer, don't be too quick to fill it in. Wait for the second listening.

36 Tick (✓) the sentences which are saying the same thing as the sentence given (A or B or both).

0 Historians think that the ruins date from the fourteenth century.
  A It is thought that the ruins are hundreds of years old. ✓
  B Experts believe the ruins to be 1,400 years old.

1 Venice is not only famous for its beauty.
  A Venice is believed to be famous simply because it's beautiful.
  B Venice is well-known for more than just being beautiful.

2 Action is being taken to defend the sinking cities.
  A People are said to be acting in defence of these cities.
  B There are people defending the cities against rising sea levels.

3 The archaeological finds are of enormous significance.
  A Archaeologists have found very large and significant items.
  B What archaeologists have uncovered is extremely important.

4 The ancient houses on the canal will not necessarily be submerged.
  A It will not be necessary to protect the oldest buildings.
  B It may be possible to prevent those buildings from flooding.

5 With enough volunteers, the site could be excavated.
  A They will be able to dig up the site if they have enough helpers.
  B Without enough helpers, it may not be possible to excavate the site.

37 [3.24] Read and listen to two extracts from two different guided tours of Chatsworth House in Derbyshire and choose from the list (1–4) what the speaker likes best about this house. There are two extra sentences.

Tour 1 Hello and welcome to Chatsworth House, perhaps the most famous stately home in the UK and certainly the pride of Derbyshire. You will have driven up to this great house across the beautiful parkland over a stone bridge which crosses the River Derwent. Did you notice the Emperor Fountain to the side of the house? The water in this amazing fountain is said to have reached a height of 90 metres, which was certainly a record when it was constructed. It is easy to see why Chatsworth is the top tourist attraction of the region.

Tour 2 Many famous people have come to Chatsworth, past and present. Among the most famous is Mary Queen of Scots, who was here both as a guest and as prisoner between 1573 and 1582. In 2005, Chatsworth House was the location used for filming Jane Austen's masterpiece *Pride and Prejudice*, in which it became the home of the handsome Mr Darcy.

1 It is popular because of the people who have been there.
2 The weather is always good.
3 The architecture is spectacular.
4 It has a wonderful park full of animals.

38 [3.25] You will hear four short extracts in which people are talking about a visit to the Roman baths in Bath. Choose from the list (1–4) what each speaker talks about.

1 Actors dressed as Romans told us stories about life in those times.
2 The baths is where Romans bathed and socialised around AD 70.
3 I drank the spa water but I have to say I didn't like the taste of it very much.
4 Visitors, including foreigners and children, can learn a lot from the audio guides.

Unit 6   65

REVISE AND ROUND UP

1 **Complete the sentences with a / an, the or –.**

0   A lot of money was stolen by ...**a**... man that ...**the**... police didn't know.
1   We rented .... apartment overlooking .... Arno which was lovely.
2   Did you see .... moon last night? I took .... great photo.
3   Al Capone, ... most wanted criminal of his time, spent years in .... prison.
4   Our visitors went to .... theatre to see .... opera by Verdi.
5   This is .... problem we were talking about in .... autumn.
6   *Rebus*, which means .... kind of puzzle, is .... name of .... fictional detective.

2 **Complete the sentences with who, which or whose.**

0   He spoke to a man ......**who**......... had been in prison for a month.
1   I read a crime story .... I found very unconvincing.
2   We visited the town .... was flooded last winter.
3   Where are the witnesses .... are going to give evidence?
4   The police spoke to the woman .... bag had been stolen.
5   Our teacher knows someone .... son is a film star.
6   Alcatraz was the prison .... was featured in the movie.

3 **Match the beginnings and ends of the sentences.**

0   [e] This spa is the place
1   [ ] We'll always remember the day
2   [ ] The children's homes are
3   [ ] I think Italy is the country
4   [ ] Will there ever be a time
5   [ ] Isn't Elba the island
6   [ ] This is where my parents lived

a   where Napoleon spent many years?
b   where Pavarotti came from.
c   when there is no violent crime?
d   when they were students.
e   where the Romans bathed.
f   when we first met.
g   where they should feel safe.

4 **Correct the mistakes.**

0   The prisoner which spoke first was very intelligent.
    The prisoner who / that spoke first was very intelligent.
1   Our guides were all actors were dressed up as Romans.
2   The man who money was taken gave his name to the police.
3   Some of the crimes they committed by were not very serious.
4   Can you show me the place when you were born?
5   The lawyer doesn't like the judge is in court today.
6   Ned Kelly killed the officer assaulted his sister.

5 **Make one sentence with a non-defining relative clause. Join the sentences with who or which.**

0   Miss Marple is an amateur detective. Miss Marple is an Agatha Christie character.
    Miss Marple, who is an Agatha Christie character, is an amateur detective.
1   Some of the students are studying law. They are all from Australia.
2   This book is fascinating. It is about an unsolved mystery.
3   The man has been proved innocent. He was accused of multiple crimes.
4   Ned Kelly's gang went on the run. They were all wanted men.
5   I found the story rather unconvincing. It is said to be true.
6   Schiphol is one of Europe's busiest airports. It lies below sea level.

6 **Rewrite the sentences to make them passive.**

0   They regularly drain the land in this region.
    The land in this region is regularly drained.
1   We speak many languages in this school.
    ....
2   They will use yurts and tents on their camping trip.
    ....
3   People are cleaning the rooms that were flooded.
    ....
4   They give hurricane warnings as early as possible.
    ....
5   We won't build the new apartments near the river.
    ....
6   Climate change will definitely affect people's lives.
    ....

7 Make questions using the words in brackets and *by*.

0 *The Girl with a Pearl Earring* is my favourite work of art. (*who / paint*?)
   Who was it painted by?
1 I really enjoyed reading *Death on the Nile*. (*who / write*?)
2 Do you know the song about the Vistula? (*who / sing*?)
3 My sister received a very strange letter. (*who / send*?)
4 They discovered Tutankhamun's mummy in the 1920s. (*who / find*?)
5 These wooden artefacts date from ancient times. (*who / make*?)
6 We have a prize-winning building in our town. (*who / design*?)

8 Rewrite the sentences so that they mean the same.

0 They could make many interesting discoveries.
   Many **interesting discoveries could be made**.
1 Unfortunately we can't share our results.
   Our ....
2 They could locate underground activity.
   Underground ....
3 We can teach children how to interpret the photos.
   Children ....
4 They believe that priceless treasures are hidden underground.
   It is ....
5 They could offer volunteers valuable training.
   Valuable ....
6 We knew that nomadic people once lived in the region.
   It was ....

9 Correct the mistakes.

0 The images will be ~~send~~ to scientists via satellite.
   sent
1 The prisoners, which crimes are varied, live in colourful wooden cottages.
2 The police inspected the missing man's wife of fraud but it couldn't be proved.
3 Ned Kelly was a violent gangster which life story has become a legend.
4 The sunken city, what was discovered last year, is of enormous significance.

CONCEPT CHECK

Read the sentences and answer the questions.

1 *The girl David met last night looked like his cousin.*

(Answer Yes / No / Maybe)

0 A meeting took place last night. **Yes**
1 David met a girl last night.
2 The girl's name was David.
3 David met his cousin last night.
4 David and the girl both like his cousin.
5 The girls had similar appearances.

2 *The man in the car crash is recovering in hospital.*

(Answer True / False)

0 A man had an accident in his car. **True**
1 We know the name of the man.
2 The accident victim was hurt in the car crash.
3 He was taken to hospital.
4 He is still a patient in this hospital.
5 He is getting better.

3 *Who were the Palaeolithic cave paintings in France painted by?*

(Answer Yes / No)

0 We know that the paintings are inside. **Yes**
1 We want to know the period in history when the paintings were done.
2 We already know which country the paintings can be found in.
3 We want to know exactly where these paintings are in that country.
4 We know who did the cave paintings.
5 We want to know who did the cave paintings.

4 *The Zeddam tower mill, dating from the fifteenth century, is believed to be the oldest windmill in the Netherlands.*

(Answer Yes / No / Maybe)

0 We know what kind of building we are talking about. **Yes**
1 This windmill has been there since the 1400s.
2 We know which country it can be found in.
3 It is the oldest windmill in the world.
4 People believe that there isn't an older windmill in the Netherlands.

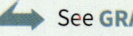

See **GRAMMAR REFERENCE**
pages 121–123

7 Glorious food

GRAMMAR PRACTICE

Zero and first conditionals

Choose the correct option.
We use the *zero / first* conditional when one action follows automatically after another.
We use the *zero / first* conditional when we talk about possible future actions.

➤ See **GRAMMAR REFERENCE** page 123

1 **Complete the sentences using the zero conditional and the verbs in brackets.**

   0 If Amy ……**eats**…… (*eat*) raw fish, she always ……**feels**…… (*feel*) sick.
   1 If you ……………… (*overcook*) vegetables, they ……………… (*lose*) their vitamins.
   2 Children ……………… (*get*) bad teeth if they ……………… (*drink*) too much cola.
   3 If you ……………… (*not / add*) any salt, bread ……………… (*be*) tasteless.
   4 Ice cream ……………… (*melt*) if you ……………… (*leave*) it in the sun.
   5 It ……………… (*be*) better if you ……………… (*cook*) the meat slowly.
   6 If Daniel ……………… (*make*) the dinner, the kitchen ……………… (*be*) a mess.

2 **Choose the correct option to make first conditional sentences.**

   0 If the baby *finishes* / *will finish* that yogurt, I'll give her some more.
   1 If it *rains* / *will rain*, we won't have a picnic outside.
   2 I *cook* / *'ll cook* if you agree to help me.
   3 If he *uses* / *will use* good olive oil, his salad will taste nicer.
   4 You'll feel healthier if you *exercise* / *will exercise* more.

3 **Make questions in the first conditional using *if*.**

   0 people / live longer / not / eat meat?
      Will people live longer if they don't eat meat?
   1 what / you / do / restaurant be fully booked?
   2 how / they / survive / not / have enough food?
   3 we all / feel better / eat superfoods?
   4 how / Bella / get here / we invite her for dinner?

Second and third conditionals

Choose the correct option.
We use the *second / third* conditional to talk about imaginary or *unlikely / impossible* events or situations in the present or future.
We use the *second / third* conditional to talk about imaginary and *unlikely / impossible* events or situations in the past.

➤ See **GRAMMAR REFERENCE** pages 123, 124

4 **Complete the second conditional sentences with the correct form of the verbs in brackets.**

   0 If I ……**had**…… (*have*) my camera with me, I ……**'d take**…… (*take*) some photos now.
   1 I ……………… (*learn*) how to make paella if I ……………… (*live*) in Spain.
   2 If Ben ……………… (*not / work*) all the time, he ……………… (*take*) more exercise.
   3 What ……………… you ……………… (*do*) if you ……………… (*find*) a wallet?
   4 If I ……………… (*have*) a million euros, I ……………… probably ……………… (*buy*) a yacht.
   5 ……………… you ……………… (*know*) where to go if you ……………… (*not / have*) a map?
   6 Katie ……………… (*help*) you if you ……………… (*ask*) her.

5 **Complete the third conditional sentences with the correct form of the verbs in brackets.**

   0 If you ……**had been**…… (*be*) more careful, you wouldn't have cut your finger.
   1 If she ……………… (*add*) more salt, the soup would have tasted better.
   2 If he had stopped eating junk food sooner, he ……………… (*be*) so ill.
   3 If her brother ……………… (*phone*) her, she wouldn't have been worried.
   4 If I had studied harder, I ……………… (*pass*) all my exams.
   5 If they had had more time, they ……………… (*cook*) the meal.
   6 If we ……………… (*run*) faster, we wouldn't have missed the train.

68   Unit 7

GRAMMAR PRACTICE

6 Put the words in the correct order to make third conditional sentences.

0   you / you / enjoyed / if / had / have / come / it / meal / a / for / would
    If you had come for a meal, you would have enjoyed it.

1   us / have / she / would / had / her / helped / if / we / asked

2   would / had / been / won / team / we / I / if / the / in / have

3   he / had / have / would / found / given / that / it / back / if / money / he

4   they / have / taken / train / had / they / the / been / if / wouldn't / tired / so

should / shouldn't have; wish

Choose the correct option.
I should *had / have* listened to my friends. I wish I *had / have* listened to them.
I shouldn't *had / have* gone on the show. I wish I *hadn't / haven't* gone there.

➡ See **GRAMMAR REFERENCE** page 124

7 Write sentences with *should / shouldn't have*.

0   we / try that new restaurant
    We should have tried that new restaurant.
1   she / not / add so much salt
2   we / peel the apples first
3   you / not / use those eggs
4   he / boil the water before drinking it

8 Respond to the situations. Use *should / shouldn't have* and the correct form of the verbs in brackets.

0   Pamela has been shopping and now she hasn't got any money. (spend)
    She shouldn't have spent all her money.
1   Our friends gave us fried fish for dinner and it wasn't nice. (grill)
2   I had a party and I forgot to tell the neighbours. (invite)
3   They missed the last bus home and had to walk. (catch)
4   Our team played really badly and we lost the match. (good)

9 Read Dan's email and complete the sentences.

Hi Bernie,
Thanks for your email. Sorry I didn't reply earlier, I've been busy. I went to the gym as usual on Monday. I don't always have a swim after working out, but on Monday I did, and in the pool, I bumped into my friend from primary school, Mesut. I didn't recognise him at first, and we both laughed about it. We agreed to meet for lunch the next day. He was late, so I ordered our sandwiches and drinks. When he arrived, we were talking so much that he didn't notice his sandwich had chicken in it. Suddenly he was very upset because … he hadn't told me … he's a strict vegan! I felt terrible about that. Fortunately he's got a very good sense of humour. Maybe you'll meet him at the club this weekend.
See you,
Dan

0   Dan **would have replied** (reply) earlier if he **hadn't been** (not / be) so busy.
1   He .... (not / meet) Mesut if he .... (not / have) a swim.
2   He .... (not / recognise) Mesut eventually if he .... (not / be) to primary school with him.
3   If he .... (not / be) late, Dan .... (not / order) for him.
4   If they .... (not / talk) so much, Mesut .... (notice) what he was eating.
5   If his food .... (not / be) vegan, Mesut .... (not / eat) it.
6   Dan wishes he .... (not / order) him a chicken sandwich: he .... (wait).
7   If Mesut .... (not / have) a good sense of humour, they .... (not / still be) friends now.
8   If Bernie .... (go) to the club at the weekend, maybe he .... (meet) Mesut.

READING SKILLS

10 Look at the photos. What do you think the guy is eating? Would you eat that?

11 [3.26] Read the text and choose the correct option to complete the sentences. Then listen and check.

1	A appetite	B appetising	C unappetising
2	A disgust	B disgusted	C disgusting
3	A relatively	B relative	C relativity
4	A safety	B safely	C safe
5	A hungry	B hunger	C hungered
6	A solve	B solution	C insoluble
7	A healthily	B unhealthy	C healthy
8	A friendly	B friendliness	C friendship
9	A product	B production	C produce
10	A appeal	B unappealing	C appealing
11	A benefits	B beneficiary	C benefit

12 What do these figures refer to in the text?

1 nine billion
2 nearly one billion
3 almost two billion
4 many thousands
5 two thousand
6 70 million

13 Answer the questions, giving two reasons in each answer.

1 Why do people in Europe rarely eat insects?
2 Why do we need to produce more food?
3 Why would eating insects be beneficial?
4 Why would or wouldn't you eat insects?

Would you eat insects?

A once-popular TV reality show featured celebrities in an Australian jungle eating food which looked very ¹............ . People found this amusing to watch, although they would never have done it themselves.

Often, the contestants had to eat insects, sometimes live insects, or spiders. To many viewers, and indeed to the contestants themselves, eating **creepy-crawlies** was one of the most ²............ things they had to do. What would you do if someone asked you to eat an insect? Although eating insects is ³............ rare in Europe, people have eaten insects for many thousands of years.

Today, almost two billion people eat insects as part of their regular diet, in places like China, Africa, Mexico, Thailand, Vietnam, Cambodia, Colombia and New Guinea. Nearly two thousand species are ⁴............ to eat. The most commonly eaten bugs are **crickets**, beetles, caterpillars, bees, wasps and ants. Would the world's food problems be solved if more of us ate insects? It is calculated that nearly one billion people around the world are already ⁵............ all the time. The world's population grows by about 70 million people every year. If the numbers keep increasing, the population will be nine billion by 2050.

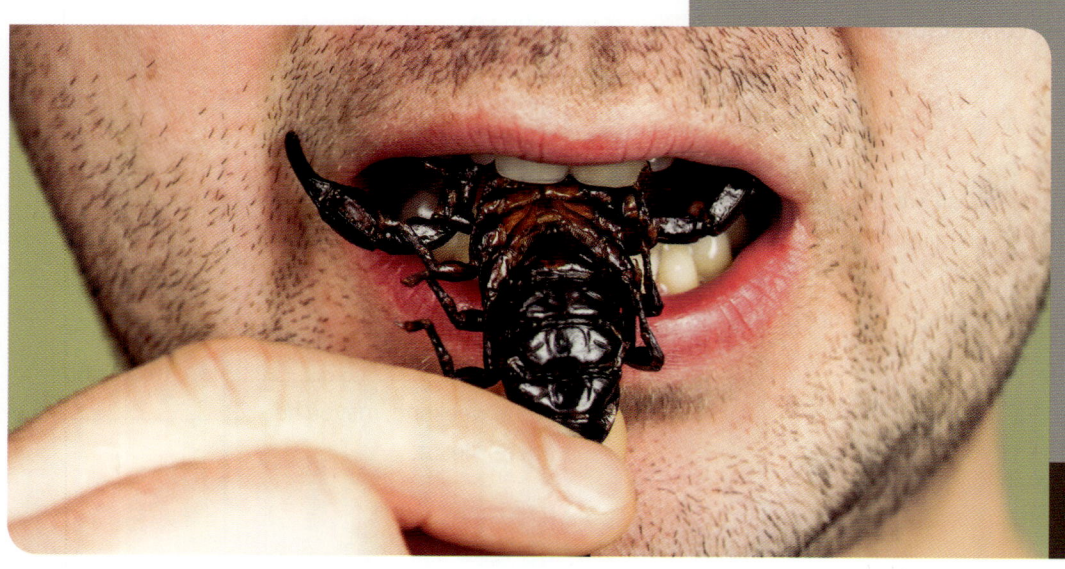

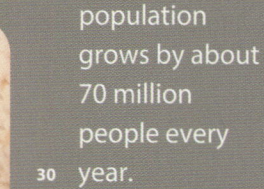

So we will need to produce almost twice as much food as we do now if we want to feed the world. Could insects be the ⁶............ to world hunger?
There is more protein and less fat in insects than there is in beef, lamb or chicken, so they are very nutritious and form part of a ⁷............ diet. Eating insects rather than other meat is more environmentally ⁸............ . Farming insects needs less land and water than farming traditional animals. Also, insects reproduce much more quickly, so food ⁹............ is more efficient. In addition, insects produce far fewer greenhouse gases than farmed animals, especially cows.
If the idea of eating insects was more ¹⁰............, perhaps our planet and everyone on it would ¹¹............ from a cheap and plentiful source of superfoods.

GLOSSARY

creepy-crawlies ➤ insects
crickets ➤ insects that makes short, loud noises by rubbing their wings together

VOCABULARY

COOKING

14 Reorder the letters to make verbs.

0	yrf	fry			
1	aetgr	....	7	opur	....
2	skhwi	....	8	ubr	....
3	iglrl	....	9	ixm	....
4	phco	....	10	dad	....
5	rist	....	11	tepaerh	....
6	keab	....	12	eepl	....

15 How many cooking actions can you find for each verb in exercise 14?

Fry: *eggs, onions, meat*

16 Complete the recipe with the words below.

> add • bake • butter • chocolate • creamy • delicious • favourite • ingredients • method • optional • roasted • stir • whisk

Crunchy cricket and chocolate cookies

⁰ *Ingredients* :
250 g flour
pinch of bicarbonate of soda
pinch of salt
240 g soft ¹........................
400 g sugar
2 eggs
300 g ²........................ pieces
150 g chopped mixed nuts (³........................)
100 g ⁴........................ crickets

⁵........................: Preheat the oven to 190 °C and rub a little oil or butter onto a metal baking tray. Mix the butter and sugar together until the mixture is ⁶........................ and smooth. ⁷........................ in the eggs. Slowly ⁸........................ the flour, with the bicarbonate of soda and the salt. ⁹........................ in the insects, chocolate chips and nuts (if used). Pour round spoonfuls of the mixture onto the baking tray and ¹⁰........................ in the oven for 10–12 minutes. Allow to cool for 10 minutes. These ¹¹........................ crunchy cookies, so easy to make, will soon be a family ¹²........................ .

Unit 7

GRAMMAR PRACTICE

Mixed conditionals

Complete the words.
Mixing third and second conditionals can show how a different **past** would have changed the **present**.

p.................... condition	p.................... result
If we had booked a table,	*we wouldn't be in this queue now.* (But we didn't book.)

→ See **GRAMMAR REFERENCE** page 124

17 Decide if the second sentence of each pair is true (T) or false (F).

0 If I had known the time, I wouldn't be late for this class.
I am late. ☑ T ☐ F

1 If you had checked your phone, you'd know the time.
You didn't check your phone. ☐ T ☐ F

2 If we'd cleared up last night, the kitchen would be tidy now.
The kitchen is tidy. ☐ T ☐ F

3 If you hadn't woken me in the night, I wouldn't be so tired now.
I'm not tired. ☐ T ☐ F

4 If the children hadn't eaten, they'd be hungry now.
The children have eaten. ☐ T ☐ F

5 If Tom worked harder, he'd have passed these exams.
He failed the exams. ☐ T ☐ F

6 If we'd known the address, we wouldn't be lost now.
We didn't know the address. ☐ T ☐ F

18 Complete the message with the words below.

> eat • ~~get~~ • had told me • hadn't invited • hadn't gone • had realised • wouldn't have eaten • wouldn't have gone • would have worn

You ask me, how was Sylvia's beach party? A disaster! Apparently I ⁰ *get* sick when I ¹ .... raw fish. I didn't know. If I ² ...., I ³ .... any. I wish I ⁴ .... at all, actually. I ⁵ .... if Sylvia ⁶ .... me personally. If she ⁷ .... it was a fancy dress party, I ⁸ .... something better. Total disaster.

Time clauses with *when, unless, until, as soon as*

Complete the sentences.
I won't drink the water .... it's clean = if it's not clean.
I won't drink any water .... I can get clean water.
.... / .... I find clean water, I'll drink it.

→ See **GRAMMAR REFERENCE** page 124

19 Complete the sentences with *when*, *if* or *unless*.

0 I won't catch that train ......*unless*...... I run.
1 I'll make the coffee .... I wake up first.
2 She wouldn't cook .... she didn't enjoy cooking.
3 .... you can pay for all that food, you shouldn't order it.
4 He won't give you meat .... he knows you're a vegetarian.
5 She'll make dinner .... she gets home.
6 I can't read this recipe .... I wear my glasses.
7 Call me .... you get home.
8 You will be sick .... you stop eating.

20 Complete the sentences using the verbs in brackets.

0 If I *had been* (be) a contestant in a reality show, I wouldn't eat insects.
1 We would be healthier if we .... (eat) more fresh fish, fruit and vegetables.
2 If she .... (not eat), she probably wouldn't have been ill.
3 I .... (serve) the dessert as soon as it's cool.
4 You shouldn't have left unless you .... (be given) permission.
5 Unless we do something, there .... (not be) enough food for everyone.

SPEAKING SKILLS

GIVING INSTRUCTIONS

21 Complete the recipe with the words below.

> add • break • Have you got •
> freeze • Next, you mix • pour • roll •
> So first, peel • What about

You want a good recipe? ¹.......................... frozen bananas with nuts and chocolate? ².......................... your bananas and cut them up. Then push a stick into each piece and freeze them. ³.......................... some yogurt and chopped nuts together. ⁴.......................... any peanut butter? OK, ⁵.......................... that, too. When the bananas are frozen, take them out and ⁶.......................... them in the nutty yogurt mixture. Freeze them again and when they're frozen, ⁷.......................... some chocolate into a bowl and melt it. Then ⁸.......................... the chocolate over the bananas and ⁹.......................... them once again. Easy!

22 Match the beginnings and ends to make checking phrases.

1	☐ Hang on,	a	say peanut butter?
2	☐ Would this	b	you said?
3	☐ Is that	c	what was that?
4	☐ Sorry, could you	d	be all right?
5	☐ Did you	e	that again?
6	☐ Is that what	f	OK?
7	☐ What was	g	just say that again?

23 Choose the correct option.

1 Have you got any eggs?
   A What about dessert?   B Yes, I think so.
2 What about cheese?
   A Did you say cheese?   B What now?
3 Grate some parmesan into a bowl.
   A Is that what you said?   B Into a … what?
4 What did you say?
   A I said, let it cool first.   B It says, let it cool first.
5 Chop the nuts into small pieces.
   A What about the nuts?
   B Hang on, what was that?
6 Preheat the oven.
   A How hot should it be?   B What should I do?
7 Spread the melted chocolate with a fork.
   A Did you say fork?   B What is a fork?

LISTENING SKILLS

A ☐ B ☐ C ☐ D ☐ E ☐

24 Read extracts of what these five people say about what they eat. Match the speakers (1–5) to the food (A–E).

Speaker 1 I'm training to run a marathon. To build up my leg muscles and improve my stamina, I have to eat plenty of carbs and protein.

Speaker 2 I'm a vegan, which is getting easier and easier these days. There are lots of vegan restaurants and cafés where people really understand about not eating animal products.

Speaker 3 It's difficult, cutting down on something that's so nice and so easy to eat … but recently I've noticed that my stomach feels very uncomfortable unless I'm careful what grains I eat.

Speaker 4 If I had more time, I'd learn to cook with whole grains and fresh vegetables. I don't eat a lot of fast food but …

Speaker 5 I loved burgers with chips when I was younger, but not any more. Now I believe that our food source should be sustainable. I'll eat fish if I know that it's been farmed organically …

25 🔊 [3.27] Listen to the five speakers and check your answers to exercise 24.

26 🔊 [3.27] Listen again. Which speaker says what?

a ☐ I think especially raw food has a lot of flavour.
b ☐ I wish I had more time to cook.
c ☐ I really like raw fish and it's full of protein and vitamins.
d ☐ I have to eat lots of pasta and potatoes.
e ☐ There are lots of gluten-free products in the supermarkets these days.

EXAM SKILLS

EXAM STRATEGY

Reading and Use of English – Gapped text

Read through the entire article with the gaps in it first. Try to get a general idea of the structure of the text and the development of the writer's ideas.
When choosing a sentence to fill the gap, carefully read the information before and after the gap so that it follows logically.

27 You are going to read an article about honey bees. Six sentences have been removed from the article. Choose from the sentences a–g the one which fits each gap 1–5. There is one extra sentence.

a A law passed by the Scottish government has made it illegal to bring any other bees onto the islands.
b Moving hives from farm to farm is believed to cause stress to the bees.
c An EU-funded research project to produce so-called *smart bees* could be the answer.
d Today they play a large role in agriculture.
e However, this vital resource in the food chain is in danger.
f In fact, it is probably the main cause for colony loss.
g Bees also pollinate the plants grown for cattle feed.

Honey bees in danger

If bees did not pollinate many hundreds of different plants, those plants would not be able to reproduce. The modern farming system that humans have developed depends on the work of bees, and without them, it would not work so efficiently. Honey bees are not native to the United States, but they were successfully introduced there from Europe. **0** ..*d*.. Farmers rely on beekeepers who move their bee colonies around to different agricultural areas, and it is in this way that their crops are pollinated.

Many foods enjoyed by humans, such as apples, cucumbers, broccoli and almonds, would have disappeared if the plants were not pollinated by bees. **1** .... It is from cows that people get most of their milk, cheese, butter, yogurt and beef. Moreover, the by-product of honey bee pollination is of course honey, which is widely used as a sweetener.

2 .... If a condition known as *colony collapse disorder* hits a beehive, every one of the all-important worker bees dies or vanishes. If this happens, the queen bee is left with only young bees that have not yet fully developed, and the hive is no longer sustainable. One survey estimated that almost 40% of beehives died in 2014 alone.

Farming methods that are used today are thought to be one of the main reasons for this decline. **3** .... Many of the bees' natural feeding areas have been lost to agriculture, and chemical pesticides are known to be harmful to bees, too.

Climate change is also a factor, but perhaps the biggest single danger to bees is disease. The disease that is most feared by beekeepers and farmers is the Varroa mite (*Varroa destructor*). As its Latin name suggests, this tiny parasite is very destructive. **4** .... The Varroa mite has been a major problem in the UK since the 1990s. Scientists are working on a solution to the Varroa problem, but meanwhile, two tiny Hebridean islands have become the UK's first sanctuary for native honey bees. The islands of Colonsay and Oronsay, off the west coast of Scotland, are home to approximately 50 honey bee colonies. These remote islands were chosen as a nature reserve because the colonies there are genetically pure and free from the Varroa parasite. **5** .... In this way, the local beekeeper hopes to protect his bees from cross-breeding and disease.

74 Unit 7

EXAM SKILLS

> **EXAM STRATEGY**
>
> **Writing – A review**
>
> The tasks in this part give you a chance to show a range of language. The main purpose of writing a review is to describe and express a personal opinion about something you have experienced. It will usually include a recommendation.

28 Read the advertisement for a review of a cookery show on TV. Which show could you write a review about?

> **REVIEWS WANTED**
>
> We are looking for reviews of a popular TV cookery show for teenagers. Choose a show to review. Your review should include information about what the show does well and what does not work so well.
> What kind of food is prepared?
> Is it a competition or a demonstration?
> Describe the presenters and the cooks. Would you recommend this show to other people your age?

29 Read the review a student wrote about a show called *Let's Cook!* Find and correct six mistakes in the review.

A popular TV cookery show at the moment is broadcast at eight on a Saturday evening, when is prime time TV. That means it will get a lot of viewers because that is when many people watch TV, but I'm not sure if it's when most teenagers are watching. So I think it's not broadcast at the best time. The format of the show is always same, which I think is quite boring. Four teenage cooks are given a box full from ingredients but they don't know what they are. The presenter is a crazy guy with big hair who makes a lot of noise, counting down from ten when the cooks can open they boxes. Then they have a short time to decide what to cook and then cook it with what's in the box. There is usually a celebrity cook who judge the best meal.

30 What does the reviewer of *Let's Cook!* not include?

1 A description.
2 An opinion.
3 A recommendation.

31 Read the advertisement for a café's review. Which café near you could you write a review about?

> **REVIEWS WANTED**
>
> We are looking for reviews of the best cafés for teenagers near where you live. Your review should include information about where the café is and what it looks like, the quality of the food and drinks, the service and the value for money. Would you recommend this café to other people your age?

32 Make a few notes about each of the points to include in your review.

- Where is the café? Can you sit outside?
- What's it like inside? Is there music / wi-fi? Are the chairs comfortable?
- Is the coffee good? What kind of food do they serve?
- Are the waiters / waitresses friendly? Or is the café self-service?
- Is it expensive?

33 Write your own review in 140–190 words in an appropriate style, using your notes from exercise 32. Would you recommend this café to your friends?

Unit 7   75

8 All in the mind

GRAMMAR PRACTICE

used to / would + infinitive without to

Choose the correct option.
We *can / can't* use *would* or *used to* when we talk about past habits which we don't do any more.
In affirmative sentences, we *can / can't* use *used to* when we describe permanent states that are no longer true. We *can / can't* use *would* in these sentences.
With both *used to* and *would*, we use the *infinitive / -ing form* of the verb that follows.

➡ See **GRAMMAR REFERENCE** page 125

1 Make sentences with *used to* and the verbs below.

be · ~~have~~ · live · play · ride · walk · wear

0 My grandparents **used to have** a black-and-white TV.
1 The children .... football outside until it got dark.
2 Our neighbour's dog .... (*not*) so aggressive.
3 .... your parents .... a uniform at school?
4 They .... (*not*) in such a big apartment.
5 My father .... his motorbike with me on the back.
6 .... your sister .... to school with you?

2 Mark the sentences in exercise 1 where *would* can replace *used to*.

3 Make questions to match the answers.

0 **Did they use to live in Amsterdam?**
   No, not Amsterdam. They used to live in Amersfoort.
1 He used to drive a Honda, not a Fiat.
2 No, she's never eaten meat.
3 Warm milk? No, and I still hate it!
4 My mum was strict, but not my dad.
5 Yes, they've always taught lots of languages here.
6 Bad dreams? I didn't have many, I'm happy to say.

4 Match the beginnings and ends of the sentences.

0 [f] The milkman used to
1 [ ] Her mother would
2 [ ] The weather used to
3 [ ] The Romans would
4 [ ] Parts of the Netherlands
5 [ ] Did the family use to meet
6 [ ] Teenagers didn't use to

a socialise in the hot baths.
b used to be under water.
c bring smartphones to school.
d make her children's clothes.
e be more predictable.
f deliver milk to the door.
g for a traditional Sunday lunch?

be / get used to + something / -ing

Choose the correct option.
We use *be used to* + something when we want to describe *being / becoming* familiar with it.
We use *get used to* + something when we want to describe *being / becoming* familiar with it.
With both *be used to* and *get used to*, we use the *infinitive / -ing form* of the verb that follows.

➡ See **GRAMMAR REFERENCE** page 125

5 Make sentences with the correct form of *be used to*.

0 we / lots of cats / animals
   We've got lots of cats, so I'm used to animals.
1 our house / busy road / traffic
2 they often / this restaurant / food
3 children / their new classroom yet?
4 we / never in hotels / camping
5 I / mountains / snow
6 she / five little brothers / a lot of noise
7 Pedro / Spanish / dinner very late
8 if / Clara / move to England / rain

76 Unit 8

GRAMMAR PRACTICE

6 🔊 **Put the words in the correct order.**

0 get / left / soon / driving / visitors / used / on / to / the
   Visitors soon get used to driving on the left.
1 my / used / can't / I / glasses / wearing / to / get / new
2 library / studying / the / is / in / to / used / Pamela
3 used / language / not / to / we're / hearing / bad
4 grandfather / used / texts / sending / has / his / got / to
5 shopping / Sundays / they / used / to / on / get / can't
6 Paris / metro / we / using / used / the / got / in / soon / to

7 🔊 **Choose the correct option.**

0 We used to (ski) / skiing in the Dolomites every winter.
1 I used to *dream / dreaming* about being an astronaut.
2 We'll never get used to *drink / drinking* tea with milk in it.
3 There didn't use to *be / being* so many adverts on TV.
4 She's slowly getting used to *live / living* alone.
5 Did you use to *babysit / babysitting* for their kids?
6 More trains used to *stop / stopping* here.

8 🔊 **Choose the correct option.**

0 Life .... very different from the way it is now.
   A use to be   (C) used to be
   B used to being
1 I'm slowly .... Ned's sense of humour.
   A getting used to   C being used to
   B used to
2 Helena could never get .... coffee.
   A use to drink   C used to drinking
   B used to drink
3 My father would always .... to school in winter.
   A skate   B to skate   C skating
4 Did you .... long hair when you were little?
   A use to having   C used to having
   B use to have
5 Doctors have to get used .... at night.
   A work   B to working   C to work
6 People .... vinegar to clean the windows.
   A used to used   B use to use   C used to use

9 🔊 **Complete the text with the words in brackets and the correct form of (get) used to or would.**

School in the 1950s

My uncle John went to school in the 1950s. They ⁰ **used to write** (*write*) on chalkboards then because of course they ¹.................... (*not / have*) interactive whiteboards. Boys in his class ².................... (*not / wear*) school uniform, but they ³.................... (*always dress*) smartly. From the age of ten, John had to ⁴.................... (*be*) in single-sex classes: girls ⁵.................... (*go*) to a different school. When I asked him: '⁶.................... your teachers .... (*be*) strict?' he laughed and told me they ⁷.................... (*carry*) canes, and they ⁸.................... (*even use*) them! I said I could ⁹.................... (*never*) that. He replied that they ¹⁰.................... (*not / like*) it much, either.

10 🔊 **Write sentences using (get) used to or would that are true for you.**

1 When I was a baby ....
2 When I was a toddler ....
3 At nursery school I ....
4 At primary school I ....
5 Last year I ....

Unit 8   77

READING SKILLS

11 Look at the picture about dreaming. Which of these things do you dream about?

12 [3.28] Read and listen to the text. Which do you think is the best title?

1. Freudian dream analysis
2. Sweet dreams
3. Dreams and their meanings
4. Dream on!

13 Read the text again and choose the correct option.

1. Sigmund Freud's theories …
   A are still accepted by psychoanalysts.
   B have been popular for millennia.
   C disagree with the interpretation of dreams.
   D are the basis of much dream theory today.

2. The main features of dreams are …
   A running, falling and flying.
   B frequently forgotten.
   C absurdity and emotional intensity.
   D not extraordinary to the dreamer.

3. All three teenagers …
   A used to remember their dreams.
   B believe in hidden meanings.
   C have had memorable dreams.
   D describe the same dreams.

4. In the writer's opinion, …
   A interpreting dreams shapes your unconscious mind.
   B asking teenagers is a proven empirical approach.
   C even the theorists still don't understand dreams.
   D having bizarre dreams is completely normal.

14 Answer these questions.

1. Can you describe a dream that you used to have when you were younger?
   ....
   ....
   ....
   ....

2. How do you interpret your dream?
   ....
   ....
   ....
   ....

Dreaming is the subject of serious scientific studies nowadays, but the interest in it is not new. Dreams have intrigued people for millennia. Yet empirical research has so far failed to **come up with** one robust theory about what our dreams mean or indeed why we dream at all.

Is it possible to understand your unconscious wishes and thoughts by interpreting dreams? Sigmund Freud certainly thought so, and his famous book *The Interpretation of Dreams* **shaped** the psychoanalytic theory of dreams for many years. More modern theories of dreams disagree with Freud's conclusions, but still many books are written about common dream symbols and what they mean.

The main characteristics of dreams are that they are frequently full of intense emotions, such as anxiety, fear or surprise. Dreams tend to be incongruous; featuring people the dreamer may or may not know, in bizarre combinations. The events in dreams are strange and often illogical, but they are accepted as normal while dreaming. They can be very clear or extremely vague but, however traumatic, 95% of what we dream is forgotten on waking.

Are there really hidden meanings in your dreams?

VOCABULARY

THE MIND

15 Use the definitions to complete the puzzle. Write your own definition for the word in the grey squares.

0 giving you hope and support
1 making you feel unhappy and without hope
2 worried and nervous; opposite of relaxed
3 calming, making you less anxious
4 easily angry or unhappy; with changing emotions
5 feeling or showing certainty
6 afraid and uneasy; opposite of untroubled
7 full of hope and confidence

⁰E	N	C	O	U	R	A	G	I	N	G
		¹D							
				²S					
³R									
				⁴M					
		⁵C							
⁶A									
		⁷P							

16 Complete the sentences with words from the crossword.

0 My mother used to get very **stressed** when she had all five of us kids under ten!
1 Her .... attitude to life has helped her through some difficult times.
2 The news of starving children in war zones is very ....
3 Amy found it very ...., doing yoga while listening to calm music.
4 I used to get really .... before an exam and would never sleep well.
5 He's .... that he will pass his driving test first time: he's had lots of practice.
6 The teacher's remarks were very ....; she said I was doing OK.
7 You never know what to expect from Harry these days, he's so ....

17 Finish the sentences about yourself.

1 The word that describes me on most days is …
2 My closest friend is usually …
3 I like being with people who are …
4 I think / don't think I'm an optimist because …

We asked three teenagers:

Marie Hidden meanings? I'm not sure. There are lots of myths about dreaming. I once read that if you have a dream about falling, and you hit the ground in your dream, you will actually die. I used to have that dream all the time and, although it wasn't very nice, I'm still alive! 30

Jason I think there might be. I take part in national snowboarding competitions, 35 and I used to get very anxious the night before. You'd think I'd dream about flying or falling but in fact I would dream about sitting an exam. I interpret that as worrying about being unprepared for a big challenge. 40

Molly Definitely. I used to have a recurrent dream about a **weird** animal chasing me. I couldn't run, I couldn't even move, I was terrified. I think that was about avoiding a problem I had in real life because when 45 I solved that problem, the dreams stopped.

GLOSSARY

come up with	▶	think of, find
shaped	▶	influenced
weird	▶	strange

Unit 8   79

GRAMMAR PRACTICE

Gerunds and infinitives (1)

Complete the rules.
We use gerunds:
- as the .... of a sentence:
  Listening to music is very relaxing.
- after some ....:
  I **can't stand going** to bed early.
- after ....:
  If you're interested **in analysing** your dreams …

We use infinitives:
- to describe ....:
  We rang up **to book** our holiday.
- after some ....:
  Are you **prepared to work** hard?

Infinitives follow some verbs and phrases, too:
If you **want to pass** the exam, …

→ See GRAMMAR REFERENCE page 125

18 Write the sentences so that they mean the same, using the gerund as the subject.

0 I usually read in bed because I find it relaxing.
   Reading in bed relaxes me.
1 I hope I get a good job; that's important to me.
2 It's healthy to eat plenty of fruit and vegetables.
3 It's impolite to text at the dinner table.
4 It can cause stress if you work too hard.

19 Match the parts and join them with the word *to*.

0 [b] She went to the post office
1 [ ] I logged onto the CNN website
2 [ ] Did you use honey or sugar
3 [ ] He took a job as a waiter
4 [ ] They drank strong black coffee

a sweeten your cake?
b collect a parcel.
c read the latest news.
d finance his studies.
e keep themselves awake.

20 Make sentences with verbs in the gerund.

0 Julia / keep / fall asleep in class
   Julia keeps falling asleep in class.
1 we / look forward to / see you tomorrow
2 our cats / always / enjoy / take a nap in the sun
3 I / not / mind / do the washing-up / sometimes
4 they / can't help / laugh at Ben's jokes

21 Complete the sentences with the prepositions below.

about ▪ ~~against~~ ▪ for ▪ in ▪ on ▪ up ▪ with

0 We decided ....**against**..... flying to Prague just for the weekend.
1 If I get tired, I can't concentrate .... doing my homework.
2 She's fed up .... hearing how clever her sister is.
3 They don't believe .... driving the children to school.
4 He rang his friend and apologised .... forgetting to buy the concert tickets.
5 My best friend worries .... failing exams but she never does.
6 Our parents gave .... eating meat years ago.

22 Choose the correct option.

0 She really likes (*listening*) / *listen* to relaxing music in the evenings.
1 We were amazed *learning* / *to learn* that the concert was free.
2 They stopped on the way *get* / *to get* some food.
3 Thank you very much for *helping* / *helped* me yesterday.
4 *Giving* / *Give* presents is even nicer than *receiving* / *receive* them.
5 She couldn't help *to feel* / *feeling* sorry for the losers.
6 He hopes *will come* / *to come* to the meeting tomorrow.

23 Complete the invitation with the verbs in the gerund or infinitive.

Hi Celia,
I hope you don't mind me ⁰ ....**writing**..... (*write*) to you; maybe you remember ¹ .... (*meet*) me years ago? Our mothers used to ² .... (*work*) together, and didn't we use to ³ .... (*go*) to the same primary school? Anyway, I was pleased ⁴ .... (*find out*) you've moved back to the area. Do you feel like ⁵ .... (*get*) together? Would you like ⁶ .... (*come*) to my party? It'd be great if you decide ⁷ .... (*join*) us! We're very easy ⁸ .... (*find*) and please feel free ⁹ .... (*bring*) a friend. You can check out the details on Facebook. Looking forward to ¹⁰ .... (*see*) you again!
   Danni x

SPEAKING SKILLS

TALKING ABOUT HABITS

24 Are the speakers talking about past or present habits? Tick (✓) the correct column.

	Past	Present
1 We never do anything remotely dangerous.	☐	☐
2 I used to be quite keen on dancing.	☐	☐
3 It's always too busy at the sports centre.	☐	☐
4 I sometimes swim after school.	☐	☐
5 I'd go when the pool was almost empty.	☐	☐
6 I used to go swimming three times a week.	☐	☐
7 Don't tell me you go skiing every weekend.	☐	☐

25 Read the conversation. Underline Mike's present habits and circle his past habits.

Wendy Hey Mike, I've been trying to call you for ages! How's things in Zurich?

Mike Hi Wendy, it's OK on the whole. Yeah, I'm getting used to living here … I suppose.

Wendy You always used to love going to the mountains. You'd go skiing twice a year. Now you can ski all the time.

Mike You're right, the skiing's great most of the time. When there's enough snow, I can get my skis out most weekends.

Wendy Brilliant! So is that what you usually do?

Mike I used to say I'd ski every free minute once I lived here, but actually, school's hard. I didn't use to have any problems, but we get so much homework here. My German's not fluent yet.

Wendy Do you always speak Swiss German now?

Mike The classes are mostly in High German, but my new friends generally talk in three or four different languages. So … I don't say much, as a rule!

Wendy Wow, I can't imagine you not saying much. I remember when you never used to stop talking!

26 Find the words or phrases in the dialogue which the speakers use to generalise.

LISTENING SKILLS

27 Look at the signs of the zodiac. Fill in the names below.

Aries • Aquarius • Cancer • Capricorn • Gemini • Leo • Libra • Pisces • Sagittarius • Scorpio • Taurus • Virgo

1 .... 2 .... 3 .... 4 ....
5 .... 6 .... 7 .... 8 ....
9 .... 10 .... 11 .... 12 ....

28 Read the questions and the options before you listen.

1 Which statement is correct?
  A All three speakers believe the zodiac predictions they read.
  B They all know the characteristics of their own star sign.
  C Only one of them is sceptical about horoscopes.

2 The person who is honest, friendly and communicates well is
  A a Leo.   B a Scorpio.   C an Aquarius.

3 The first speaker thinks
  A she is confident enough to be a teacher.
  B her parents wouldn't agree to her being a teacher.
  C authoritarian people shouldn't be teachers.

4 The second speaker wants to believe in his horoscope because he
  A knows he's competitive in sports.
  B likes the idea of becoming a secret agent.
  C enjoys annoying his sister.

5 The third speaker thinks
  A Valentine's Day is significant.
  B horoscopes are too general.
  C lots of predictions are inappropriate.

29 [3.29] Listen to three people talking about their star signs. Answer the questions in exercise 28.

30 [3.29] Listen again and check your answers.

Unit 8 81

ACADEMIC SKILLS

PROOFREADING YOUR WORK

31 Decide if the sentences are true (T) or false (F). Correct the false ones.

0. Proofread your writing as soon as you've done it. [T] [✓]
   Wait a little while before proofreading.
1. Be careful not to rely on your spell checker. [T] [F]
2. Use a dictionary to check spellings. [T] [F]
3. Don't print it out to proofread it. [T] [F]
4. Read it out loud to yourself. [T] [F]
5. Check punctuation, word order, spelling and grammar separately. [T] [F]

32 Correct the punctuation mistakes.

0. If you finish early read your work through carefully,
   If you finish early, read your work through carefully.
1. They went to visit the roman baths last saturday.
2. 'Thank you for helping me, she said, warmly
3. Generally speaking, the best month to visit isnt may.
4. The people, that we met, were very friendly.
5. Dutch school's don't have parking for teacher's cars.

33 Put the words in brackets in the correct position.

0. He goes swimming after school. (*often*)
   He **often** goes swimming after school.
1. We hardly see our old neighbours now. (*ever*)
2. It's too crowded in town on Saturdays. (*always*)
3. As a rule, they go to school by bike. (*general*)
4. Do any of these new apps work? (*actually*)
5. After a while, he was able to speak English. (*again*)

34 Correct two spelling mistakes in each sentence.

0. We weren't very ~~ungry~~ because we'd already ~~heaten~~. **hungry; eaten**
1. The dates you suggist are not possibile for me, sorry.
2. He gave up runing after his motorbike accidente.
3. After a longe illness, she looked tin and pale.
4. I'm busy so pleas don't west my time.
5. My grandfather used to be a famose psicoanaliste.

35 Correct two grammar mistakes in each sentence.

0. After years of ~~be~~ a vegetarian, he's got used to ~~eat~~ meat again. **being; eating**
1. He lives in the same house since 50 years.
2. I would be very happy if you would come with myself.
3. She was extremely interesting in learn another language.
4. What you normally do if school finishes every day?
5. Far less animals are been hunted these days.

36 Proofread the text and correct the 22 mistakes.

WHY BELIEVE IN HOROSCOPES?

According to the experts: the majority people who read newspaper horoscopes are believing the prediction if its positive but ignore it if its negative. I believe this being true. I've been checking my own since years but I've always see it as just a bit of funny. Thinking that all other person born on 22nd or twenty-first of august has the same characteristics as me is total rubbish. However, a cheerfull horoscope could make you feel happyer if you're depressing if you wake up.
And furthermore, a pessimistic prediction such like "You have an accident' might be useful warning for you to be more careful crossing road.

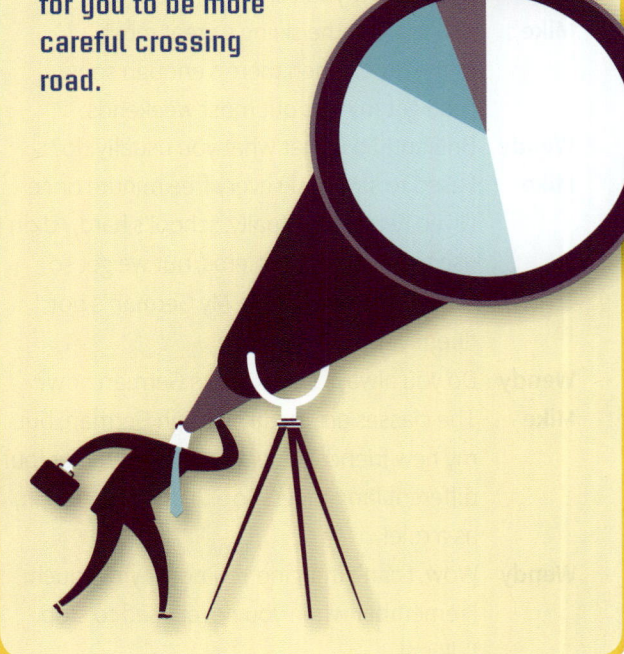

37 Write a text of about 100 words with the same heading and proofread it.

EXAM SKILLS

> **EXAM STRATEGY**
>
> **Listening – Multiple choice**
>
> Read the questions first, to give you an idea of what kind of information you are listening for. Try to answer the questions in your own words before choosing an option, then decide which option is closest to your own answer.

38 Read the questions. What kind of information are you listening for in each question?

0 <u>When</u> did Irena decide she wanted to be a dancer?
   A What made her decide.
   B What she decided to be.
   C) The time when she decided.
1 How did the boys win the tennis doubles final?
   A What they won.   C The way they won.
   B Who won.
2 Why was Tina so disappointed by her exam result?
   A Her reaction.   C The reason for her
   B The way she reacted.   reaction.
3 How many extra hours did Mr Fletcher work last week?
   A When he worked.
   B How long he worked.
   C The amount of additional work time.
4 What did the angry customer say when she returned to the shop?
   A The words she spoke. C How she felt.
   B What she took back.

39 🔴 [3.30] Listen to an interview with a teenage violinist talking about her family. Choose the correct option.

0 Why did Christina first take up playing a musical instrument?
   A Her parents were both professional musicians.
   B She wanted to compete against her brothers.
   C) It seemed the accepted thing to do in her family.
1 Why did she decide to play the violin?
   A Stringed instruments were better than brass for girls.
   B The decision wasn't really made by her.
   C Her first Chinese instrument didn't cost much.
2 What did Christina say about her relationship with her mother?
   A It was crazy at first.
   B In the end it was discouraging.
   C It was fair and friendly.
3 Why did she think about giving up playing?
   A She wanted more time to go to her brothers' concerts.
   B Her friends used to hang around waiting for her.
   C Practising the violin took too much of her time.
4 What stopped Christina from giving up?
   A She wasn't bright enough to do anything else.
   B Her parents expected her to continue.
   C She was a very good player for her age.
5 What did winning a scholarship mean to Christina?
   A She was more motivated to play and improve.
   B She could see her own friends every Saturday.
   C She was no longer competing against her mother.

> **EXAM STRATEGY**
>
> **Speaking – Long turn / Extended discourse**
>
> For this part of the exam, you have to speak for one minute without interruption. Practise timing yourself while you are speaking, so that you get a feeling for how much you can say in a minute. The task is to talk about two photos. You are not expected to describe them in detail, but compare them and give your own reaction to them.

40 Look at the photos and make notes in answer to the questions.

1 Name at least two ways in which these situations are similar.
2 Think of at least two ways in which they are dissimilar.
3 What are the people in the photos enjoying most?
4 What are your reasons for the preference you expressed?
5 Could you talk about these two photos for one minute?

Unit 8   83

REVISE AND ROUND UP

1 🔊 **Choose the correct option to make zero and first conditional sentences.**

0 We won't buy processed food if there *is* / *will be* fresh food on the market.
1 If she *changes* / *will change* her lifestyle, she'll probably be fitter.
2 When will we arrive if we *leave* / *will leave* after breakfast?
3 What will they eat if they *don't like* / *won't like* meat?
4 If you *freeze* / *will freeze* chocolate, it goes hard.
5 This recipe doesn't work if you *don't use* / *won't use* salt.
6 She *comes* / *'ll come* tomorrow if she has time.

2 🔊 **Match the beginnings and ends to make second conditional sentences.**

0 [f] If she went on a diet,
1 [ ] If we employed a cook,
2 [ ] He would open his own café
3 [ ] If I had more time,
4 [ ] Would this coffee taste better
5 [ ] If they didn't breathe polluted air,
6 [ ] This meal would cost a lot more

a if he had the money.
b if we had it in a restaurant.
c they would be healthier.
d if it was a bit stronger?
e we would eat very well.
f would she look like a model?
g I wouldn't spend it in the kitchen.

3 🔊 **Complete the answers using the third conditional.**

0 'He hurt his leg playing football. Did he fall?'
'Yes, he **wouldn't have hurt** his leg if he hadn't fallen.'
1 'Julia looked happy. Did her husband remember her birthday?'
'Yes, she .... so happy if he had forgotten it.'
2 'Those teenagers were very fit. Did they eat well as children?'
'I'm sure they .... so fit if they'd eaten only junk food.'
3 'How was your holiday? Was the weather nice?'
'No, I'm afraid the holiday .... better if we'd had nicer weather.'
4 'You took a quick lunch break yesterday. Were you very busy?'
'Yes, if we hadn't been so busy, we .... a longer lunch break.'
5 'You cooked steaks? Didn't you know they were vegetarians?'
'If I had known that, I .... meat.'
6 'Why did Oliver arrive so late? Didn't he have his car?'
'Yes, he did, and he .... on time if his car hadn't broken down.'

4 🔊 **Make sentences using the words in brackets and *should* / *shouldn't have* or *I wish*.**

0 The old cinema building was really beautiful. (*knock down*)
They shouldn't have / I wish they hadn't knocked it down.
1 He put a handful of salt in the spaghetti sauce! (*pinch*)
2 The refugees were drinking dirty water. (*boil*)
3 Those children were rude to their teacher. (*apologise*)
4 My sister's never learnt to swim. (*younger*)
5 I feel sick after eating two chocolate cakes. (*any*)
6 We went to bed very late last night. (*earlier*)

5 🔊 **Complete the sentences with *unless*, *until* or *as soon as*.**

0 Belinda goes for a run **as soon as** she wakes up.
1 .... you leave now, you'll miss the start of the film.
2 She waited for him .... six o'clock, but he didn't come.
3 I'll call you back .... I've finished my dinner.
4 Old Mrs Howe won't hear you .... you speak louder.
5 He didn't like olives .... he went to live in Spain.
6 You won't get what you want .... you say *please*.

6 🔊 **Put the words in the correct order.**

0 marathon / year / she / to / a / every / used / run
She used to run a marathon every year.
1 until / play / we / dark / outside / got / it / would
2 school / to / trousers / boys / wear / to / used / short
3 use / computers / didn't / schools / to / have
4 child / you / pets / have / use / a / did / to / as / ?
5 week / play / mothers / would / bingo / once / our / a
6 dreams / remember / I / use / didn't / to / my

7 🔊 Complete the sentences with the *-ing* form of the verbs below.

> be • drive • eat • ~~live~~ • speak • wear • work

0   It took ages to get used to ……**living**…… in the city.
1   I'm not used to ………………… to a large audience.
2   She's getting used to ………………… in a new school.
3   You get used to ………………… in heavy traffic.
4   Doctors have to get used to ………………… at night.
5   We're not really used to ………………… Indian food.
6   He'll soon get used to ………………… contact lenses.

8 🔊 Choose the correct option.

0   I can't stand *lose* / (*losing*) my phone.
1   Do you feel like *come* / *coming* out tonight?
2   Are you sure that device is safe to *use* / *using*?
3   They decided not to *go* / *going* on holiday.
4   She apologised for *break* / *breaking* a glass.
5   We were lucky enough to *win* / *winning* a prize.
6   I don't mind *to walk* / *walking* in the rain.

9 🔊 Complete the sentences with the prepositions below.

> about • at • for • from • in • of • ~~on~~

0   Our friends insisted ……**on**…… paying for the meal.
1   She was very excited ………… flying to New Zealand.
2   The court found him guilty ………… stealing the money.
3   I really must thank him ………… being so kind.
4   They used to be very good ………… skateboarding.
5   I hope he succeeds ………… passing that exam.
6   Eating well might prevent you ………… getting ill.

10 🔊 Choose the correct option.

Hi Sandy,
I wish ⁰ *I were* / (*I'd been*) able to join you yesterday. I should ¹ *have called* / *had called* you, sorry. I ² *had* / *would have* come if I hadn't been so stressed. If I don't keep studying hard, ³ *I'll* / *I'd* fail my next exam, and that'll be a catastrophe! I always ⁴ *used* / *got used* to be top of my class. Now I have to ⁵ *use* / *get used* to being with really bright students. Wish me luck and see you soon.
Harry xx

CONCEPT CHECK

Read the sentences and answer the questions.

1 *If Kit had gone to bed earlier, he wouldn't have overslept.*

(Answer Yes / No / Maybe)

0   Kit went to bed late. **Maybe**
1   He didn't go to bed as early as he should have done.
2   He didn't sleep well.
3   He slept later than he wanted to.
4   Going to bed earlier would have meant waking at a better time.

2 *I wish I hadn't drunk so much coffee.*

(Answer True / False)

0   This is something I wished in the past. **False**
1   This is something I wish now.
2   I'm drinking coffee now.
3   I drank a lot of coffee in the recent past.
4   I now regret drinking the coffee I drank.

3 *She won't forgive him unless he says sorry.*

(Answer Yes / No / Possibly)

0   She is angry with him about something. **Yes**
1   He knows she is angry with him.
2   She wants him to apologise.
3   He is going to apologise.
4   She will excuse him if he says sorry.

4 *I'd never get used to living anywhere without wi-fi.*

(Answer True / False / Don't know)

0   In the past I lived somewhere without wi-fi.
    Don't know
1   I didn't use to live anywhere with wi-fi.
2   I have to get used to living without wi-fi now.
3   I would be happy if I lived somewhere without wi-fi.
4   I could never accept living somewhere without wi-fi.

➡ See **GRAMMAR REFERENCE**
pages 123–125

9 Business rules

GRAMMAR PRACTICE

Gerunds and infinitives (2)

Choose the correct option.
Some verbs take both the gerund and the infinitive.
With some verbs, the meaning *stays the same* / *changes*:
continue, start, begin, prefer, like, love, hate.
With other verbs, the meaning *stays the same* / *changes*:
remember, forget, regret, try, stop, mean.

➡ See **GRAMMAR REFERENCE** page 125

1 Complete the sentences with the verbs below. Use either the gerund or infinitive forms.

buy • chat • leave • read • save • talk • work

0 Do you usually prefer <u>to talk / talking</u> to your bank manager in person or on the phone?
1 She's always loved .... clothes when they're cheap in the sales.
2 You should start .... up your pocket money for your next holiday.
3 I hate .... on Sundays; it should be a day of rest.
4 People began .... the theatre before the end of the play.
5 Do you like .... books about famous bank robbers?
6 The girl at the back continued .... after the teacher had asked for silence.

2 Make sentences with the words given.

0 I / not / like / get up early / weekend
   I don't like getting up early at the weekend.
1 you / start / eat / before your guests arrive / last night?
2 we / usually / prefer / not / buy / concert tickets online
3 it / continue / rain / all through yesterday night
4 he / begin / work / as an apprentice / in 2015
5 they / hate / revise for exams / since the start of term
6 I / always love / be able / transfer money online
7 It / start / snow / a couple of hours ago
8 I / hate / not be able to sleep / before an important exam

3 Choose the correct option.

0 I must remember .... my friend's birthday present.
   A posting   B post   **C to post**
1 She spoke sharply but she didn't mean .... rude.
   A being   B to be   C be
2 The teacher asked for silence but they still didn't stop ....
   A shouting   B to shout   C shouted
3 We regret .... you that this bank is closing soon.
   A informed   B to inform   C inform
4 She's trying .... the document but the printer's broken.
   A printing   B to print   C print
5 Don't forget .... the lights when you leave.
   A to switch off   B switching   C to switch on
6 I regret .... these shoes, they're so uncomfortable.
   A to buy   B buy   C buying

4 Choose the correct option.

0 I regret selling my skateboard.
   A I wish I hadn't sold it.
   B I'm not sorry I sold it.
1 He'll never forget hearing Mandela speak.
   A It will always be a memory.
   B He can't remember it.
2 We stopped to have lunch in the café.
   A We don't eat there any more.
   B We ate there.
3 I remember saying sorry.
   A I know I apologised.
   B I never forget to apologise.
4 He introduced himself and went on to give his lecture.
   A He said his name first.
   B He started his lecture first.
5 I regret to tell you that your account is overdrawn.
   A I'm sorry that I told you.
   B I'm sorry but you should know.
6 The driver stopped to send a text.
   A She was texting while driving.
   B She texted after stopping.

GRAMMAR PRACTICE

Reporting verbs

Choose the correct option.
Verbs like *tell*, *ask*, *order*, *command*, *warn*, *persuade*, *remind* follow this pattern:
verb + direct object + gerund / infinitive with *to*:
- The bank manager **persuaded** her **to open** a new account.
- I heard Annie **asking** the teacher **to help** her with the translation.

→ See GRAMMAR REFERENCE page 126

5 Complete the questions with the words below.

ask ▪ commanding ▪ ~~order~~ ▪ persuaded ▪ remind ▪ tell ▪ warned

0 Why did the captain ......**order**...... the soldiers to attack?
1 Who .... you to buy such expensive speakers?
2 Why didn't you .... me to pay the credit card bill when I forgot?
3 Did he .... you to leave nicely or was he rude?
4 Do your parents usually .... you not to stay out late?
5 Is the group leader .... us to move on or wait here?
6 Has nobody ever .... you not to charge your phone in the bath?

6 Rewrite the direct speech into indirect speech.

0 He said to me: 'Don't show anyone else your PIN.'
He told **me not to show anyone else my PIN**.
1 She said to the customer: 'If I were you, I'd open a new account.'
She persuaded ....
2 The bank robber said to us: 'Put your hands on your head!'
The robber commanded ....
3 My IT expert said: 'Don't use your date of birth as your password.'
He warned ....
4 The policewoman told him: 'You shouldn't put your wallet in your back pocket.'
The officer advised ....

7 Rewrite the sentences so that they mean the same. Use the correct form of the words in brackets.

0 She waited for him until the last bus arrived. (*continue*)
She continued to wait for him until the last bus arrived.
1 He wishes he hadn't spent all his savings. (*regret*)
2 The old man asked us the way to the bank. (*how*)
3 Seeing The Beatles will always be in my memory. (*forget*)
4 'Don't forget to lock up your bike,' her dad said. (*remind*)
5 I forgot to cash the cheques you gave me. (*remember*)
6 She advised us to take dollars on holiday. (*should*)

8 Choose the correct verbs to complete the bank's advice.

HOW TO KEEP YOUR MONEY SAFE ONLINE

Online banking is an easy and secure way ⁰(*to manage*) / *managing* your money. Any bank will advise you ¹*to protect* / *protecting* your personal information. Of course you need ²*to keep* / *keeping* your financial information safe.
- Remember not ³*to reveal* / *revealing* your passwords to anyone.
- Avoid ⁴*to use* / *using* a password that's easy ⁵*to guess* / *guessing*, like the name of your pet.
- And don't forget ⁶*to log out* / *logging out* of your online banking account as soon as you've finished ⁷*to access* / *accessing* it.
- Your bank will probably advise you ⁸*to check* / *checking* for unusual transactions, and warn you ⁹*to contact* / *contacting* them if you suspect someone of ¹⁰*to hack* / *hacking* your account.

Unit 9 87

READING SKILLS

9 Are there any words in the word cloud that you don't know? If so, look them up.

success · advertise · past · corporate · story · share · motivation · creativity · strategy · teamwork · successful · inspiration · achievement · skill · business · analysis · efficiency · lean · career · experience · determination · coaching · marketing · development · plan · education · presentation · win · idea · performance · progress · advice · leadership · professional · innovation · confidence · people · management

10 [3.31] Read and listen to the text. What do all four success stories have in common?

11 Now answer the questions. For questions 1–10, choose from the stories (A–D). The stories may be chosen more than once.

Which success story …
1 is about a multinational business?
2 tells us about a local success?
3 started decades ago?
4 got a positive reaction on social media?
5 began at a musical event?
6 had small beginnings in someone's home?
7 depended on a customer vote?
8 turned a disability into a unique selling point?
9 is run by people who gave up their day jobs?
10 has a name chosen by satisfied customers?

SUCCESS

Success doesn't always come easily. Bill Gates' first company, Traf-O-Data, was a complete failure, yet his later achievements were phenomenal. Richard Branson, the legend behind the Virgin group of companies, is dyslexic, and with no support at school he underachieved academically. So what does it take to overcome setbacks and become a successful business? Here are four success stories, big and small.

A Amanda Hopkins started in a small way, making lunches for the staff in a local office. She would make sandwiches in her kitchen and deliver them by bike. Her customers called her *the food angel*, the name stuck and the business grew. A year later, in 2016, Amanda had a small café and a Food Angel van for her deliveries.

B Georgia Duffy dreamed of opening her own small bookshop. One day she decided to quit her job as a radiographer to follow her passion. Georgia opened Imagined Things in the town of Harrogate, UK, in July 2017. However, the bookshop did not make much money and on June 26th, 2018, Georgia tweeted that she had had the 'worst day ever' of sales. She did not expect a big response to the tweet but, suddenly, people started placing orders, making donations and sending messages of support. Georgia was amazed! The bookshop is now doing much better and Georgia hopes its success will continue.

C There's nothing small and local about a drinks company called Innocent, but how did they begin? A group of friends sold healthy fruit smoothies at a music festival in 1999. They put up a sign, asking customers if they should give up their jobs to start a **smoothie** business. There were two large bins, one said Yes and one No, for people to put their empty cups in. By the end of the weekend, the Yes bin was full and it was not long before Innocent Smoothies were the world market leader.

D Two childhood friends from New York, Jerry and Ben, opened an ice-cream parlour in Burlington, Vermont, in 1978. As Ben suffered from a lack of a sense of smell or taste, he added texture to the ice creams, giving them their characteristic *chunks* of chocolate, nuts and so on. Decades later, Ben & Jerry's operates globally as a subsidiary of the Dutch / British conglomerate Unilever.

GLOSSARY
smoothie ➤ cold fruit drink made with milk or yoghurt

STORIES!

VOCABULARY

MONEY AND BUSINESS

12 Match the definitions to the words.

0. [i] an amount or level of payment
1. [ ] to receive money as payment for work
2. [ ] to take or move out or back, or to remove
3. [ ] to get something from someone with the intention of giving it back
4. [ ] an arrangement with a bank to put in and remove money and the bank keeps a record of it
5. [ ] money that is borrowed from a bank
6. [ ] a small plastic card that can be used as payment, the money leaving your bank account automatically
7. [ ] a machine from which you can take money out of your bank account using a special card
8. [ ] to need to pay something to someone who has lent money to you
9. [ ] the money that is used in a particular country

a bank account
b bank loan
c borrow
d cash machine
e currency
f debit card
g earn
h owe
i rate
j withdraw

13 Correct the mistakes.

0. I need some money, please can you ~~borrow~~ me £10? **lend**
1. The interest rates have been shrinking this month.
2. He wins some extra pocket money by walking people's dogs.
3. I lent some euros from my friend so I'll have to pay him back.
4. Her hairdresser raised her business by opening a second salon.
5. You should try falling the size of your bank loan.
6. The charge of a cup of coffee is getting ridiculous.

Unit 9   89

GRAMMAR PRACTICE

have / get something done

Choose the correct option.
We use *have* or *get something done* to talk about something that somebody does *to* / *for* us.
We can also use *have* or *get something done* to talk about something unpleasant that is done *to* / *for* us.

➡ See **GRAMMAR REFERENCE** page 126

14 Complete the sentences with the correct form of the verbs below.

assess ▪ make ▪ pay ▪ print ▪
~~repair~~ ▪ search ▪ translate

0 Where did you get your bike ....**repaired**.... ?
1 They have their wages ……………… directly into their accounts.
2 She got the letter ……………… from Danish into English.
3 Charlie had a new suit ……………… for his sister's wedding.
4 They had their luggage ……………… at the airport.
5 I'm getting my essay ……………… by both my teachers.
6 Why are you having those photos ……………… ?

15 Make sentences with the correct forms of *have something done*.

0 Joanna / hair / cut / yesterday
Joanna had her hair cut yesterday.
1 they / usually / passports / check / gate
2 we / online account / hack / since January
3 she / hope / book / publish / next year
4 our company / website / build / soon
5 your boss / just / her office / decorate again?
6 I / my credit card / steal / last night

16 Choose the correct option.

0 The zip on your coat is broken.
 (A) Yes, I must have it repaired.
  B Yes, I've had it repaired.
1 Is that scooter safe to drive?
  A Yes, I'll have to test it.
  B Sure, I've had it tested.
2 Are you preparing all the party food yourself?
  A Yes, I'll get it delivered.
  B No, I'll get it delivered.

3 We've lost our front door key.
  A Why not make another one?
  B Why not get another one made?
4 Why was your company registered for business?
  A We had to do it by law.
  B We had it done by law.
5 You really should read Branson's biography.
  A Who was it published by?
  B Who had it published?
6 Our company website was written by me.
  A Yes, I know you'd had it written.
  B Yes, I know you wrote it.

17 Rewrite the sentences so that they mean the same.

0 Jamie's bags were opened by the customs officer.
 Jamie had ….**his bags opened**…. by the customs officer.
1 The bank manager closed my friend's account.
 My friend ……………… by the bank manager.
2 We have to ask someone to make a spare key.
 We have to get ……………… .
3 I need the optician to check my eyesight.
 I need to have ……………… .
4 The Browns' new house has been built in France.
 The Browns ……………… .
5 We asked an events manager to organise our conference.
 We got ……………… .
6 A burglar stole all my aunt's jewellery.
 My aunt ……………… .

18 Find five mistakes in this email.

I've had my job application accepted and the interview will be tomorrow – help! I never liked going to interviews but I will love to work for this bank. I really want to get this job. I'm worried about them asking me difficult questions. Mum advised me to wear a good suit and cut my hair. She also suggested preparing for the interview by study the company website. Have you got any tips for me?

90 Unit 9

SPEAKING SKILLS

INTERVIEWING

19 Complete the sentences with the words below.

> actually ▪ honest ▪ interesting ▪
> put ▪ repeat ▪ see ▪ start

1 Let me ...., you're from London College, aren't you?
2 Let's .... with your reasons for studying IT.
3 I think, ..., that the course would be right for me.
4 How can I .... it? We need 100% commitment.
5 I'm not sure, to be ....
6 Sorry, could you .... that, please?
7 OK, that's an .... question!

20 Choose the correct option.

1 How did you hear about us?
  A Well, I saw an advert.
  B Right, I saw an advert.
2 I'd like you to meet my colleague.
  A Look, all right.
  B Oh, all right.
3 Can you come for an interview today?
  A I mean, I'm not free.
  B The thing is, I'm not free.

21 Reorder the conversation.

a ☐ Really? Tell me about the ones you've worked for.
b ☐ They were all animal charities. Have you ever heard of the CatTrust?
c ☐ 1 Good morning. I'm Ms Williams, head of PR. Could you tell me why you want to work in a bank?
d ☐ I'm interested in money. I've done some voluntary accountancy for charities.
e ☐ Cats are my hobby, but I really want to have a career in finance.
f ☐ Why do you want to work for a bank, if you're so interested in cats?
g ☐ Their work is all about rehoming cats, which I think is important.
h ☐ I haven't, to be honest. Can you describe it?

LISTENING SKILLS

22 Complete the advice. Use the strategy box on page 92 to help you.

Listening for detail: true / false questions
In some exams, you have to decide if a statement is ¹......................... or ²......................... . This involves listening for ³......................... . Read each statement ⁴......................... . Look out for ⁵......................... – for example, you might see a word you have heard (or a ⁶.........................), but the statement could still be ⁷......................... . Remember that you are answering according to what the speaker says, not '⁸.........................'. Listen again and ⁹......................... .

23 Look at the picture. Melissa wants to advertise her new babysitting business. What words do you think she will use to describe herself?

24 [3.32] **Listen to Melissa talking to a friend. Check your answer to exercise 23.**

25 [3.32] **Now listen again and decide if the sentences are true (T) or false (F). Correct the false ones.**

1 Melissa has already started her babysitting business. T F
2 Jake thinks it's a bad idea. T F
3 She has a plan for times when she cannot work. T F
4 Melissa is confident about her organising skills. T F
5 She is already thinking about her future study and job prospects. T F
6 Melissa wants to work with special needs children. T F
7 She babysits for families who are not developing normally. T F
8 She has had a business plan worked out. T F

EXAM SKILLS

> **EXAM STRATEGY**
>
> **Reading and Use of English – Multiple matching**
>
> You will need to practise skimming and scanning texts quickly for specific information. Ask yourself why a particular part of the text matches the question.

26 For each word given, choose the word (A, B or C) that is *not* similar in meaning.

0 assistance
   A aid
   (B) investment
   C support
1 uninterested
   A different   B indifferent   C unconcerned
2 supplementary
   A additional
   B extra
   C superfluous
3 inspired
   A talented   B motivated   C encouraged
4 irritated
   A cross
   B unreasonable
   C annoyed
5 content
   A successful   B satisfied   C pleased
6 anxious
   A uneasy
   B furious
   C nervous
7 overdue
   A late   B unpaid   C borrowed

27 Read four extracts about people complaining because their holidays went wrong. For questions 1–7, choose from the four speakers (A–D).

Which person:

0 [C] had bad conditions?
1 [ ] was disappointed with the food?
2 [ ] enjoyed the water sports?
3 [ ] found the accommodation terrible?
4 [ ] was disturbed by noise?
5 [ ] felt the holiday was not good value?
6 [ ] had health problems?
7 [ ] was confused by the language?

A It took me about a year to save up enough money for this holiday and even so, I did not stay in the best hotel. In fact, the hotel I found was amazing and not overpriced and the owners were friendly. They didn't speak much English but there was a lot of shouting and sign language and we managed to make ourselves understood. The problem actually came after I'd been swimming and scuba diving in the sea. I adored that, so I was really frustrated when I came down with an ear infection – probably from the water. It was terribly painful and it put a stop to all activities for the rest of my stay.

B The place I stayed had been recommended by a close friend, who is a very keen chef and a great cook. The town was renowned for its incredible restaurants and indeed the ones I tried lived up to their reputation. They weren't cheap but I don't mind paying for excellence. However, the self-catering apartment was disappointing, to say the least. The facilities were very poor and the bathroom was frankly disgusting. I don't expect to have to clean the toilet before I use it, especially if I've been charged a lot of rent for it. The owners can expect some very harsh words from me on *Trip Adviser*.

C Growing up in Scotland, I learnt to ski at a very young age: waterskiing on the lakes and downhill skiing in the mountains. My trip to the Swiss Alps was to be the holiday of a lifetime, and it cost a small fortune as well, so you can imagine how annoyed I was when I arrived to find no snow! It was cloudy and wet but warm – in fact, the weather I'd left in Scotland had been better. And not only that: when I tried to explain to our tour guide that I needed to go higher to get good skiing, he had trouble understanding my schoolboy German. He used a dialect of Swiss German that was unintelligible, even to some of the locals!

D A city break in Paris for my birthday – what a lovely surprise! My friends had joined together to pay for my train tickets and a shared room. We found our accommodation charming, though to be honest none of us slept very well because the sounds of the water system banging away all night kept us all awake. The weather was unexpectedly cold for the time of year, too, but nobody minded. We weren't exactly there to enjoy river trips on the Seine or any other outdoor sporting activity. No, we were there for the culture and for the food, for which of course the French are famous. Disappointment number one was that, as a vegetarian, I was quite restricted in choices on most menus. I have enough of the language to know what words like *escargot* and *tripes* mean!

EXAM SKILLS

28 You are going to read an article about four young entrepreneurs. For questions 1–9, choose from the four people (A–D). The people may be chosen more than once.

Which entrepreneur:

0 **B** took out a small loan to start the business?
1 ☐ was not motivated by money?
2 ☐ was advised to start a business by a family friend?
3 ☐ achieved success in spite of rejection?
4 ☐ started a business from what was just a hobby?
5 ☐ became motivated by the creativity of others?
6 ☐ mentions a learning difficulty?
7 ☐ was unsuccessful academically?
8 ☐ admits to being an obsessive IT enthusiast?
9 ☐ relies on computer hardware?

A Adam: educational app designer

I've always been academic, by which I mean that I've never had any trouble with my studies. I've been lucky enough to get high grades without having to work very hard. My younger brother, on the other hand, has struggled with a condition called dyscalculia, commonly known as *number blindness*. Most people have heard of dyslexia but being unable to make sense of numbers is not so well known. So I always helped my brother with his studies and that gave me the idea for the app I wrote. I sell it with a personalised tutoring programme and it can be done online, at home, anywhere you like. There were no set-up costs and I didn't need any financial support. I'm now at university but I'm also running my own business, which is growing and increasingly successful.

B Susie: web developer

When other girls in my class were designing new hairstyles or discussing the latest fashion, at the age of nine or ten, I was learning HTML and CSS. At that time, these were the basic building blocks of web design. I suppose I was a computer geek and programming is what I still love doing. I'd learnt JavaScript before I went to secondary school. So it isn't perhaps surprising that I started developing websites, initially just for fun and for myself. It was a family friend who pointed out that there was a market out there. Lots of people need to have web pages designed for all sorts of different reasons, but not all of them want to do it themselves or know how to do it. I followed business advice and had to borrow a little money, but the main support I needed was encouragement.

C Marcus: director of JustExchange.com

JustExchange.com is a business I started while I was still at school, and now I employ over 20 people. Formal education bored me, and to be honest I was keener on gardening and growing things. Most of the kids in my class were ambitious for the lifestyles their parents had – or better! I wasn't particularly interested in making money, which is ironic because actually my company is financially rather successful. It all started with a simple bartering idea. I needed to get my bike repaired, a friend who repaired bikes needed help in the garden … so we exchanged services and JustExchange.com was born. We bartered anything from dog walking to singing lessons to cake making and the business has grown. I love its simplicity.

D Olivia: jewellery maker

I was doing an online design course at the same time as training to be a nursery school teacher. Teaching was the safe career option my parents had chosen for me: design was what I really wanted to do but didn't have the courage to commit myself to. I did some work experience with young kids which gave me a brilliant idea. We were using old computer components, bits of metal and plastic, to make sculptures. Little children are incredibly inventive and I suddenly thought what amazing jewellery I could make, basically with pieces of old junk. I took my idea to an investment expert at the bank who rejected my idea as just that – rubbish. Despite that setback, I started making bracelets, necklaces and rings from old computer parts and I've never looked back. My jewellery is now worn by celebrities all over the world, I even get royalty and I don't need to teach any more.

Unit 9

10 Conflict

GRAMMAR PRACTICE

Revision of modals

Complete the rules with the verbs below.

can / can't ▪ have to ▪ must ▪
should / shouldn't have ▪ will / won't be able to

- We use .... to say someone has or doesn't have an ability. In the past, we use *could / couldn't* or *was / wasn't able to*. To speak about the future, we use ....
- We use .... and *have to / don't have to* say that something is or isn't necessary. When we use the future, we need a form of ....
- To talk about the best or right thing to do, we use *should / shouldn't* in the present and .... in the past.
- We use .... to talk about something that is prohibited or an order.

➤ See **GRAMMAR REFERENCE** page 126

1 🔊 Complete the sentences with *can, can't, could* or *couldn't*.

0 I ...**couldn't**... ride a bike until I was five.
1 How many instruments .... you play?
2 .... you speak French before you moved to Paris?
3 We .... come tonight, sorry. We're busy.
4 I .... imagine living in a refugee camp, can you?
5 .... today's politicians prevent wars or not?
6 She .... hear the music, it wasn't loud enough.

2 🔊 Complete the sentences with the verbs below.

finish ▪ join ▪ log on ▪ train ▪ ~~travel~~

0 People weren't able to ...**travel**... so easily in the past.
1 Will you be able to .... us for dinner?
2 Without the password, she wasn't able to .... earlier.
3 He'll be able to .... as an engineer if he joins the army.
4 I was able to .... my project yesterday.

3 🔊 Respond with the correct form of *should / shouldn't* (*have*) and the words in brackets.

0 She didn't reply to Jo's invitation and now it's too late. (*straight away*)
   She ...**should have replied straight away**...
1 He was attacked on the way home but told nobody. (*police*)
   He ....
2 Come on, we're going to be late for the lesson. (*hurry*)
   We ....
3 Oliver's bike was stolen last night. (*lock*)
   He ....
4 That car nearly knocked me down! (*careful*)
   The driver ....
5 Their team didn't play very well. (*better*)
   They ....
6 We got lost trying to find your house. (*map*)
   You ....

4 🔊 Choose the correct option.

0 The food was free. We (*didn't have to*) / *mustn't* pay for it.
1 You *don't have to / must* wash those cups, they're clean.
2 They *mustn't / didn't have to* shout or they'll wake the baby.
3 He *has to / had to* help his parents next weekend.
4 You *mustn't / don't have to* drink cola, it's so bad for you.
5 We *don't have to / had to* meet our guest yesterday.
6 *Don't you have to / Mustn't you* shower before you swim?

5 🔊 Choose the correct option.

0 She was in trouble for using bad language.
   (A) She shouldn't be rude.
   B She couldn't be rude.
1 The flood waters rose but they were lucky.
   A They were able to escape.
   B They won't be able to escape.
2 Sorry, but I've already been invited to a party next Saturday.
   A I shouldn't have come to yours.
   B I won't be able to come to yours.

94 Unit 10

GRAMMAR PRACTICE

3 When we arrived, all the washing-up had been done.
   A We mustn't do it.
   B We didn't have to do it.
4 He missed the train which left a few minutes early.
   A He wasn't able to catch it.
   B He can't catch it.

Modals of deduction

Complete the rules.

past: modal + ... + past participle	present: modal + ... without *to*
It **must** .... **been** terrifying.	Her story **must** .... true.
It **can't** .... **been** easy.	It **can't** .... possible.
She **may / might / could** .... **died**.	We **may / might (not)** .... safe now.

➡ See GRAMMAR REFERENCE page 127

6 📶 **Complete the sentences with *must* or *can't*.**

0 Bill ......*can't*...... be skiing, I've just seen him in class.
1 That book .... be mine, it's got your name on it.
2 Nobody's answering the door, they .... be out.
3 You .... possibly be hungry, you've just eaten!
4 Lina looks pale and thin. She .... be ill.
5 My calculation .... be right, I've checked it twice.
6 It .... be safe to live in a war zone.

7 📶 **Make sentences. Use *must / can't have* and the correct form of the words in brackets.**

0 That clock is wrong. (*it / stop*)
   It must have stopped.
1 She didn't move when the phone rang. (*she / hear*)
2 I don't see any fruit in your shopping bag. (*you / buy*)
3 He didn't get off the six o'clock train. (*he / miss*)
4 There's still lots of birthday cake left. (*the children / finish*)
5 This note isn't in Henry's handwriting. (*he / write*)
6 We found a wallet in the park. (*someone / drop*)

8 📶 **Match the parts.**

0 [f] We weren't in when the postman came.
1 [ ] I can't find my phone.
2 [ ] The apartment is very quiet.
3 [ ] Nigel hasn't replied to my text yet.
4 [ ] There aren't any concert tickets left.
5 [ ] James doesn't look happy.
6 [ ] Our teacher went to Thailand last summer.

a It must be a good band.
b Everyone must have gone out.
c That must have been exciting.
d He can't have passed his exam.
e I might have left it on the bus.
f He may have left the parcel outside.
g He might not have got it.

9 📶 **Order the dialogue.**

GIRL HIT BY TEXTING DRIVER

[ ] A Yes, he was shocked. But then he shouldn't have been using his phone and driving!
[ ] B He must have called an ambulance.
[ ] A He had to do that. He won't be able to keep his driver's licence now. He might even go to prison.
[1] B Was she badly hurt? The driver must have been really shocked.
[ ] A Well, he shouldn't have been on the phone.
[ ] B The girl could have died. She might be badly injured. That driver must feel terrible.

READING SKILLS

10 Look at the text and the photo. Who might Alicia be?

1. A film reviewer.
2. An advice columnist.
3. A fashion journalist.
4. A homework mentor.

11 [3.33] Read and listen to the text. Was your answer to exercise 10 correct?

12 Choose from the sentences a–g the one which fits each gap (1–6). There is one extra sentence.

a. They may be right but I don't think so.
b. She must have known how hurt I would be.
c. They should have shown you more respect.
d. But what would you have done?
e. Their behaviour was very aggressive but I didn't do anything.
f. Your parents should have been more supportive.
g. A quiet word from you to someone older might be advisable.

13 Answer these questions.

1. What would your advice to Penny have been?
   ....
2. How would you have advised Jane?
   ....
3. Do you think advice columns are more interesting for girls than for boys? Explain your answer.
   ....
4. Do you ever read advice columns like this? Why / Why not?
   ....
5. Would you ever write to an advice column with a problem you had? Why / Why not?
   ....

Ask Alicia

16 May

I'm 16, in my GCSE exam year at school, and my little brother started at my school last term. I don't see much of him of course, and at first he seemed fine. However, recently he keeps saying he's sick and that can't be true. I thought he must be worried about his lessons, but he said the work was OK and told me it was nothing to do with me.
Then the other day I noticed a group of bullies intimidating him on the bus. [1].......... Perhaps I should have said something at the time, but I didn't. I didn't want to make things worse for him. I'm sure he wouldn't like his big sister **sticking up for him**. [2].......... ? Please advise!
Penny

Your brother should have been more assertive but that can't be easy when you're confronted with bigger boys. It must have been hard for you to **witness**, but you probably couldn't have helped in that situation. [3].......... It would be better if your brother was able to speak about his lack of self-confidence to your parents, for example, or a teacher.

96 Unit 10

15 July

I've known my best friend since primary school, but she fell out with me three days ago. It has truly broken my heart. My parents say I'm not old enough to know how that feels. ⁴............ That's not all, though. She's now friends with another group of girls at school who don't like me. I feel so hurt because I used to tell her everything.
She might have guessed what this would do to me. ⁵............ I won't be able to face her or her new friends now.
What should I do?

Jane

This must be painful. It's bad enough when a relationship ends, but falling out with your best friend is even worse. ⁶............ *Perhaps they are too old to remember how it feels to be a teenager. This is the time to turn to some of your other friends. They will be there for you, and in time, you will surely find another best friend.*

GLOSSARY
- **sticking up for him** ➤ defending him
- **witness** ➤ see something happen

VOCABULARY

WAR AND CONFLICT

14 Complete the crossword.

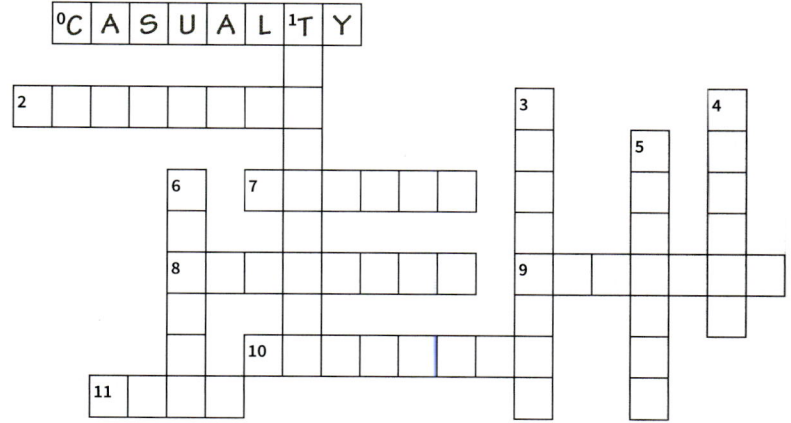

⁰C A S U A L ¹T Y

Across:
- 0 person injured or killed in war
- 2 person who still lives in spite of danger
- 7 person who uses explosives
- 8 person who is not in the army
- 9 person physically hurt
- 10 person who uses violence to hurt someone
- 11 the military force of a country

Down:
- 1 person who uses (threats of) violence for political reasons
- 3 people who fight in an army
- 4 people who agree officially to help and support in war
- 5 person who escapes from their country because of war
- 6 person hurt or killed because of the actions of others

15 Choose the correct option.

- 0 A war (broke out) / blew up in 1918.
- 1 The soldiers *defended* / *defeated* their native country bravely.
- 2 The city of Troy did not *surround* / *surrender* during the siege.
- 3 The Conservatives were *beaten* / *lost* in the last UK election.
- 4 Menelaus pretended to *capture* / *withdraw* his troops.
- 5 Our troops were ordered to *terrorise* / *attack* the city at dawn.
- 6 The injured soldier had *shot* / *fought* himself in the foot.
- 7 The soldiers *injured* / *invaded* the city in 1963.

Unit 10   97

GRAMMAR PRACTICE

Permission and obligation: *can / can't, be allowed to, let, be supposed to*

Choose the correct option.

Permission:
- You *can / can't* say that.
- Talking isn't *allowed / let* in here.
- You are *allowed / let* to talk in here.
- They will *allowed / let* me speak.

Obligation:
- I am *supposed / let* to leave.

➡ See **GRAMMAR REFERENCE** page 127

16 Make sentences to match the signs.

0 You're not allowed to swim here.

17 Rewrite the sentences, using *be allowed to* or *let*.

0 I was allowed to walk to school when I was nine.
   My mum *let me walk to school when I was nine*

1 We were all allowed to leave class early today.
   Our teacher ....

2 Our parents let us stay up late last night.
   We ....

3 Under-tens weren't allowed to use the hotel gym.
   The hotel owner ....

4 Harry will be allowed to go and talk to the pilot.
   The pilot ....

5 I wasn't allowed to take three bags onto the plane.
   The airline staff ....

6 I don't think the waiter will let you eat your sandwich here.
   You ....

18 Choose the correct option.

0 *Am I allowed /* (*Can*) I ask you a personal question?
1 You *supposed / 're not allowed to* skateboard here: read the sign!
2 In the past, people *were allowed to / can't* smoke in the cinema.
3 *Can / Let* I sit next to you?
4 You're *not allowed to / supposed to* drive a car without a licence.
5 Is it true that visitors *can't / aren't let* walk on the grass?
6 Mum says my brother has homework so he *is supposed / isn't allowed* to go out.

19 Answer these questions.

1 When were you first allowed to go shopping with a friend?
2 What are you supposed to do to help at home?
3 When does your teacher let you have your mobile in class?
4 Who is allowed to stay out later, you or your best friend?

20 Complete the text with the correct modal verbs.

This morning the alarm was ⁰ **supposed** to go off at 7am, but unfortunately the battery had run out. So I woke up late. I arrived at the exam hall at 9.05 but the teacher said that nobody was ¹............................. to enter after 9.00 am. I told her what had happened with my phone and eventually she ²............................. me enter. She told me to go and sit at the back, but I asked if I was ³............................. to sit at the front. We were ⁴............................. to answer the questions using a black pen, but I only had a blue pen. We weren't ⁵............................. to use a calculator and anyone caught using one would fail. The exam was ⁶............................. to be two hours long, but most of us found it quite easy, so the teacher ⁷............................. us leave as soon as we had finished. That was the final exam and I'm glad they are over. My parents say I ⁸............................. take some driving lessons if I pass everything.

98 Unit 10

SPEAKING SKILLS

EXPRESSING ANNOYANCE

21 Match the beginnings and ends to make sentences that show annoyance.

0 **g** Monica keeps
1 ☐ Frank is always
2 ☐ I wish he
3 ☐ Sorry, but it's just
4 ☐ Her singing drives
5 ☐ How come
6 ☐ You should

a you always get top marks?
b wouldn't play his music so loud.
c me mad.
d talking about himself.
e not on.
f see how untidy the kitchen is.
g complaining about her homework.

22 Tick (✓) the correct column: sympathising (S) or agreeing (A). You may sometimes tick both columns.

		S	A
1	I know!	☐	☐
2	Too right!	☐	☐
3	Poor you.	☐	☐
4	Hard luck!	☐	☐
5	That's true.	☐	☐
6	Same here.	☐	☐
7	That's not fair.	☐	☐
8	Oh, tell me about it!	☐	☐

23 Complete with phrases from exercise 22. There may be more than one answer.

Leila I'm completely exhausted.
Jed ¹........................ I am, as well.
Leila I get far too much homework.
Jed ²........................ . I get lots too. It's no fun studying for exams.
Leila ³........................ . I guess they are important, though.
Jed ⁴........................ . But I've got a weekend job too.
Leila ⁵........................ . You have to work weekends? ⁶........................ .
Jed ⁷........................ . But if you think that's bad, I've been dropped from the football team.
Leila That is ⁸........................ . Well, at least you'll have more time for your homework …

LISTENING SKILLS

24 Complete the advice about listening for detail. Use the words below.

> check ▪ distracted ▪ focus ▪ key ▪
> numbers ▪ pauses ▪ trick ▪ words

Read each question carefully. Underline ¹........................ words, for example *how*, *why*, *when*. They will help you ²........................ on what to listen for. Don't be ³........................ by unnecessary information – it's there to ⁴........................ you! Listen out for ⁵........................ and spellings. Don't answer in sentences – just a few ⁶........................ . Answer each pair of questions in the ⁷........................ between recordings, if you can. Then listen again and ⁸........................ .

25 Look at the photos. What do they all have in common?

26 [3.34] Listen to the boy speaking and match the pictures from exercise 25 to the recordings.

☐ Recording 1
☐ Recording 2
☐ Recording 3

27 [3.34] Listen again and answer the questions. Write no more than three words for each answer.

1 A When did England invade Scotland?
   B Who played William Wallace in the film, *Braveheart*?
2 A Where did the Battle of Hastings take place?
   B How long is the Bayeux Tapestry?
3 A What symbol represented the House of York?
   B Who won the War of the Roses?

Unit 10

ACADEMIC SKILLS

WRITING A CONCLUSION

28 Choose the correct option.

The ⁰(conclusion)/ title of an essay should contain a brief summary of the ¹main / opening points. It ²should / shouldn't include your personal opinion, with a quick ³argument / justification for it. It ⁴does not have / has to be more than a few sentences long. Try to echo your ideas in the opening paragraph and, if appropriate, the ⁵title / summary of your essay.

29 Tick (✓) the words and expressions that are useful in a conclusion.

- [✓] To conclude, …
- [ ] In conclusion, …
- [ ] Finally, …
- [ ] To sum up, …
- [ ] In my opinion, …
- [ ] I think / believe …
- [ ] Let me begin by … ,
- [ ] However, …
- [ ] Moreover, …
- [ ] For reasons that I will give, …
- [ ] Therefore, …

30 Read the essay title below. Try to complete the introduction and make notes for paragraphs 2 and 3.

Title	Do video games about wars make war look exciting? What is your opinion?
Introduction	Many people say that video games in which battles take place make war look fun and exciting. On the other hand, there are plenty of people who believe that virtual reality is, by definition, not real life and so there is no harm in video games …
Paragraph 2	....
Paragraph 3	....

31 Read another essay title. Make notes in the same way.

Title	Write about a film you have seen which you will never forget.
Introduction	Some films are purely entertainment, and can be very creative and moving while at the same time being relaxing and enjoyable. You often forget such films, even if you enjoyed them at the time. Other films stay with you for a long time and are impossible to forget. The film that has made a lasting impression on me is …
Paragraph 2	....
Paragraph 3	....

32 Now read a third essay title. Make notes for the introduction and paragraphs 2 and 3.

Title	Write an essay for an English school magazine about what people in your country are and are not allowed to do at the age of 16. What would you change if you could?
Introduction	....
Paragraph 2	....
Paragraph 3	....

33 Now write two conclusions (for exercises 31 and 32). Follow the steps below.

1. Think of your main points.
2. Give a short summary.
3. Express your own viewpoint.

EXAM SKILLS

> **EXAM STRATEGY**
>
> **Speaking – Collaborative task**
>
> In this part of the exam, you will be given a discussion question with some written prompts to give you ideas. You have to express and justify your opinion. You will do this with another candidate: don't be afraid to *agree to disagree* politely – in fact, this is often a good way to move the discussion forward. The language of negotiation and collaboration will be useful here.

34 [3.35] Read and listen to how an examiner starts a discussion.

'Now, I'd like you to talk about something together for two minutes. I'd like you to imagine that your school is going to start a Counselling Club to encourage young pupils to come to older students with their problems. Your discussion question is:

What kind of person might be a good counsellor?
Here are some ideas to help your discussion.'

35 Look at the ideas and make notes on what you might say about the question in exercise 34.

GOOD COUNSELLOR: popular, shy, academic, was bullied when younger, thoughtful, confident, cool, has younger siblings

36 [3.36] Now listen to two students talking about the question the examiner asked. Write down two ways in which they agree and two ways in which they disagree with each other.

Agreeing: *Yes, I agree …*
Disagreeing: *I'm not so sure about that …*

> **EXAM STRATEGY**
>
> **Writing – A story**
>
> If you choose to write a story for this part of the writing exam, it is important to engage the interest of your reader. You have to have a clear storyline linking to the first sentence, which you will be given. Remember to use the prompts you are given, too, and use a variety of narrative tenses.

37 Complete the extracts of two stories with the correct tense of the verbs in brackets: past simple, past continuous or past perfect.

A Tom **0** ...*knew*... (*know*) that it **1** .... (*rain*) a lot overnight. It **2** .... still .... (*rain*) a little when he **3** .... (*open*) his front door and **4** .... (*step*) out into the garden. The grass **5** .... (*feel*) wet under his bare feet. The early morning air was still but suddenly he **6** .... (*hear*) a voice that he **7** .... (*think*) he **8** .... (*recognise*).

B The grass **9** .... (*appear*) flat and brown where the circus tent **10** .... (*stand*). Marie **11** .... (*have*) a strange sensation as she **12** .... (*reach*) the empty site. Meeting the clowns and acrobats **13** .... (*be*) such fun! She **14** .... (*walk*) slowly away when she **15** .... (*catch*) sight of a small shining object on the ground in front of her.

38 Choose one of the extracts and write another 100 words to complete it.

39 Read this exam question and make notes on how you would complete it. Then write your story in no more than 200 words.

You have seen this announcement for a new English-language magazine for young people.

> **STORIES WANTED**
>
> We are looking for stories for our new English-language magazine for young people. Your story must begin with this sentence:
> *When I woke up that morning, I wasn't expecting anything unusual to happen …*
>
> Your story must include:
> a present / a misunderstanding.

Unit 10 101

REVISE AND ROUND UP

1 **Make sentences with either the gerund or infinitive forms.**

0 it / continue / snow / all through the night
It continued to snow / snowing all through the night.
1 we / start / cook dinner / ten minutes ago
2 Rob / begin / speak / when he was two
3 I / prefer / live / in the city
4 she / like / buy books / from a bookshop
5 they / love / ski / since they were small
6 we / hate / work late / on Fridays

2 **Complete the sentences with the correct form of the verbs in brackets.**

0 I'm really sorry that I forgot ......**to ring**....... (ring) you back.
1 She'll never forget .... (see) Adele at Glastonbury.
2 If you don't have his work number, try .... (call) his mobile.
3 I tried very hard .... (open) the door but it was locked.
4 We regret .... (tell) you that your bank account is empty.
5 Do you remember .... (play) in the street when you were young?
6 He very much regrets .... (get) angry in front of his children.

3 **Rewrite the direct speech into indirect speech. Use an appropriate reporting verb.**

0 police officer / terrorists: 'Drop your weapons right now!'
The police office commanded the terrorists to drop their weapons.
1 bank manager / me: 'It's not safe to write down your password.'
2 captain / troops: 'Surrender peacefully!'
3 tourist / us: 'Can you show me the way to the cathedral, please?'
4 teacher / him: 'Don't forget to hand in your work on time.'
5 friend / me: 'You really should train for a half marathon.'
6 parents / her: 'Don't worry too much about your exams, dear.'

4 **Make questions with the correct forms of** *have / get something done*.

0 when / that hotel / new swimming pool / build?
When did that hotel have / get a new swimming pool built?
1 where / you / usually / shoes / repair?
2 how often / he / hair cut?
3 you / ever / your computer / steal?
4 why / she / her bags / check / yesterday?
5 how many times / they / their house / decorate?
6 when / you / your passport / renew?

5 **Complete the sentences with** *can't be* **or** *must be*.

0 'I haven't heard the people upstairs for days.'
'They ......**must be**...... on holiday.'
1 'I've lost my mobile charger.'
'Where have you looked? It .... here somewhere.'
2 'There was another attack last night.'
'I know. It .... terrifying to live in a war zone.'
3 'He's brought up all those kids on his own.'
'Yes, it .... easy, being a single dad.'
4 'Are you coming? It's half past ten.'
'Oh no, it .... that time already!'
5 'Is this burger yours or Phil's?'
'It .... Phil's, I don't eat meat.'
6 'Edward says you owe him 20 euros.'
'That .... right. I never borrow money.'

6 **Choose the correct option.**

0 Come on, we (*mustn't*) / *don't have to* be late for class.
1 It's a brilliant book about war, you really *should* / *shouldn't* read it.
2 She feels unwell. She *shouldn't have eaten* / *should eat* so much.
3 We'll go without Rachel if she *can't* / *will be able to* come.
4 You *can* / *have to* be over 18 or they won't let you in.
5 I *should have written* / *should write* to my grandad and now I wish I had.
6 He *won't be able to* / *doesn't have to* help me, I can do it alone.

102 Units 9–10

7 📶 Complete the sentences with the words below.

~~allowed to~~ ▪ can ▪ can't ▪ let ▪ not allowed to ▪
not supposed to ▪ supposed to

0   Am I ..*allowed to*.. bring my dog into the café?
1   Jess, ... I borrow your iPad to check my mail?
2   She was .... be here by now. Where is she?
3   Our parents didn't .... us stay out late on a weekday.
4   American women were .... vote until 1920.
5   He .... continue playing because he's had a red card.
6   You're .... wear your shoes in a mosque.

8 📶 Choose the correct option.

0   'My father lost his best friend in the war.'
    'That *mustn't have been* / (*can't have been*) easy.'
1   'My little cousin fell into the river and she can't swim.'
    'Oh no, she *must have drowned / might have drowned*.'
2   'They regret not telling their neighbours about the party.'
    'They *may have warned / should have warned* them.'
3   'The enemy troops surrounded the city for months.'
    'The siege *must have been / didn't have to be* terrifying.'
4   'The time of the lesson has changed from ten to nine o'clock.'
    'That's OK, I *will be able / won't be able* to come earlier.'
5   'Those young men all volunteered for the army.'
    'Their choice; they *didn't have to join / mustn't join* up.'
6   'I know a really good joke about the Trojan horse.'
    'I think you *may have told / should have told* me already.'

9 📶 Add the missing words.

0   Will you ∧ able to come tonight? **be**
1   Where to? I'm supposed to my homework.
2   You must heard, there's a meeting at eight.
3   I remember now. You should have reminded.
4   Sorry, I forgot to tell you, but I telling you now.
5   I won't be allowed come.

CONCEPT CHECK

Read the sentences and answer the questions.

1 *He really regrets not learning to drive.*

(Answer Yes / No / Maybe)

0   He has learnt to drive. **No**
1   He hasn't learnt to drive.
2   He wants to learn to drive now.
3   He is sorry that he learnt to drive.
4   He is sorry that he didn't learn to drive.
5   He now wishes that he had learnt to drive.

2 *William cooked today so he doesn't have to help with the washing-up.*

(Answer True / False / Don't know)

0   William always cooks. **Don't know**
1   He usually helps with the washing-up.
2   He must help with the washing-up today.
3   He mustn't help with the washing-up.
4   He's excused from the washing-up because he cooked.
5   He can help with the washing-up if he wants to.

3 *Pamela must have missed that bus.*

(Answer True / False)

0   Pamela was supposed to catch a bus. **True**
1   She was expected to catch a particular bus.
2   She hasn't arrived when expected.
3   She has very probably missed that bus.
4   We know why she missed the bus.
5   We can deduce she missed it because she's not on it.

4 *Betsy left the cat outside in the snow all night. He could have frozen to death.*

(Answer Yes / No / Maybe)

0   The cat didn't come inside overnight. **Yes**
1   It was a very cold night.
2   The cat is no longer outside.
3   There had been a possibility that he wouldn't survive.
4   The speaker blames Betsy for risking the cat's life.
5   The cat has died of the cold.
6   The cat has survived a cold night outside.

➡ See **GRAMMAR REFERENCE**
pages 125–127

WORDLIST

STARTER A
blues (n) /bluːz/
classical (n) /ˈklæs.ɪ.kəl/
electronic (n) /ˌɪ.lekˈtrɒn.ɪk/
folk (n) /fəʊk/
jazz (n) /dʒæz/
pop (n) /pɒp/
rock (n) /rɒk/

STARTER B
basketball (n) /ˈbɑː.skɪt.bɔːl/
climbing (n) /ˈklaɪ.mɪŋ/
cycling (n) /ˈsaɪ.klɪŋ/
diving (n) /ˈdaɪ.vɪŋ/
football (n) /ˈfʊt.bɔːl/
horse riding (n) /ˈhɔːs ˌraɪdɪŋ/
rowing (n) /ˈrəʊ.ɪŋ/
running (n) /ˈrʌn.ɪŋ/
skating (n) /ˈskeɪ.tɪŋ/
skiing (n) /ˈskiː.ɪŋ/
swimming (n) /ˈswɪm.ɪŋ/
tennis (n) /ˈten.ɪs/

STARTER C
bike (n) /baɪk/
boat (n) /bəʊt/
bus (n) /bʌs/
car (n) /kɑːr/
ferry (n) /ˈfer.i/
lorry (n) /ˈlɒr.i/
motorbike (n) /ˈməʊ.tə.baɪk/
plane (n) /pleɪn/
ship (n) /ʃɪp/
taxi (n) /ˈtæk.si/
tram (n) /træm/
Tube (n) /tjuːb/
underground (n) /ˌʌn.dəˈɡraʊnd/
van (n) /væn/

STARTER D
accountant (n) /əˈkaʊn.tənt/
actor (n) /ˈæk.tər/
architect (n) /ˈɑː.kɪ.tekt/
builder (n) /ˈbɪl.dər/
carpenter (n) /ˈkɑː.pɪn.tər/
dentist (n) /ˈden.tɪst/
electrician (n) /ˌɪl.ekˈtrɪʃ.ən/
engineer (n) /ˌen.dʒɪˈnɪər/
lawyer (n) /ˈlɔɪ.ər/
lecturer (n) /ˈlek.tʃər.ər/
mechanic (n) /məˈkæn.ɪk/
pilot (n) /ˈpaɪ.lət/
plumber (n) /ˈplʌm.ər/
soldier (n) /ˈsəʊl.dʒər/
surgeon (n) /ˈsɜː.dʒən/
vet (n) /vet/

STARTER E
corner shop (n) /ˈkɔː.nər ʃɒp/
delicatessen (n) /ˌdel.ɪ.kəˈtes.ən/
department store (n) /dɪˈpɑːt.mənt ˌstɔːr/
supermarket (n) /ˈsuː.pəˌmɑː.kɪt/
chain store (n) /tʃeɪn stɔːr/

UNIT 1
block (v) /blɒk/
blog (n) /blɒɡ/
blogger (n) /ˈblɒɡ.ər/
brain scan (n) /breɪn skæn/
call (v) /kɔːl/
comic (n) /ˈkɒm.ɪk/
comment (n) /ˈkɒm.ent/
dating site (n) /ˈdeɪtɪŋ saɪt/
drug addiction (n) /drʌɡ əˈdɪk.ʃən/
empathise (with) (v) /ˈem.pə.θaɪz/
essay (n) /ˈes.eɪ/
face-to-face (adj) /ˌfeɪs.təˈfeɪs/
follow (v) /ˈfɒl.əʊ/
follower (n) /ˈfɒl.əʊ.ər/
journalist (n) /ˈdʒɜː.nə.lɪst/
leaflet (n) /ˈliː.flət/
magazine (n) /ˌmæɡ.əˈziːn/
mental health (n) /ˈmen.təl helθ/
message (n) /ˈmes.ɪdʒ/
message board (n) /ˈmes.ɪdʒ.bɔːd/
newspaper (n) /ˈnjuːzˌpeɪ.pər/
novelist (n) /ˈnɒv.əl.ɪst/
post (v) /pəʊst/
report (n) /rɪˈpɔːt/
share (v) /ʃeər/
social media (n) /ˈsəʊ.ʃəl ˈmiː.di.ə/
text (v) /tekst/
troll (v) /trəʊl/
update (v) /ʌpˈdeɪt/
website (n) /ˈweb.saɪt/

UNIT 2
amazing (adj) /əˈmeɪ.zɪŋ/
appalling (adj) /əˈpɔː.lɪŋ/
astonishing (adj) /əˈstɒn.ɪ.ʃɪŋ/
awareness (noun) /əˈweə.nəs/
awful (adj) /ˈɔː.fəl/
bedding (n) /ˈbed.ɪŋ/
brilliant (adj) /ˈbrɪl.i.ənt/
catchy (adj) /ˈkætʃ.i/
delighted (adj) /dɪˈlaɪ.tɪd/
deliver (v) /dɪˈlɪv.ər/
disgraceful (adj) /dɪsˈɡreɪs.fəl/
disgusting (adj) /dɪsˈɡʌs.tɪŋ/
dreadful (adj) /ˈdred.fəl/
extraordinary (adj) /ɪkˈstrɔː.dɪn.ər.i/
fantastic (adj) /fænˈtæs.tɪk/
headline (n) /ˈhed.laɪn/
horrifying (adj) /ˈhɒr.ɪ.faɪ.ɪŋ/
jingle (n) /ˈdʒɪŋ.ɡl/
lavishly furnished (adj) /ˈlæv.ɪʃli ˈfɜː.nɪʃt/
lodge (v) /lɒdʒ/
magnificent (adj) /mæɡˈnɪf.ɪ.sənt/
miraculous (adj) /mɪˈræk.jʊ.ləs/
misleading (adj) /ˌmɪsˈliː.dɪŋ/
nutrition (noun) /nuˈtrɪʃ·ən/
obesity (noun) /əʊˈbiː.sə.ti/
ridiculous (adj) /rɪˈdɪk.jʊ.ləs/
scandalous (adj) /ˈskæn.dəl.əs/
shocking (adj) /ˈʃɒk.ɪŋ/
stove (n) /stəʊv/
stunning (adj) /ˈstʌn.ɪŋ/
suitable (adj) /ˈsuː.tə.bl̩/
superior (adj) /suːˈpɪə.ri.ər/
target (v) /ˈtɑː.ɡɪt/
tempting (adj) /ˈtemp.tɪŋ/
terrified (adj) /ˈter.ə.faɪd/
towel (n) /taʊəl/
wonderful (adj) /ˈwʌn.də.fəl/

UNIT 3
bottle bank (n) /ˈbɒt.l̩ bæŋk/
bridge the gap (n) /brɪdʒ ðiː ɡæp/
climate change (n) /ˈklaɪ.mɪt ˌtʃeɪndʒ/
fair trade (n) /ˌfeəˈtreɪd/
farmers' market (n) /ˈfɑː.məzˌmɑː.kɪt/
greenhouse gas (n) /ˈɡriːn.haʊs ɡæs/
homegrown (adj) /ˌhəʊmˈɡrəʊn/
knock-on effect (n) /ˌnɒk.ɒn ɪˈfekt/
landfill site (n) /ˈlænd.fɪl saɪt/
leftovers (n) /ˈleftˌəʊ.vəz/
minimum wage (n) /ˈmɪn.ɪ.məm weɪdʒ/
rickshaw (n) /ˈrɪk.ʃɔː/

WORDLIST

seasonal food (n) /ˈsiː.zən.əl fuːd/
share (n) /ʃeərz/
standard of living (n) /ˈstæn.dəd əv ˈlɪv.ɪŋ/
vegetable patch (n) /ˈvedʒ.tə.bl̩ pætʃ/
waste disposal (n) /weɪst dɪˈspəʊ.zəl/
wealthy (adj) /ˈwel.θi/
working conditions (n) /ˈwɜː.kɪŋ kənˈdɪʃ.ənz/

UNIT 4
ageing (n) /ˈeɪ.dʒɪŋ/
alien (n) /ˈeɪ.li.ən/
artificial intelligence (AI) (n) /ˌɑː.tɪˌfɪʃ.əl.ɪnˈtel.ɪ.dʒənts (eɪ.ˈaɪ)/
astronaut (n) /ˈæs.trə.nɔːt/
census (n) /ˈsen.səs/
cloud storage service (n) /klaʊd ˈstɔː.rɪdʒ ˈsɜː.vɪs/
collision (n) /kəˈlɪʒ.ən/
conscious (adj) /ˈkɒn.ʃəs/
cyberspace (n) /ˈsaɪ.bə.speɪs/
driverless car (n) /ˈdraɪ.və.ləs kɑːr/
eradication (n) /ɪˌræd.ɪˈkeɪ.ʃən/
galaxy (n) /ˈɡæl.ək.si/
genetic engineering (n) /dʒəˈnet.ɪk ˌen.dʒɪˈnɪə.rɪŋ/
hack (v) /hæk/
humanoid (n) /ˈhjuː.mə.nɔɪd/
mankind (n) /mænˈkaɪnd/
merge (v) /mɜːdʒ/
outdated (adj) /ˌaʊtˈdeɪ.tɪd/
robot (n) /ˈrəʊ.bɒt/
sensor (n) /ˈsen.sər/
space colony (n) /speɪs ˈkɒl.ə.ni/
starship (n) /stɑː.ʃɪp/
struggling (v) /ˈstrʌɡ.lɪŋ/
telepathy (n) /təˈlep.ə.θi/
time machine (n) /taɪm məˈʃiːn/
vinyl (n) /ˈvaɪ.nəl/
virtual reality (n) /ˌvɜː.tju.əl.riːˈæl.ə.ti/

UNIT 5
accused (n) /əˈkjuːzd/
arrest (v) /əˈrest/
bar (n) /bɑːr/
charge (v) /tʃɑːdʒ/
court (n) /kɔːt/
crime scene (n) /kraɪm siːn/
defendant (n) /dɪˈfen.dənt/
evidence (n) /ˈev.ɪ.dəns/
fake (v) /feɪk/
fraud (n) /frɔːd/
guilty (adj) /ˈɡɪl.ti/
innocent (adj) /ˈɪn.ə.sənt/
insurance (n) /ɪnˈʃɔː.rəns/
investigate (v) /ɪnˈves.tɪ.ɡeɪt/
judge (n) /dʒʌdʒ/
jury (n) /ˈdʒʊə.ri/
lock up (v) /ˈlɒk.ʌp/
mourn (v) /mɔːn/
offence (n) /əˈfens/
paddle (v) /ˈpæd.l̩/
pass sentence (n) /pɑːs ˈsen.təns/
pickpocket (n) /ˈpɪkˌpɒk.ɪt/
police station (n) /pəˈliːsˌsteɪ.ʃən/
prosecute (v) /ˈprɒs.ɪ.kjuːt/
question (v) /ˈkwes.tʃən/
release (v) /rɪˈliːs/
reoffend (v) /ˌriː.əˈfend/
shoplifter (n) /ˈʃɒpˌlɪftər/
surround (v) /səˈraʊnd/
suspect (n) /ˈsəsˌpekt/
suspect (v) /səˈspekt/
swear an oath (phr) /sweər ən əʊθ/
trial (n) /traɪəl/
unravel (v) /ʌnˈræv.əl/
valuables (n) /ˈvæl.jʊ.bl̩z/
verdict (n) /ˈvɜː.dɪkt/
witness (n) /ˈwɪt.nəs/

UNIT 6
acrylic (n) /əˈkrɪl.ɪk/
bone (n) /bəʊn/
brick (n) /brɪk/
bury (v) /ˈber.i/
clay (n) /kleɪ/
coal (n) /kəʊl/
concrete (n) /ˈkɒŋ.kriːt/
copper (n) /ˈkɒp.ər/
cotton (n) /ˈkɒt.ən/
diamond (n) /ˈdaɪə.mənd/
fabric (n) /ˈfæb.rɪk/
flooded (adj) /ˈflʌd.ɪd/
glass (n) /ɡlɑːs/
gold (n) /ɡəʊld/
grass (n) /ɡrɑːs/
kick off (phr v) /ˈkɪk.ɒf/
lead (n) /liːd/
leather (n) /ˈleð.ər/
line (v) /laɪn/
linen (n) /ˈlɪn.ɪn/
loot (v) /luːt/
lycra (n) /ˈlaɪ.krə/
marble (n) /ˈmɑː.bl̩/
metal (n) /ˈmet.əl/
mud (n) /mʌd/
nylon (n) /ˈnaɪ.lɒn/
oil (n) /ɔɪl/
paper (n) /ˈpeɪ.pər/
plastic (n) /ˈplæs.tɪk/
polyester (n) /ˌpɒl.iˈes.tər/
rock (n) /rɒk/
rubber (n) /ˈrʌb.ər/
sand (n) /sænd/
sea bed (n) /ˈsiː.bed/
silk (n) /sɪlk/
silver (n) /ˈsɪl.vər/
sink (v) /sɪŋk/
slate (n) /sleɪt/
steel (n) /stiːl/
stone (n) /stəʊn/
uncover (v) /ʌnˈkʌv.ər/
water (n) /ˈwɔː.tər/
wood (n) /wʊd/
wool (n) /wʊl/

UNIT 7
add (v) /æd/
apple core (n) /ˈæp.l̩ kɔːr/
bake (v) /beɪk/
boil (v) /bɔɪl/
breadcrumbs (n) /ˈbred.krʌm/
buttery (n) /ˈbʌt.ər.i/
chop (v) /tʃɒp/
comfort food (n) /ˈkʌm.fət fuːd/
cool (v) /kuːl/
crumbly (adj) /ˈkrʌm.bli/
cut (v) /kʌt/
fork (n) /fɔːk/
from scratch (pʰr) /frɒm skrætʃ/
fry (v) /fraɪ/
grate (v) /ɡreɪt/
grill (v) /ɡrɪl/
grow up (phr v) /ɡrəʊ ʌp/
handful (n) /ˈhænd.fʊl/
life expectancy (n) /laɪf ɪkˈspek.tən.si/
longevity (n) /lɒnˈdʒev.ə.ti/
mix (v) /mɪks/
mixture (n) /ˈmɪks.tʃər/
ovenproof dish (n) /ˈʌv.ən.pruːf dɪʃ/

Wordlist 105

WORDLIST

peel (v) /piːl/
pinch (n) /pɪntʃ/
pour (v) /pɔːr/
preheat (v) /ˌpriːˈhiːt/
raisin (n) /ˈreɪ.zən/
roast (v) /rəʊst/
rub (v) /rʌb/
serve (v) /sɜːv/
slice (v) /slaɪs/
spread (v) /spred/
steam (v) /stiːm/
stir (v) /stɜːr/
stunning (adj) /ˈstʌn.ɪŋ/
sweetened (adj) /ˈswiː.tənd/
toast (v) /təʊst/
whisk (v) /wɪsk/

UNIT 8

alter (v) /ˈɒl.tər/
anxiety (n) /æŋˈzaɪ.ə.ti/
anxious (adj) /ˈæŋk.ʃəs/
cheerful (adj) /ˈtʃɪə.fəl/
confidence (v) /ˈkɒn.fɪ.dəns/
confident (adj) /ˈkɒn.fɪ.dənt/
consciousness (n) /ˈkɒn.ʃəs.nəs/
counselling (n) /ˈkaʊn.səl.ɪŋ/
depress (v) /dɪˈpres/
depressed (adj) /dɪˈprest/
depressing (adj) /dɪˈpres.ɪŋ/
depression (n) /dɪˈpreʃ.ən/
encourage (v) /ɪnˈkʌr·ɪdʒ/
encouragement (n) /ɪnˈkʌr.ɪdʒ.mənt/
encouraging (adj) /ɪnˈkʌr.ɪ.dʒɪŋ/
fade (v) /feɪd/
increase (v) /ɪnˈkriːs/
low (adj) /ləʊ/
meditation (n) /ˌmed.ɪˈteɪ.ʃən/
mental health (n) /ˈmen.təl helθ/
mood (n) /muːd/
negative (adj) /ˈneg.ə.tɪv/
optimism (n) /ˈɒp.tɪ.mɪ.zəm/
optimistic (adj) /ˌɒp.tɪˈmɪs.tɪk/
peer pressure (n) /ˈpɪə.preʃ.ər/
positive (adj) /ˈpɒz.ə.tɪv/
reduce (v) /rɪˈdjuːs/
relax (v) /rɪˈlæks/
relaxation (n) /ˌriː.lækˈseɪ.ʃən/
relaxed (adj) /rɪˈlækst/
relaxing (adj) /rɪˈlæk.sɪŋ/

self-confidence (n) /ˌselfˈkɒn.fɪ.dəns/
self-esteem (n) /ˌself.ɪˈstiːm/
stress (n) /stres/
stress (v) /stres/
stressed (adj) /strest/
stressful (adj) /ˈstres.fəl/

UNIT 9

afloat (adj) /əˈfləʊt/
armbands (n) /ˈɑːm.bændz/
back (v) /bæk/
bad posture (n) /bæd ˈpɒs.tʃər/
bank account (n) /ˈbæŋk.əˌkaʊnt/
bank loan (n) /bæŋk ləʊn/
board game (n) /ˈbɔːdˌɡeɪm/
borrow (v) /ˈbɒr.əʊ/
cash machine (n) /ˈkæʃ məˌʃiːn/
charge (n) /tʃɑːdʒ/
charge interest (phr) /tʃɑːdʒ ˈɪn.trəst/
comment (n) /ˈkɒm.ent/
conclusion (n) /kənˈkluː.ʒən/
cost (v) /kɒst/
cross (your) arms (phr) /krɒs ɑːmz/
currency (n) /ˈkʌr.ən.si/
debit card (n) /ˈdeb.ɪtˌkɑːd/
deciding factor (n) /dɪˈsaɪ.dɪŋ ˈfæk.tər/
demonstration case (n) /ˌdem.ənˈstreɪ.ʃən keɪs/
details (n) /ˈdiː.teɪlz/
dramatic (adj) /drəˈmæt.ɪk/
earn (v) /ɜːn/
exchange rate (n) /ɪksˈtʃeɪndʒˌreɪt/
eye contact (n) /aɪ ˈkɒn.tækt/
fidget (v) /ˈfɪdʒ.ɪt/
hand gesture (n) /hænd ˈdʒes.tʃər/
handshake (n) /ˈhænd.ʃeɪk/
knowledge (n) /ˈnɒl·ɪdʒ/
lend (v) /lend/
mock (v) /mɒk/
offer a job (phr) /ˈɒf.ər ə dʒɒb/
over the counter (phr) /ˈəʊ·vər ðə ˈkaʊn.tər/
owe (v) /əʊ/
paragraph (n) /ˈpær.ə.ɡrɑːf/
pay (v) /peɪ/
pitch (n) /pɪtʃ/
raise prices (phr) /reɪz praɪsɪz/
scene (n) /siːn/

sequence (n) /ˈsiː.kwəns/
smile (n) /smaɪl/
strap (n) /stræp/
tangled hair (adj) /ˈtæŋɡld heər/
tense (n) /tens/
trendy (adj) /ˈtren.di/
wheels (n) /wiːlz/
withdraw cash (phr) /wɪðˈdrɔː kæʃ/

UNIT 10

ally (n) /ˈæl.aɪ/
attack (v) /əˈtæk/
attacker (n) /əˈtæk.ər/
battle (v) /ˈbæt.l̩/
beat (v) /biːt/
blow up (v) /ˈbləʊ.ʌp/
bomb (v) /bɒm/
bomber (n) /ˈbɒm.ər/
break out (phr v) /ˈbreɪk.aʊt/
capture (v) /ˈkæp.tʃər/
casualty (n) /ˈkæʒ.ju.əl.ti/
civilian (n) /sɪˈvɪl.i.ən/
conquer (v) /ˈkɒŋ.kər/
defeat (v) /dɪˈfiːt/
defend (v) /dɪˈfend/
fall out (phr v) /fɔːl aʊt/
fight (v) /faɪt/
fighter (n) /ˈfaɪ.tər/
hit (v) /hɪt/
injure (v) /ˈɪn.dʒər/
injured (adj) /ˈɪn.dʒəd/
innocent (adj) /ˈɪn.ə.sənt/
invade (v) /ɪnˈveɪd/
peaceful (adj) /ˈpiːs.fəl/
refugee (n) /ˌref.juˈdʒiː/
shoot (v) /ʃuːt/
siege (n) /siːdʒ/
soldier (n) /ˈsəʊl.dʒər/
stick up for yourself (phr v) /stɪk ʌp fɔːr/
surrender (v) /sərˈen.dər/
survivor (n) /səˈvaɪ.vər/
terrified (adj) /ˈter.ə.faɪd/
terrorise (v) /ˈter.ər.aɪz/
terrorist (n) /ˈter.ə.rɪst/
victim (n) /ˈvɪk.tɪm/
victorious (adj) /vɪkˈtɔː.ri.əs/
withdraw an army (phr) /wɪðˈdrɔː ən ˈɑː.mi/
wounded (adj) /ˈwuːn.dɪd/

WORDLIST

LITERATURE SKILLS 1
guardian (noun) /ˈɡɑː.di.ən/
invaluable (adj) /ɪnˈvæl.jə.bəl/
invalid (noun) /ˈɪn.væl.ɪd/
scrape (noun) /skreɪp/
tedious (adj) /ˈtiː.di.əs/
will (noun) /wɪl/

LITERATURE SKILLS 2
breath (n) /breθ/
dial (n) /ˈdaɪ.əl/
hang onto (phr v) /hæŋ ˈɒn.tu/
lever (n) /ˈliː.vər/
rise (v) /raɪz/
set (v) /set/
stretch away (phr v) /stretʃ əˈweɪ/
twilight (n) /ˈtwaɪ.laɪt/

LITERATURE SKILLS 3
ivy (n) /ˈaɪ.vi/
settle in (phr v) /ˈset.l̩ ɪn/
shed (n) /ʃed/
struggle (n) /ˈstrʌɡ.l̩/
term (n) /tɜːm/

LITERATURE SKILLS 4
daisy-chain (n) /ˈdeɪ.zi tʃeɪn/
dip down (phr v) /dɪp daʊn/
hedge (n) /hedʒ/
pick (v) /pɪk/
pop down (phr v) /ˈpɒp.daʊn/
waistcoat-pocket (n) /ˈweɪs.kəʊt ˈpɒk.ɪt/
well (n) /wel/

LITERATURE SKILLS 5
foe (noun) /fəʊ/
give way to (verb) /ɡɪv weɪ tə/
heap (noun) /hiːp/
impostor (noun) /ɪmˈpɒs.tər/
knave (noun) /neɪv/
make allowance for (verb) /meɪk əˈlaʊ.əns fər/
pitch-and-toss (noun) /pɪtʃ ənd tɒs/
sinew (noun) /ˈsɪn.juː/
stoop (noun) /stuːp/
triumph (noun) /ˈtraɪ.əmf/

CLIL A
bug (n) /bʌɡ/
close-up (n) /ˈkləʊs.ʌp/
flea (n) /fliː/
mould (n) /məʊld/
nudge (v) /nʌdʒ/
raw (adj) /rɔː/
tissue (n) /ˈtɪʃ.uː/

CLIL B
offspring (n) /ˈɒf.sprɪŋ/
pandemic (n) /pænˈdem.ɪk/
shape (v) /ʃeɪp/
smallpox (n) /ˈsmɔːl.pɒks/

CLIL C
GP (general practitioner) (n) /ˌdʒiːˈpiː/
lice (n) /laɪs/

CLIL D
consumption (noun) /kənˈsʌmp.ʃən/
flee (noun) /fliː/
medication (noun) /ˌmed.ɪˈkeɪ.ʃən/
monotonous (noun) /məˈnɒt.ən.əs/
relieve (verb) /rɪˈliːv/
therapist (noun) /ˈθer.ə.pɪst/
unconsciously (adv) /ʌnˈkɒn.ʃəs.li/
unwind (verb) /ʌnˈwaɪnd/

CLIL E
affluent (adj) /ˈæf.lu.ənt/
migraine (n) /ˈmiː.ɡreɪn/
outbreak (n) /ˈaʊt.breɪk/
rodent (n) /ˈrəʊ.dənt/

WRITING EXPANSION 1
adventurous (adj) /ədˈven.tʃər.əs/
enthusiastic (adj) /ɪnˌθjuː.ziˈæs.tɪk/
excited (adj) /ɪkˈsaɪ.tɪd/
fearless (adj) /ˈfɪə.ləs/
inquisitive (adj) /ɪnˈkwɪz.ɪ.tɪv/
lazy (adj) /ˈleɪ.zi/
nervous (adj) /ˈnɜː.vəs/
unimaginative (adj) /ˌʌn.ɪˈmædʒ.ɪ.nə.tɪv/

WRITING EXPANSION 3
although (conj) /ɔːlˈðəʊ/
because (of that) (conj) /bɪˈkəz/
finally (adv) /ˈfaɪ.nə.li/
firstly/first of all (adv) /ˈfɜːst.li ˈfɜːst əv ɔːl/
for example (phr) /fɔːr ɪɡˈzɑːm.pl/
for this reason (phr) /fɔːr ðɪs ˈriː.zən/
however (adv) /ˌhaʊˈev.ər/
in addition (phr) /ɪn əˈdɪʃ.ən/
moreover (adv) /ˌmɔːˈrəʊ.vər/
not only that (phr) /nɒt ˈəʊn.li ðæt/
on the one hand (phr) /ɒn ðiː wʌn hænd/
on the other hand (phr) /ɒn ðiː ˈʌð.ər hænd/
secondly (adv) /ˈsek.ənd.li/
so (that) (conj) /səʊ/
therefore (adv) /ˈðeə.fɔːr/

VOCABULARY EXTENSION 1
assist (v) /əˈsɪst/
build (v) /bɪld/
compose (v) /kəmˈpəʊz/
consult (v) /kənˈsʌlt/
design (v) /dɪˈzaɪn/
direct (v) /daɪˈrekt/
entertain (v) /ˌen.təˈteɪn/
interpret (v) /ɪnˈtɜː.prɪt/
invent (v) /ɪnˈvent/
lecture (v) /ˈlek.tʃər/
manage (v) /ˈmæn.ɪdʒ/
narrate (v) /nəˈreɪt/
navigate (v) /ˈnæv.ɪ.ɡeɪt/
produce (v) /prəˈdjuːs/
sail (v) /seɪl/
translate (v) /trænsˈleɪt/

WORDLIST

VOCABULARY EXTENSION 2

angry (adj) /ˈæŋ.gri/
astonishing (adj) /əˈstɒn.ɪ.ʃɪŋ/
awful (adj) /ˈɔː.fəl/
bad (adj) /bæd/
big (adj) /bɪg/
boiling (adj) /ˈbɔɪlɪŋ/
brilliant (adj) /ˈbrɪl.i.ənt/
clean (adj) /kliːn/
clever (adj) /ˈklev.ər/
cold (adj) /kəʊld/
delicious (adj) /dɪˈlɪʃ.əs/
difficult (adj) /ˈdɪf.ɪ.kəlt/
dirty (adj) /ˈdɜː.ti/
exhausted (adj) /ɪgˈzɔː.stɪd/
expensive (adj) /ɪkˈspen.sɪv/
extortionate (adj) /ɪkˈstɔː.ʃən.ət/
fascinating (adj) /ˈfæs.ɪ.neɪ.tɪŋ/
filthy (adj) /ˈfɪl.θi/
freezing (adj) /ˈfriː.zɪŋ/
funny (adj) /ˈfʌn.i/
furious (adj) /ˈfjʊə.ri.əs/
gorgeous (adj) /ˈgɔː.dʒəs/
hilarious (adj) /hɪˈleə.ri.əs/
hot (adj) /hɒt/
huge (adj) /hjuːdʒ/
hungry (adj) /ˈhʌŋ.gri/
impossible (adj) /ɪmˈpɒs.ɪ.bl̩/
interesting (adj) /ˈɪn.trəs.tɪŋ/
pretty (adj) /ˈprɪt.i/
ridiculous (adj) /rɪˈdɪk.jʊ.ləs/
scary (adj) /ˈskeə.ri/
silly (adj) /ˈsɪl.i/
skinny (adj) /ˈskɪn.i/
small (adj) /smɔːl/
spotless (adj) /ˈspɒt.ləs/
starving (adj) /ˈstɑː.vɪŋ/
surprising (adj) /səˈpraɪ.zɪŋ/
tasty (adj) /ˈteɪ.sti/
terrifying (adj) /ˈter.ə.faɪ.ɪŋ/
thin (adj) /θɪn/
tiny (adj) /ˈtaɪ.ni/
tired (adj) /taɪəd/

VOCABULARY EXTENSION 3

act (v) /ækt/
action (n) /ˈæk.ʃən/
conservation (n) /ˌkɒn.sə.ˈveɪ.ʃən/
conserve (v) /kənˈsɜːv/
destroy (v) /dɪˈstrɔɪ/
destruction (n) /dɪˈstrʌk.ʃən/
free (adj) /friː/
freedom (n) /ˈfriː.dəm/
happiness (n) /ˈhæp.i.nəs/
happy (adj) /ˈhæp.i/
homeless (adj) /ˈhəʊm.ləs/
homelessness (n) /ˈhəʊm.ləs.nəs/
hunger (n) /ˈhʌŋ.gər/
miserable (adj) /ˈmɪz.ər.ə.bl̩/
misery (n) /ˈmɪz.ər.i/
pollute (v) /pəˈluːt/
pollution (n) /pəˈluː.ʃən/
poor (adj) /pɔːr/
poverty (n) /ˈpɒv.ə.ti/
produce (n) /ˈprɒd.juːs/
produce (v) /prəˈdjuːs/
progress (v) /prəˈgres/
progress (n) /ˈprəʊ.gres/
protect (v) /prəˈtekt/
protection (n) /prəˈtek.ʃən/
protest (n) /ˈprəʊ.test/
protest (v) /prəˈtest/
renew (v) /rɪˈnjuː/
renovation (n) /ˌren.əˈveɪ.ʃən/
thirst (n) /θɜːst/
thirsty (adj) /ˈθɜː.sti/
unemployed (adj) /ˌʌn.ɪmˈplɔɪd/
unemployment (n) /ˌʌn.ɪmˈplɔɪ.mənt/
waste (v) /weɪst/
waste (n) /weɪst/
wealth (n) /welθ/
wealthy (adj) /ˈwel.θi/

VOCABULARY EXTENSION 4

find out (phr v) /faɪnd aʊt/
get in touch with (phr v) /get ɪn tʌtʃ wɪð/
go over (phr v) /gəʊ ˈəʊ.vər/
leave out (phr v) /liːv aʊt/
look at (phr v) /lʊk ət/
put off (phr v) /pʊt ɒf/
set up (phr v) /ˈset.ʌp/
take out (phr v) /ˈteɪk.aʊt/
think about/over/through (phr v) /θɪŋk əˈbaʊt/
turn down (phr v) /ˈtɜːndaʊn/

VOCABULARY EXTENSION 5

accusation (n) /ˌæk.jʊˈzeɪ.ʃən/
defence (n) /dɪˈfens/
investigation (n) /ɪnˌves.tɪˈgeɪ.ʃən/
jail (n) /dʒeɪl/
offence (n) /əˈfens/
penalty (n) /ˈpen.əl.ti/
proof (n) /pruːf/
prosecution (n) /ˌprɒs.ɪˈkjuː.ʃən/
rehabilitation (n) /ˌriː.həˌbɪl.ɪˈteɪ.ʃən/
statement (n) /ˈsteɪt.mənt/
suspect (n) /səˈspekt/
trial (n) /traɪəl/

VOCABULARY EXTENSION 6

accessible (adj) /əkˈses.ə.bl̩/
agricultural (adj) /ˌæg.rɪˈkʌl.tʃər.əl/
coastal (adj) /ˈkəʊ.stəl/
crowded (adj) /ˈkraʊ.dɪd/
humid (adj) /ˈhjuː.mɪd/
mountainous (adj) /ˈmaʊn.tɪ.nəs/
palatial (adj) /pəˈleɪ.ʃəl/
peaceful (adj) /ˈpiːs.fəl/
picturesque (adj) /ˌpɪk.tʃərˈesk/
polluted (adj) /pəˈluː.tɪd/
touristy (adj) /ˈtʊə.rɪ.sti/
traditional (adj) /trəˈdɪʃ.ən.əl/
tropical (adj) /ˈtrɒp.ɪ.kəl/

VOCABULARY EXTENSION 7

bitter (adj) /ˈbɪt.ər/
bland (adj) /blænd/
chewy (adj) /ˈtʃuː.i/
creamy (adj) /ˈkriː.mi/
crisp (adj) /krɪsp/
crumbly (adj) /ˈkrʌm.bli/
crunchy (adj) /ˈkrʌn.tʃi/
dry (adj) /draɪ/
fresh (adj) /freʃ/
greasy (adj) /ˈgriː.si/
hard (adj) /hɑːd/
juicy (adj) /ˈdʒuː.si/
light (adj) /laɪt/
lumpy (adj) /ˈlʌm.pi/
milky (adj) /ˈmɪl.ki/
moist (adj) /mɔɪst/

WORDLIST

oily (adj) /'ɔɪ.li/
peppery (adj) /'pep.ər.i/
rich (adj) /rɪtʃ/
salty (adj) /'sɒl.ti/
smooth (adj) /smuːð/
soft (adj) /sɒft/
soggy (adj) /'sɒg.i/
sour (adj) /saʊər/
spicy (adj) /'spaɪ.si/
stale (adj) /steɪl/
sticky (adj) /'stɪk.i/
sugary (adj) /'ʃʊg.ər.i/
sweet (adj) /swiːt/
tasteless (adj) /'teɪst.ləs/
tasty (adj) /'teɪ.sti/
watery (adj) /'wɔː.tər.i/

VOCABULARY EXTENSION 8

mind (n) /maɪnd/

VOCABULARY EXTENSION 9

carry out (phr v) /'kær.i.aʊt/
close down (phr v) /kləʊz daʊn/
come up with (phr v) /kʌm ʌp wɪð/
give up (phr v) /gɪv ʌp/
set up (phr v) /'set.ʌp/
sort out (phr v) /'sɔːt.aʊt/
take off (phr v) /'teɪk.ɒf/
think over (phr v) /θɪŋk 'əʊ.vər/
try out (phr v) /'traɪ.aʊt/
weigh up (phr v) /weɪ ʌp/

VOCABULARY EXTENSION 10

battle (n) /'bæt·l/
battle (v) /'bæt·l/

IRREGULAR VERBS

base form	past simple	past participle
be	was / were	been
beat	beat	beaten
become	became	become
begin	began	begun
bend	bent	bent
bet	bet	bet
bite	bit	bitten
bleed	bled	bled
blow	blew	blown
break	broke	broken
bring	brought	brought
build	built	built
burn	burned / burnt	burned / burnt
burst	burst	burst
buy	bought	bought
catch	caught	caught
choose	chose	chosen
come	came	come
cost	cost	cost
cut	cut	cut
deal	dealt	dealt
dig	dug	dug
do	did	done
draw	drew	drawn
dream	dreamed / dreamt	dreamed / dreamt
drink	drank	drunk
drive	drove	driven
eat	ate	eaten
fall	fell	fallen
feed	fed	fed
feel	felt	felt
fight	fought	fought
find	found	found
fly	flew	flown
forbid	forbade	forbidden
forget	forgot	forgotten
forgive	forgave	forgiven
freeze	froze	frozen
get	got	got
give	gave	given
go	went	gone
grow	grew	grown
hang	hung	hung
have	had	had
hear	heard	heard
hide	hid	hidden
hit	hit	hit
hold	held	held
hurt	hurt	hurt
keep	kept	kept
know	knew	known
lay	laid	laid
lead	led	led
learn	learned / learnt	learned / learnt
leave	left	left
lend	lent	lent
let	let	let
lie	lay	lain

base form	past simple	past participle
lie	lied	lied
light	lit	lit
lose	lost	lost
make	made	made
mean	meant	meant
meet	met	met
pay	paid	paid
put	put	put
read /ri:d/	read /red/	read /red/
ride	rode	ridden
ring	rang	rung
rise	rose	risen
run	ran	run
say	said	said
see	saw	seen
seek	sought	sought
sell	sold	sold
send	sent	sent
set	set	set
sew	sewed	sewn / sewed
shake	shook	shaken
shine	shone	shone
shoot	shot	shot
show	showed	shown
shrink	shrank	shrunk
shut	shut	shut
sing	sang	sung
sink	sank	sunk
sit	sat	sat
sleep	slept	slept
smell	smelled / smelt	smelled / smelt
speak	spoke	spoken
spell	spelled / spelt	spelled / spelt
spend	spent	spent
split	split	split
spread	spread	spread
spring	sprang	sprung
stand	stood	stood
steal	stole	stolen
stick	stuck	stuck
sting	stung	stung
stink	stank	stunk
strike	struck	struck
swear	swore	sworn
sweep	swept	swept
swim	swam	swum
swing	swung	swung
take	took	taken
teach	taught	taught
tear	tore	torn
tell	told	told
think	thought	thought
throw	threw	thrown
understand	understood	understood
wake	woke	woken
wear	wore	worn
win	won	won
write	wrote	written

Grammar Reference

STARTER A

Adverbs of frequency

We often use the present simple tense with adverbs of frequency such as *always*, *usually*, *often*, *sometimes*, *hardly ever*, and *never*.

Form and use

We use adverbs of frequency to talk about the frequency of an action.
Always means 100% of the time and *never* means 0% of the time.
Never is used with affirmative sentences even though it has a negative meaning.
The adverbs are usually placed in between the subject and the verb.
- He <u>always</u> listens to music.
- She <u>never</u> eats meat.

But they are placed **after** the verb *be*.
- He is <u>often</u> late.

We use the question *How often* to ask about frequency.
- How often do you get up early? I <u>always</u> get up early.

In negative sentences, adverbs of frequency usually precede the main verb but follow the auxiliary.
- He doesn't <u>always</u> play football.

But they always follow the verb *be*.
- He isn't <u>usually</u> late.

In interrogative forms, adverbs of frequency follow the subject of the sentence.
- Does Kelly <u>often</u> play football on Saturdays?

Expressions of frequency

We also talk about frequency using expressions of frequency.

Form

Expressions of frequency are usually placed at the end of the sentence:
- I go to the gym every day.
- I play football once a week.

These are the most common expressions following the frequency question *How often*:
- once / twice / three times a week / a month / a year
- every day
- two times a week
- on Saturdays / Tuesdays
- in the morning / afternoon / evening
- at weekends

Present simple v present continuous

present simple	present continuous
They usually **come** for the day.	This year we**'re camping**.

Use

The present simple is used for habitual actions, while the present continuous is used for actions happening now.
- He often gets up late. / He is getting up at the moment.

The present simple is used for permanent actions, while the present continuous is used for temporary actions.
- Jane lives in Australia. / Jane is living in London at the moment.

We use different time expressions to identify the different tense forms:

present simple	present continuous
- always	- at the moment
- usually	- now
- often	- this evening
- sometimes	- this weekend
- hardly ever	- today
- never	- tonight
- every day	
- once / twice a week	
- on Saturdays	
- at the weekends	

VERBS OF STATE AND VERBS OF PERCEPTION

We don't usually use the present continuous with state verbs. Some examples are *be*, *believe*, *hate*, *know*, *like*, *love*, *understand*, *think*, *want*, *remember*.
- I believe in you.
- I don't understand the question.

However, there are occasions when we can use the present continuous if we are referring to an action.
- What do you think of this programme? (opinion)
- What are you thinking of? (action)

We don't usually use the present continuous with verbs of perception like *taste*, *sound*, *smell*, *look*.
- That coat looks good on you.
- The lasagne tastes wonderful.

STARTER B

Past simple v past continuous

past simple	past continuous
Ellie **won** her first two medals when she was 13.	Ellie **was wearing** a big coat.

We often use the past simple and the past continuous together to describe the relationship between two actions. The past continuous is used to describe a continuous action or to *set the scene* for a shorter completed action.
- A bee **stung** Jane <u>when</u> she **was sitting** in the garden.

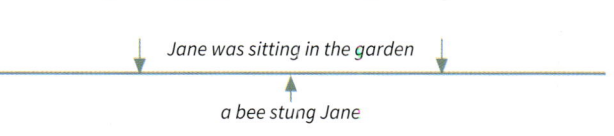

Jane was sitting in the garden

a bee stung Jane

Grammar Reference 111

GRAMMAR REFERENCE

We can use *when*, *while* and *as* to describe situations in which one event interrupts another. *While* and *as* are followed by the past continuous, *when* is followed by the past simple.
- *Mr Neale was sitting in the airport **when** he received the phone call.*
- ***While** the couple were walking, they met Jamie.*

We can use the conjunctions *while* and *as* to join two sentences describing simultaneous actions.
- ***While** we were talking in the garden, a bee was flying from flower to flower.*

Past simple: Regular and irregular verbs

affirmative		
I / You / He / She / It / We / You / They	regular verbs	deliver**ed** it.
	irregular verbs	bro**ke** it.
negative			
---	---	---	---
I / You / He / She / It / We / You / They	did not / didn't	regular verbs	like it.
		irregular verbs	have it.
questions			
Did	I / you / he / she / it / we / you / they		like it?
short answers			
Yes, I / you / he / she / it / we / they **did**.			
No, I / you / he / she / it / we / they **didn't**.			

Form

The regular past simple is formed by adding *-ed* to the base form of the verb.
- *play → play**ed**; visit → visit**ed***

There are some spelling variations:

- Verbs that end in -e:	live → live**d**; arrive → arriv**ed**
- Verbs that end in consonant + -y:	marry → marr**ied**; try → tr**ied**
- Verbs that end in vowel + consonant:	stop → stop**ped**; travel → travel**led**; regret → regret**ted**

The past simple of irregular verbs can be completely different from their base form:
- *have → had; swim → swam*, etc.

The form does not change for all subjects.
The interrogative and negative forms of the past simple are obtained by adding *did* and *did not* to the clause. These forms do not change for all subjects.
Did and *did not* are followed by the base form of the verb.
Short answers use the auxiliary form *Yes, I did. / No, I didn't*.
In short answers, only the negative can be contracted.
For a list of irregular verbs see page 284.

Use

The past simple is used for:
completed actions in the past:
- *We studied together yesterday.*
a completed period in the past:
- *He played football for six months.*
narrative tenses:
- *He checked his email, then contacted his boss.*

Expressions of past time

We often use time expressions with the past simple to state when something happened. Some common time expressions include the following:
- *last week / month / year*
- *at ten / twelve o'clock*
- *in 1492 / 2012*
- *last night*
- *ten minutes / two hours / six weeks ago*
- *on Sunday / Monday (morning, afternoon, evening)*
- *yesterday*
- *last July / summer*

We place the time expressions at the beginning or end of the sentence.
- *My uncle and aunt emigrated to Australia last year.*
- *Last year, my uncle and aunt emigrated to Australia.*

Look!: we do not use *the* with these time expressions:
✗ *He came home from hospital the last week.*

STARTER C

Perfect tenses

- *He's **applied** to medical school.*
- *He's **been studying** really hard.*

PRESENT PERFECT

affirmative		
I / You	have / 've	
He / She / It	has / 's	left.
We / You / They	have / 've	
negative		
I / You	have not / haven't	
He / She / It	has not / hasn't	left.
We / You / They	have not / haven't	
questions		
Have	I / you	
Has	he / she / it	left?
Have	we / you / they	
short answers		
Yes, he / she / it **has**.		
Yes, I / you / we / they **have**.		
No, he / she / it **hasn't**.		
No, I / you / we / they **haven't**.		

112 Grammar Reference

GRAMMAR REFERENCE

Form

The present perfect is formed using *have / has* + the past participle of the main verb.
Regular verbs generally form their past participles by adding *-d*, *-ed* or *-ied*: arriv**ed**, finish**ed**, stud**ied**.
However, many of the verbs we use most frequently are irregular and have irregular participles:

do → done; *lose → lost*; *write → written*

We form the interrogative by inverting *have / has* with the subject.

- *Have they finished their homework? Yes, they have.*

The short answers are formed using the *have / has* structure.
We form the negative by adding *not* to the *have / has* structure.

- *They haven't seen John for a while.*

Use

We use the present perfect:

- to relate the past with the present:
  Matt's lost his glasses. (He hasn't got them now.)
- to talk about events that took place at an unspecified time in the past:
  Have you ever visited France?

PRESENT PERFECT WITH *EVER* AND *NEVER*

We use the present perfect with the adverbs *ever* and *never*. They go before the main verb. *Ever* is normally used in questions to ask about events. It goes immediately before the past participle.

- *Have you ever seen Rihanna?*
  (This is asking about an event in an unspecified time in someone's life.)

Never is used in affirmative sentences to express a negative sentiment.

- *He has never held a snake.*

PAST SIMPLE V PRESENT PERFECT

Both the past simple and the present perfect are used to express events and actions in the past. The main differences are:

- we use the past simple for events that are finished in a specified time in the past.
  - *He went to school yesterday.*
  - *He moved to Turkey in 2015.*
- we use the present perfect to describe events that finished in an unspecified time in the past.
  - *He has lost his phone.*
    (We don't know when, but he hasn't got it now.)
  - *What's wrong with Jack? He's broken his ankle.*
    (We don't know when.)

In these cases, the action is more important than the time.

- we use the present perfect when the effects of the action are still present now.
  - *Oh, look at Phil. He's cut his hair.*
    (We can see the effects now, even though we don't know when it happened.)
- we use the present perfect when the action began in the past but is still continuing now.
  - *He has lived in London for five years.*
    (He still lives in London now.)

- we can see the difference between the two tenses in a dialogue like this:

Lily   Have you ever lived in a different country?
Linda   Yes, I have. I lived in Chile.
Lily   When did you live there?
Linda   I lived there in 2005. It was great.

In this case, the first question is present perfect, because the speaker is asking about an unspecified time in Linda's life. Linda's answer is in the past simple because she lived in Chile some time ago and is now back in the UK. Her time in Chile is finished at a specific time in the past.

Expressions of past time

Expressions of past time help us a lot to identify the difference between the two tenses:

past simple (specified time)	present perfect (unspecified time)
- yesterday	- already
- **last** week / month / year	- yet
- at the weekend	- just
- on my birthday	- never
- one day / two weeks / three months **ago**	- ever
	- **this** week / month / year
	- for / since
	- today

PRESENT PERFECT WITH *FOR / SINCE*

We use the present perfect with *for* and *since* to say how long something has been happening.
We use *for* referring to periods of time (*an hour, two weeks, three months, ten years,* etc.) to talk about duration and *since* with a specific moment in time or to indicate the start of a period (*two o'clock, yesterday morning, Thursday, November, 1995, July,* etc.).

- *My sister and her husband have been married for five years.*
- *Jane has been at the library since two o'clock today.*

Look at the list below. This shows the main expressions used with each form.

for	since
- a long time	- yesterday
- **a** week / month / year	- I was born
- three / four days	- **last** week / month / year
- a few months	- last summer
- five minutes	- 2016
- the past year	- Monday 16th June
- **the last few** days / weeks / months	- 5:30 pm
	- then

BEEN / GONE

Been and *gone* are the past participles of the verbs *be* and *go*. There are some differences in the meanings of these forms.

- *I've been to the shops. Here's the milk.*

Grammar Reference

GRAMMAR REFERENCE

(This means that the person has visited the shops but is now back at home. The person is now present and shows the milk.)
- 'Where is Joan?' 'She's gone to the shops.'
(This means that Joan is not at home because she is still at the shops.)

PRESENT PERFECT WITH JUST, ALREADY AND YET

affirmative (+ just, already)		
I / You	have / 've	just / already left.
He / She / It	has / 's	
We / You / They	have / 've	
negative (+ yet)		
I / You	have not / haven't	left yet.
He / She / It	has not / hasn't	
We / You / They	have not / haven't	
questions (+ yet)		
Have	I / you	left yet?
Has	he / she / it	
Have	we / you / they	
short answers		
Yes, I / you / we / they **have**. Yes, he / she / it **has**. No, I / you / we / they **haven't**. No, he / she / it **hasn't**.		

We can use the adverbs *just*, *already* and *yet* with the present perfect. They go before the main verb (in between *have / has* and the past participle).
- *Olive has just had a baby girl.*
(It happened very recently.)
- *Dani has already posted the news online.*
(He has done this faster or before was originally expected.)

Just and *already* normally take the affirmative form. We only use *yet* with present perfect questions and negative statements. It goes at the end of the sentence. If we say *yet*, we are expecting something to happen.
- *Has your sister moved house yet?*
(We thought she was moving soon.)
- *I haven't done my homework yet.* (But I will do it soon.)

PRESENT PERFECT CONTINUOUS

affirmative		
I / You	have / 've	been travelling.
He / She / It	has / 's	
We / You / They	have / 've	
negative		
I / You	have not / haven't	been travelling.
He / She / It	has not / hasn't	
We / You / They	have not / haven't	
questions		
Have	I / you	been travelling?
Has	he / she / it	
Have	we / you / they	
short answers		
Yes, I / you / we / they **have**. Yes, he / she / it **has**. No, I / you / we / they **haven't**. No, he / she / it **hasn't**.		

Form
The present perfect continuous is formed with *have / has* + the past participle of the verb *be* + *-ing* form.

Use
We use the present perfect continuous for activities that have recently stopped or have just stopped. There is a connection with the present or now.
- *You're wet. Have you been swimming?* (You're wet now.)
- *Claire is very tired. She hasn't been sleeping well.*
- *I've been talking to Joe about the problem and he agrees with me.*
- *It's been raining all day long!*

We can use *for* and *since* with the present perfect continuous when we ask the question *How long…?* The activity is still happening or have just finished.
- *How long has Alex been playing on his tablet? He's been playing on his tablet for an hour.*

We use the present perfect continuous for actions that are repeated over a period of time.
- *Will is a great pianist. He's been playing since he was six.*
- *Jenny speaks Spanish well. She's been learning it for ten years.*

Present perfect simple v present perfect continuous

The present perfect and the present perfect continuous refer to actions or situations that started in the past and are still happening or have just ended:
- we use the present perfect continuous to emphasise the action, its duration or intensity.
    - *Silvia's hands are covered in paint – she's been painting a mural.*
    (She probably hasn't finished it yet.)
- we use the present perfect simple to emphasise the result or the repetitions of the action.
    - *Silvia has painted the mural – it's full of lots of bright colours.*
    (She's finished painting it.)
- we don't use the present perfect continuous with state verbs. We use the present perfect continuous with *How long …?* because we are interested in duration.

GRAMMAR REFERENCE

- *How long have you been learning English? I've been learning English for six years.*

We use the present perfect with *How much*, *How many* and *How many times…?*

- *How much of the book have you read?*
- *How many people have visited the web page this week?*
- *How many times have they been to your house this week?*

STARTER D

Future simple and first conditional

WILL / WON'T

affirmative		
I / You / He / She / It / We / You / They	will / 'll	go.
negative		
I / You / He / She / It / We / You / They	will not / won't	go.
questions		
Will	I / you / he / she / it / we / you / they	go?
short answers		
Yes, I / you / he / she / it / we / they **will**. No, I / you / he / she / it / we / they **won't**.		

Form

The future simple is formed with *will* + the infinitive without *to*. *Will* is invariable and does not change with all subject forms. The affirmative is *will* and the negative is formed by adding *not*, *will not* or *won't* as a contracted form.
In questions, *will* is placed before the subject of the sentence. There are no other auxiliary forms.

Use

We use *will* in the following ways:
- to make predictions based on our opinions:
  - *Come and listen to my new CD. You'll love it.*
  - *I don't think you'll like that cake. It's got raisins in it and you hate them!*
- when we make a spontaneous decision at the time we are speaking:
  - *'I've got to go out to get some eggs.' 'I'll come with you.'*
- when we offer to do something:
  - *Finish your work. I'll cook lunch.*
  - *Don't worry about the tickets. I'll go and pick them up.*
- when we make a promise:
  - *I won't tell anyone. I promise.*
- for certain events that we know will happen:
  - *I'll be 18 next week! It's my birthday on Tuesday.*

FIRST CONDITIONAL

affirmative
If I **have** enough money, I**'ll buy** a new car. I**'ll buy** a new car if I **have** enough money.
negative
If it **doesn't rain**, we**'ll go** to the beach. We**'ll go** to the beach if it **doesn't rain**. If it **rains**, we **won't go** to the beach. We **won't go** to the beach if it **rains**.
questions
Will you **drive** to the station if it **rains** tomorrow? If it **rains** tomorrow, **will** you **drive** to the station?
short answers
Yes, I **will**. / No, I **won't**.

Form

The first conditional is formed as follows:

conditional clause	**result clause**
If + present simple,	future simple
result clause	**conditional clause**
future simple	*if* + present simple

The clauses can be inverted, with the *if* clause coming second, but in this case we omit the comma.
The negative form can be in the first or second clause or in both clauses.
- *We won't go to the match if our team isn't playing.*

Use

We use the first conditional to talk about situations which are possible in the present or the future as long as the condition upon which they rely happens. In this way, there is a definite possibility that the event will happen.
- *If I pass my exams, I will go to university.*
- *We will show you how to install that program if you don't know how to do it.*
- *She won't buy the dress if they don't give her a discount.*

IF, WHEN, AS SOON AS, UNLESS, UNTIL WITH THE FIRST CONDITIONAL

conditional clause	result clause
If it **rains**, **When** it **rains**, **As soon as** it **rains**, **Unless** it **stays** dry,	we **will come** home.
result clause	conditional clause
We **will stay** at the fair	**until** it **rains**.

Grammar Reference 115

GRAMMAR REFERENCE

Form and use

In the first conditional, *if* can be replaced by other words with a similar meaning such as *when, as soon as, unless* and *until*. They follow the same form as *if*:

conditional clause	result clause
If / when / as soon as / unless / until + present simple,	future simple

- **I'll lend** you my book **as soon as** I **finish** reading it.
- **When** it **stops** raining, we**'ll start** the game again.
- We **will carry** on the game **until** it **rains.**

Unless means *if not*.
- She'll make the cake tonight **if** she **isn't** tired.
- She'll make the cake tonight **unless** she**'s** tired.

STARTER E

Subject and object questions

Questions change depending on whether they refer to the subject or the object of the sentence.
- *Who did you see yesterday? I saw Jack.*

In this question, the question word *who* refers to *Jack* – the object of the sentence. For this reason, we use the auxiliary verb, *did*.
- *Who saw Jack? I saw Jack.*

In this question, the question word *who* refers to *I* which is the subject of the sentence. We do not use the auxiliary forms. Subject questions are usually only referred to with question words, *who* and *what*.
- **What** caused the accident? **The fire** caused the accident.
- **Who** called the fire brigade? **James** called the fire brigade.
- **What** did you see at the house? I saw **a huge fire**.
- **Who** did you call? I called **the fire brigade**.

Direct and indirect questions

Most questions invert the subject and verb, but sometimes we want to make questions more formal. We use expressions like this:

- *Could you tell me …*
- *Do you know …*
- *I wonder …*
- *I don't know …*
- *The question is …*
- *Would you mind telling me …*

In this case, the main question is indirect, this means it is inside the other question. Because of this, it follows the order of statements (with the verb after the subject).
- *How much is the coffee?*
  *Can you tell me **how much the coffee is**?*

Similarly if we have auxiliary forms, they are not used.
- *Where did you go last night?*
  *Can you tell me **where you went last night**?*

UNIT 1

Past tenses review

PAST SIMPLE V PAST CONTINUOUS

past continuous	past simple
Buildings **were** still **shaking**	**when** the rescue efforts **started**.
While survivors **were** still **appearing** from the ruins, offers of help **were flooding** in.	Newspapers **were** out of date before they **left** the printing presses.

We often use the past simple and the past continuous together to describe the relationship between two actions. The past continuous is used to describe a continuous action or to *set the scene* for a shorter completed action.

- *A bee **stung** Jane **when** she **was sitting** in the garden.*

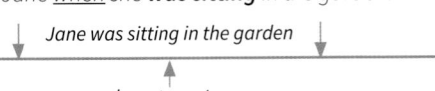

     ↓ Jane was sitting in the garden ↓
     ↑
     a bee stung Jane

- *The phone **rang** while I **was having** a shower.*

We can use *when, while* and *as* to describe situations in which one event interrupts another. *While* and *as* are usually followed by the past continuous, *when* is usually followed by the past simple.
- *Mr Neale was sitting in the airport **when** he received the phone call.*
- ***While** the couple were walking, they met Jamie.*

We can use the conjunctions *while* and *as* to join two sentences describing simultaneous actions.
- ***While** we were talking in the garden, a bee was flying from flower to flower.*

PAST SIMPLE V PRESENT PERFECT

Both the present perfect and the past simple are used to express events and actions in the past. The main differences are:

– we use the past simple for events that are finished in a specified time in the past.
- *He went to school yesterday.*
- *He moved to France in 2015.*

– we use the present perfect to describe events that finished in an unspecified time in the past.
- *He has lost his phone.*
  (We don't know when, but he hasn't got it now.)
- *What's wrong with Jack? He's broken his ankle.*
  (We don't know when.)

In these cases, the action is more important than the time.

– we use the present perfect when the effects of the action are still present now.
- *Oh, look at Phil. He's cut his hair.* (We can see the effects now, even though we don't know when it happened.)

– we use the present perfect when the action began in the past but is still continuing now.
- *He has lived in London for five years.*
  (He still lives in London now.)

– we can see the difference between the two tenses in a dialogue like this:

116   **Grammar Reference**

Lily	Have you ever lived in a different country?
Linda	Yes, I have. I lived in Chile.
Lily	When did you live there?
Linda	I lived there in 2005. It was great.

In this case, the first question is in the present perfect, because the speaker is asking about an unspecified time in Linda's life. Linda's answer is in the past simple because she lived in Chile some time ago and is now back in the UK. Her time in Chile is finished at a specific time in the past.

Expressions of past time

Expressions of past time help us a lot to identify the difference between the two tenses:

past simple
(specified time)
- *yesterday*
- *last* week / month / year
- *at the weekend*
- *on my birthday*
- *one day / two weeks / three months* **ago**

present perfect
(unspecified time)
- *already*
- *yet*
- *just*
- *never*
- *ever*
- *this* week / month / year
- *for / since*
- *today*

Past simple v past perfect

past perfect		
affirmative		
I / You / He / She / It / We / You / They	had	done.
negative		
I / You / He / She / It / We / You / They	had not / hadn't	done.
questions		
Had	I / you / he / she / it / we / you / they	done?
short answers		
Yes, I / you / he / she / it / we / they **had**.		
No, I / you / he / she / it / we / they **hadn't**.		

Form

The past perfect is formed using *had* + the past participle of the main verb.
The negative form adds *not* to the auxiliary form *had* and for the interrogative form *had* is inverted before the subject. There are no other auxiliaries used.

Use

We use the past perfect to talk about two past events when we want to make it clear which event happened first. We use the past perfect for the first event and the past simple for the second event.
- John **had finished** his homework when someone **knocked** on the door.
  (John finished his homework. Then someone knocked on the door.)

GRAMMAR REFERENCE

UNIT 2

Direct and reported speech

When we transfer direct speech to reported, we make some changes to the sentence.

TENSE CHANGES

In general the verb tenses go back one tense, as in the table.

direct speech	reported speech
Present simple He **is** well.	**Past simple** He **was** well.
Present continuous He **is doing** well.	**Past continuous** He **was doing** well.
Past simple He **went** home.	**Past perfect** He **had gone** home.
Past continuous He **was going** home.	**Past perfect continuous** He **had been going** home.
Present perfect He **has done** well.	**Past perfect** He **had done** well.
Present perfect continuous He **has been working** long.	**Past perfect continuous** He **had been working** long.
Future – *will* He **will / won't** come.	**Conditional** – *would* He **would / wouldn't** come.
can He **can** come.	*could* He **could** come.
must He **must** come.	*had to* He **had to** come.
has to He **has to** come.	*had to* He **had to** come.

PRONOUNS AND ADJECTIVES

Apart from changing the verb tenses, we also have to remember to change the personal pronouns and possessive adjectives where necessary.
- '*I go skiing every winter,*' Jake said.
  Jake said that he went skiing every winter.
- '*I'm really excited – my story is in the school newspaper,*' Edwina said.
  Edwina said she was really excited because her story was in the school newspaper.

We can omit the word *that* in reported speech.

TIME CHANGES

When we are reporting speech, we often make other changes related to time.

- *this* morning / afternoon / evening / week → *that* morning / afternoon / evening / week
- *today* → *that* day
- *tonight* → *that* night
- *next* week / month / year → *the following* week / month / year
- *yesterday* → *the day before*

Grammar Reference 117

GRAMMAR REFERENCE

- **last** summer / week / → **the** summer / week /
  month / year   month / year **before**
- '*I uploaded my post **this morning**,*' Fran said.
  Fran said that she had uploaded her post **that morning**.
- '*Did you go away **last summer**?*' Claudia asked.
  Claudia asked me if I had been away **the summer before**.

SAY AND TELL

When we report what someone has said we use *say* if there is no direct object and *tell* if there is an object.
- She **said** that she wanted to study journalism.
- She **told me** that she wanted to study journalism.

Reported speech: Questions

direct speech	reported speech
When did you buy it?	She asked me when I had bought it.
Do you have the receipt?	She asked me if / whether I had the receipt.

To report questions, we make the same tense changes as in reported statements.
When we are reporting *Yes / No* questions (i.e., questions without question words), we use *if* or *whether* before the reported clause and we use the statement form rather than the question form.
- '***Did you read** that story?*' Martin asked.
  Martin asked **if / whether I had read** the story.
- '***Have you read** the papers today?*' Kirsten asked.
  Kirsten asked **if / whether I had read** the papers that day.

When we report questions which have question words (*Who*, *What*, *How*, etc.), we use the question word in the reported question. The word order is the same as for reported statements.
- '***Where are you going** on holiday?*' Melinda asked.
  Melinda asked **where I was going** on holiday.
- '***How much did the printer cost**?*' Joshua asked.
  Joshua asked **how much the printer had cost**.

Reported speech: Commands

We use the structure **tell somebody to do something** to report commands.
- '*Turn down the TV,*' Lauren said.
  Lauren told me to turn down the TV.

If the command is negative, then we use the structure **tell somebody not to do something**.
- '*Don't forget to buy some milk,*' my mum said.
  My mum told me not to forget to buy some milk.

Reported speech: Requests

We use the structure **ask somebody to do something** to report requests.
- '*Please answer the phone,*' my dad said.
  My dad asked me to answer the phone.

If a request is in the negative form, then we use the structure **ask somebody not to do something**.
- '*Don't tell my parents,*' Emily said.
  Emily asked me not to tell her parents.

UNIT 3

Revision of comparative and superlative adjectives

spelling variations	
Regular adjectives:	+ -er / -est
Adjectives ending in -y:	~~y~~ + -ier / -iest
Adjectives ending in -e:	+ -r / -st
Adjectives ending in vowel + consonant:	double the final consonant
Two-syllable (+) adjectives:	add *more* / *most*
Some two-syllable adjectives:	have two forms -er / -est and *more* / *most*

adjectives	comparative	superlative
small	small**er than**	**the** small**est**
happy	happ**ier than**	**the** happ**iest**
nice	nic**er than**	**the** nic**est**
big	big**ger than**	**the** big**gest**
expensive	**more** expensive **than**	**the most** expensive
clever	clever**er than** / **more** clever **than**	**the** clever**est** / **the most** clever

irregular adjectives		
adjectives	comparative	superlative
good	better than	the best
bad	worse than	the worst
far	further / farther than	the furthest / farthest

Qualifiers

In order to qualify comparative adjectives we can add adverbials like **much**, **a lot**, **far**, **even**, **a little**, **a little bit**.
- He's **much younger** than me.
- My brother is **a little older** than me.
- That watch is **a lot more expensive** than the one in the catalogue.
- Their house is **far bigger** than ours.

With superlative adjectives, we can add **by far**.
- He's **by far the best** student in the class.
- They're **by far the wealthiest** people in our street.

LESS THAN AND THE LEAST

The comparative and superlative form of *little* is *less* and *the least*. This comparative and superlative form acts in the same way as other comparative and superlative forms.
- That house is less expensive than the one we saw yesterday. It's the least expensive house in the street.

Grammar Reference

GRAMMAR REFERENCE

(NOT) AS ... AS

We use (not) as … as to compare equivalent aspects of two things.
- The apple is (not) as heavy as the banana.
- The boy is not as tall as his brother.

We can also use not so … as in the same way, but not in positive sentences and questions.

Comparatives and superlatives with nouns

We form the comparative of nouns by using words like *more*, *fewer* and *less*. We also need to consider countable and uncountable nouns.
- There are **more** cars here than in Scotland.
- There are **fewer** cars at lunchtime than in the rush hour.
- There is **more** money in this purse than in that one.
- There is **less** money in Africa than in the US.

Qualifiers

We also use qualifiers such as *much*, *a lot*, *far*.
- There are **much fewer** cars at lunchtime than in the rush hour.
- There is **a lot less money** in Africa than in the US.
- There are **far more** cars here than in Scotland.

We form superlatives of nouns by using words like *the most*, *the fewest*, *the least*. We also use qualifiers as *by far* to add intensity.
- There are **the most** cars in Mexico City.
- There are **the fewest** cars on the Isle of Skye.
- There is **the least money** in Bangladesh.
- There is **by far the most cars** in Mexico City.
- There is **by far the least money** in Bangladesh.

too many / too much, too few / too little, (not) enough + nouns

Countable
- There **are too many** souvenirs. (excess)
- There **are too few** souvenirs. (insufficient)
- There **aren't enough** souvenirs. (insufficient)

Uncountable
- There **is too much** space. (excess)
- There **is too little** space. (insufficient)
- There **isn't enough** space. (insufficient)

Form and use

Too many / too much means there is an excess of items.
Too many is used with countable nouns and *too much* is used with uncountable nouns.
Too few / too little means there isn't enough of something.
Too few is used with countable nouns and *too little* is used with uncountable nouns.

Not enough is used with both countable and uncountable nouns and means there is an insufficient amount of something.

Qualifiers

As with other comparative and superlative forms we can use qualifiers here by using expressions such as *much*, *a lot of*, *far*.
- There are **far too many** cars in this city.
- There is **much too little** space in my suitcase.

Comparative and superlative adverbs

With regular adverbs, we use *more / less* to make a comparative comparison, and *the most / the least* for a superlative comparison.
- He works **more quickly than** me.
- He studies **less carefully than** his brother.
- He works **the most quickly**.
- He studies **the least quickly**.

With irregular adverbs, comparative and superlative are formed in this way:
- **faster**, **better**, **further**, **worse than** for comparative adverbs.
- **the fastest**, **the best**, **the worst** for superlative adverbs.

Qualifiers

As with adjectives, there are qualifiers we can use with comparatives and superlatives of adverbs. For comparatives, we can use *much*, *far*, *a lot*, *even*, *a little* and for superlatives we can use *by far*.

UNIT 4

Future predictions: will v may / might

affirmative		
I / You / He / She / It / We / You / They	will / 'll	go.
negative		
I / You / He / She / It / We / You / They	will not / won't	go.
questions		
Will	I / you / he / she / it / we / you / they	go?
short answers		
Yes, I / you / he / she / it / we / they **will**. No, I / you / he / she / it / we / they **won't**.		

will	may / might
With reasonable care photos **will last** indefinitely.	Your grandparents' photos **may fade**.
With new technology, the contents **won't be** accessible.	It **might happen** in the near future.

Grammar Reference 119

GRAMMAR REFERENCE

Form and use

Will, *may* and *might* are all modal verbs. This means they are invariable in all forms, they are not used with auxiliary verbs and they are followed by verbs in the base form.

- *Jack will come to the party. They won't listen to you. Will he help us?*
- *Her dad might drive her to the party. We may see her there. They might not come this evening.*

WILL / MAY / MIGHT FOR FUTURE POSSIBILITY

We use the modal verbs *may*, *might* and *will* to express possibility. *Will* is used when we believe something will definitely happen in the future. *May* and *might* are used to say that something is possible. Usually you can use *may* or *might*.

- *Tim may / might help you. He studied science.*
- *We may not / might not go to the cinema tonight. We have an exam tomorrow. (We aren't sure, we will possibly go.)*
- *We won't go to the cinema tonight. We have an exam tomorrow. (We know we aren't going.)*

Future perfect

affirmative	
I / You / He / She / It / We / You / They	will / 'll have forgotten you.
negative	
I / You / He / She / It / We / You / They	will not / won't have forgotten you.
questions		
Will	I / you / he / she / it / we / you / they	have forgotten you?
short answers		
Yes, I / you / he / she / it / we / they **will**.		
No, I / you / he / she / it / we / they **will not / won't**.		

Form

We form the future perfect with *will have* and the past participle form of the main verb.

Use

We use the future perfect to talk about things that will or will not be finished before a certain time in the future.

- *Let's do our homework now. Then we'll have finished **before the tennis match starts**.*
- ***In September**, I will have studied English for three years.*

Expressions of time

We often use words and expressions with this verb form:
- *by Friday / Monday / next week*
- *by the time*
- *in (the next / an) hour*
- ***By the time** we get to the stadium, the match **will have started**.*
- ***In three years' time**, you **will have worked** there for 10 years.*

Revision of future

+	I **will be** 17 next week. It's my birthday! I**'m having** a party on Saturday 23rd September. This evening I**'m going to try** and buy some balloons.
−	I **won't invite** John, he's not my friend anymore! I**'m not cutting** my hair this week, that's next Friday. I**'m not going to buy** any food. Everyone is bringing something.
?	**Will** Jasmine **come** to my party? Yes, she **will**, if she's free. **Are** you **preparing** a cake for me? Yes, I **am**. I**'m cooking** it this evening. **Are** they **going to bring** some food with them? Yes, **they are**. That's their intention at least.

WILL / WON'T

We use the future simple to make predictions based on our opinions.

- *Come and listen to my new CD. You'll love it.*

We often use *will* with the following words and expressions: *be sure, expect, probably, think*.

- *I'm sure the teacher will sympathise with your problems.*
- *She doesn't think her parents will mind.*

When we want to make a negative sentence with **think** + **will**, the *not* goes with *think*, not with *will*.

- ✓ *She **doesn't think** her parents **will** let her go horse riding.*
- ✗ ~~She thinks her parents won't let her go horse riding.~~

We often use *will* when we make a decision at the time we are speaking.

- *'I've got to go out to get some spaghetti and some tomatoes.' 'I'll come with you.'*

We also use *will* when we offer to do something.

- *Finish your work. I'll cook lunch.*
- *Don't worry about the tickets. I'll go and pick them up.*

BE GOING TO

We use *be going to* and a main verb to talk about future plans and intentions.

- *I'm going to get my ears pierced next week.*
- *They're not going to spend the summer in Calpe this year.*
- *Are you going to make a cake for my birthday?*

We can use *be going to* to make predictions when there is strong present or past evidence that something is going to happen.

- *The temperature is already 20 ºC and it's only 8 am. It's going to be really hot today.*
- *Mum's going to be angry because I haven't tidied my room.*

PRESENT CONTINUOUS

We use the present continuous to talk about future events which are already planned.

- *The vet's operating on my dog next week.*
- *'Are we all meeting at Paco's house on Friday?' 'That's right. That's the plan.'*

GRAMMAR REFERENCE

When we use the present continuous to talk about the future, there is usually a reference to time, either in the sentence or in the context.
- *What are you doing?* (now) *I'm finishing my homework.*
- *Are you doing anything on Friday?* (future) *Yes, I'm meeting Monica.*

Future continuous

affirmative	
I / You / He / She / It / We / You / They	will / 'll be playing tennis.
negative	
I / You / He / She / It / We / You / They	will not / won't be playing tennis.
questions	
Will	I / you / he / she / it / we / you / they	be playing tennis?
short answers	
Yes, I / you / he / she / it / we / they **will**.	
No, I / you / he / she / it / we / they **will not / won't**.	

Form
The future continuous is formed with *will + be + -ing* form.

Use
We use the future continuous to talk about actions that will be in progress at a specific point in the future.
- *This time next week, we'll be packing our cases for our holiday.*
- *When I'm 20, I'll be studying Fine Arts at university.*

We also use the future continuous to talk about a future event which has already been decided.
- *They'll be going away next week.*
- *Jo won't be coming to the party because he's got to babysit.*

Expressions of time
We often use these words and expressions with this verb form:
by Friday / Monday / next week
by the time
in (the next / an) hour
- **By the time** *we get home, they***'ll be playing** *video games.*
- **This time next week**, *you* **will be lying** *on a beach in Taormina.*

UNIT 5

Defining relative clauses

Defining relative clauses make clear which person or thing we are talking about. They are essential to understand the meaning of the sentence. Without them, the sentence doesn't make sense.
- *The students* **who** *cheated in the exam won't get any marks.*
- *The man* **who** *is over there is my maths teacher.*

RELATIVE PRONOUNS IN DEFINING RELATIVE CLAUSES

who / that	refers to people	The boy **who** / **that** lives next door goes to my school.
which / that	refers to things	The car **which** is parked in my drive belongs to my sister.
where	refers to places	That's the house **where** I was born.
whose	refers to possession	Jane is the girl **whose** friend was arrested.
when	refers to time	That's the month **when** I start school.

We can omit the relative pronoun when the person or thing being defined is the object of the sentence. However, it is not wrong if it is inserted.
- *That's the dress (***which** / **that***) I bought for my wedding.*

Non-defining relative clauses

Unlike defining relative clauses, non-defining relative clauses are clauses that are not essential to understand the sentence. They give us extra information, but the sentence will still make sense without them. Look at these examples.
- *Harry Houdini, whose real name was Ehrich Weiss, was born in Hungary.*
- *That's the woman who bought our old house.*

In the first sentence, you can omit the information about Houdini's real name. The sentence will still make sense:
- *Harry Houdini was born in Hungary.*

But the second sentence is nonsense without the information after *who*.

When we add a non-defining relative clause, we always use a comma before and after the clause. If the clause comes at the end of the sentence, it is preceded by a comma and ends in a full stop.
- *The Prado Museum, which is visited by thousands of people every year, is in Madrid.*
- *Alex's favourite video game is Minecraft, which was created by a Swedish programmer.*

In non-defining relative clauses we use **who** for people and **which** for things. We don't use **that**.
- *Harry Houdini, who is my hero, came from Hungary.*
- *The Tower of London, which is very popular with tourists, is located on the north bank of the River Thames.*

Unlike defining relative clauses, we cannot omit the relative pronoun in a sentence.

Articles: *a / an*, *the*, no article

A / AN

We use the indefinite article *a / an* with a singular countable noun when we use it for the first time.

Grammar Reference 121

GRAMMAR REFERENCE

We use *a* for nouns beginning with a consonant and *an* with nouns which begin with a vowel. The exceptions to this are:
- nouns beginning with the /ju/ sound also take *a*: *a university*
- nouns beginning with a silent /h/ also take *an*: *an hour*.

THE

We use the definite article *the*:
- with singular and plural nouns if they have been mentioned before:
  - *I turned into **a** road on my left. It was **the** road where I lived.*
- with certain geographical names, names of some countries, mountain ranges, rivers, seas:
  - ***the** Andes, **the** Pacific ocean, **the** Alps, **the** USA, **the** United Kingdom*
- with certain organisations, dates, expressions of time:
  - *the police, the 1930s, the 21st century, in the morning / afternoon / evening*
- with things which are unique:
  - *the earth, the sun, the truth*
- with superlatives:
  - *the best song, the most interesting book*

NO ARTICLE

We don't use any article:
- with certain towns, cities, the names of most countries, lakes:
  - *The greatest city is London.*
  - *I live in France.*
  - *They live near Lake Geneva.*
- with plural countable nouns when we are talking about them in general:
  - *I don't like pop music.*
- with possessive adjectives:
  - ✓ *I live with my mother.*
  - ✗ *I live with the my mother.*
- with certain expressions:
  - *go to bed, at sea, in hospital, have lunch*

UNIT 6

The passive: *be* + past participle

The passive is formed by using the verb *be* in the same tense as the normal verb and the past participle of the main verb.
The verb tenses remain the same.
When we form the passive construction, the object of the active sentence becomes the subject of the passive one.

Present simple: The earth quake **shakes** the buildings.
→ The buildings **are shaken** by the earthquakes.
Present continuous: They **are teaching** the children to read.
→ The children **are being taught** to read.
Future simple: They **will build** houses for everyone.
→ Houses **will be built** for everyone.
Past simple: She **wrote** the best seller in a week.
→ The best seller **was written** in a week.
Past continuous: He **was building** the road for a long time.
→ The road **was being built** for a long time.
Present perfect: He **has painted** several paintings in his life.
→ Several paintings **have been painted**.
Past perfect: They **had performed** the play outside.
→ The play **had been performed** outside.

Look!: We cannot use the passive with the present perfect continuous, future continuous or past perfect continuous.

questions	
active	Where **do** they **display** the flags?
passive	Where **are** the flags **displayed**?
active	When **did** they **discover** the city?
passive	When **was** the city **discovered**?
active	Who **saw** the play?
passive	Who **was** the play **seen by**?

BY

When we use the passive voice, if we say who or what was responsible for the action, we use the preposition *by*.
- *That theatre is owned by a famous actor.*
- *Many people were affected by the Second World War.*

We do not use *by* + agent when it is obvious who performed the action. For example, we would not usually say: *He was arrested by the police.* We would say: *He was arrested.* We would not use *by* + agent in this case, as only the police can arrest people.

Passive with *can / can't / could / couldn't*

We form the passive with *can / could* by using the infinitive of the verb *be* + past participle of the main verb.
- They **can write** the book in a week. → The book **can be written** in a week.
- They **could build** the house in 6 months. → The house **could be built** in 6 months.

Verbs with two objects

Some verbs can be followed by two objects in the passive. The two objects usually refer to a person and a thing. When these sentences are transformed into the passive, there are two possibilities.

Active: They **gave** the best comedian a prize.
Passive: The best comedian **was given** a prize.
A prize **was given** to the best comedian.

The most common verbs which are followed by two objects are: *give, lend, offer, pay, promise, refuse, send, show, tell.*

Passive with *say, believe, know, think*

With most verbs of thinking, believing or saying there are two possible passive constructions. The personal passive and the impersonal passive. In the impersonal passive we start the construction with *It*, while in the personal passive, we start with the subject.
- **It is** often **said that** birds are free.
- Birds **are** often **said to be** free. (*to be* = infinitive)

- *It is known that* their numbers have declined.
- Their numbers *are known to have declined*.
  (*to have declined* = passive infinitive)

These are the most common verbs used in this way: *believe, consider, estimate, expect, feel, know, predict, presume, report, say, suppose, think, understand*.

Question tags

When we want to confirm that what we are saying is true, we often use question tags at the end of the statement. Our intonation will tell the listener how sure we are of the information. If the intonation with the tag question falls, it means we are very sure; if the intonation rises, it means we are less sure. We form question tags by using the main verb or its auxiliary and making the opposite of the main statement. So if a statement is negative, the question tag is positive; if the main statement is positive, the question tag is negative. We use a pronoun to represent the subject of the sentence.

- *Jane is* my friend, *isn't she?*
- *Jack leaves* on the 1 pm train, *doesn't he?*
- *You don't want* an ice cream, *do you?*
- *They left* yesterday, *didn't they?*
- *Sally has gone* home, *hasn't she?*
- *They will help* us, *won't they?*
- *Sarah could come* along, *couldn't she?*
- *You're getting married* tomorrow, *aren't you?*

Look!: The question tag for *Let's* is *shall we?*
The question tag for *I am* is *aren't I?*
The question tag for *I'm not* is *am I?*

Echo questions

We use echo questions to reply to a statement, often in the form of surprise, or to carry on the conversation. Like tag questions, they are formed using the basis of the auxiliary verb. However, unlike tag questions, they do not change form from negative or positive, but keep the same form as the main statement.

- 'Their house *has got* a swimming pool.' '*Has it?*'
- 'Jake *went* to France last week.' '*Did he?*'
- 'Becky and Liz *have gone* on holiday.' '*Have they?*'

UNIT 7

Conditionals

zero	*If* we **start** life with 'good' genes, we **have** the best possible advantage.
first	*If* their research **proves** this theory, rosemary **will** probably **become** the next 'superfood'.
second	We **would** all **be** healthier and fitter *if* we **breathed** such clean air.
third	*If* they **had grown up** in a different place, they **would** probably still **have lived** long and healthy lives.

GRAMMAR REFERENCE

ZERO CONDITIONAL

conditional clause	result clause
If + present simple,	present simple

We use the zero conditional to talk about things which are generally or always true.

- *If you heat water to 100 °C, it boils.*
- *If you mix yellow and blue, you get green.*

These forms can be inverted: present simple + *if* + present simple

- *Water boils if you heat it to 100 °C.*
- *You get green if you mix yellow and blue.*

We can replace *if* with *when* in zero conditional sentences.

- *When you heat water to 100 °C, it boils.*
- *When you mix yellow and blue, you get green.*

We also use the zero conditional with imperatives and modals to talk about possible future events.

- *If you go to England next week, bring me back some tea.*
- *If you want to pass your driving test, you should get more lessons.*

FIRST CONDITIONAL

conditional clause	result clause
If + present simple,	future simple
result clause	**conditional clause**
future simple	*if* + present simple

We use the first conditional to talk about situations which are possible in the present or the future as long as the condition upon which they rely happens. In this way, there is a definite possibility that the event will happen.

- *If I pass my exams, I will go to university.*
- *We will show you how to install that program if you don't know how to do it.*
- *She won't buy the dress if they don't give her a discount.*

SECOND CONDITIONAL

conditional clause	result clause
If + past simple,	conditional
result clause	**conditional clause**
conditional	*if* + past simple

We use the second conditional to talk about unreal or hypothetical situations.

- *If they had more money, they would buy the computers now.*
- *They would help the poor if they had more money.*

Second conditional v first conditional

> **First conditional**
> *If* **it's** a girl, we**'ll call** her Poppy. *If* **it's** a boy, we**'ll call** him Jack.
> **Second conditional**
> *If* **I won** the lottery, **I'd buy** a Ferrari.

The first conditional talks of situations that are in the future but probable / likely to happen. The woman is pregnant, she will have a boy or a girl. That is a fact.

Grammar Reference 123

GRAMMAR REFERENCE

The second conditional talks of hypothetical situations. They may never be probable. I may never win the lottery, it's very unlikely.

THIRD CONDITIONAL

conditional clause	result clause
If + past perfect,	would have + past participle
result clause	conditional clause
would have + past participle	if + past perfect

We use the third conditional to talk about things in the past that did or did not happen and what would have happened if we had done something different. We cannot change the consequences of the actions.
- If he hadn't started working in Bristol, he would never have met his future wife.
(But he did work there and now he's married.)
- I wouldn't have left my job if the bosses hadn't been so unfair.
(But they were unfair and I have now left.)

should / shouldn't have
- I missed the train because I left too late. I **should have left** earlier.
- I'm sick now because I ate too many chocolates. I **shouldn't have eaten** all those chocolates.

We use should / shouldn't have + past participle to criticise or express regret about a past action. There is nothing we can do to change this situation.

wish + past tenses

wish + past simple (for present regret)
I wish I **had** the chance to do it again.
I wish I **could** go on the show again.
wish + past perfect (for past regret)
I wish I'**d cooked** something else.
I wish I'**d learnt** some more recipes.

Use
We use wish to talk about how we would like a present or past situation to be different.
When we are referring to a present situation, the structure is wish + past simple / continuous.
- There are no cheap restaurants near where I live. I wish there were some cheap restaurants near where I live. (It's unlikely, but it is possible there may be some in the future.)
- I wish I could cook, but I'm a disaster in the kitchen. (I may learn to cook in the future.)

When we are referring to a past situation, we use wish + past perfect simple / continuous.
- Those trousers look awful on me. I wish I hadn't bought those trousers. (But I did buy them.)
- We didn't get a good view of the castle because it was raining. I wish it hadn't been raining. (But it was raining.)

Mixed conditionals

Mixed conditional sentences are sentences which use a mixture of second and third conditionals because we want to express things we did in the past that might have present consequences or to express past events that may be the result of present facts.
- If I **hadn't eaten** all the cake, I **wouldn't feel** sick now!
(Past action: you ate all the cake. Present consequence: you feel sick now.)
- If I **didn't have to go** to hospital, I **would have booked** the holiday to Ibiza.
(Present fact: I have to go to hospital. Past consequence: I wasn't able to book the holiday.)

Time clauses with *when*, *unless*, *until*, *as soon as*

conditional clause	result clause
When I **stop** the training, **As soon as** my jeans **fit**, **Unless** I **know** they're from happy hens,	I'**ll need** to be careful. I'**ll stop** my diet! I **won't eat** those eggs.
result clause	conditional clause
I **won't eat** any more crisps	**until** my jeans **fit** me again.

Form and use
If can be replaced by other words with a similar meaning such as *when*, *as soon as*, *unless* and *until*. They follow the same form as *if*:

conditional clause	result clause
if / as soon as / unless / when / until + present simple / present perfect,	future simple

- I'll lend you my book **as soon as** I've finished reading it.
- **When** it stops raining, we'll start the game again.
- We will carry on the game **until** it rains.

Unless means *if not*.
- She'll make the cake tonight **if** she is**n't** tired.
- She'll make the cake tonight **unless** she's tired.

Conditional sentences sometimes contain other modal verbs than *will*, *would* and *would have*:
- instead of *will*: *can*, *may*, *might*
- instead of *would*: *could*, *might*
- instead of *would have*: *could have*, *might have*

The modal verbs *can* and *could* may also appear in the *if* clause.

Even if is used to make the condition more emphatic.
- She won't go to Mark's wedding even if he invites her.

We often use *or* or *otherwise* in conditional sentences.
- You've got to study or / otherwise you won't be going to university.

GRAMMAR REFERENCE

UNIT 8

used to / would + infinitive without to

affirmative	negative
Watching TV **used to be** a communal activity.	They **didn't use to switch on** immediately.
questions	short answers
Did your grandmother **use to have** a TV?	Yes, she **did**. No, she **didn't**.

Form and use

We use *used to* when we want to express something that happened regularly in the past, but no longer happens.
- *Freddie used to read all the business news online.*
- *Did you use to ride your bike every day?*
- *I didn't use to like ice cream!*

We don't use *for* with *used to* when we are talking about a state.
- ✓ *I used to live in Durham.*
- ✗ *I used to live in Durham for five years.*

We also use *used to* for something that was true, but isn't true anymore.
- *Evie used to have very long hair when she was a child. Now it's short.*

We can also use *would / wouldn't* + base form to talk about a habit or repeated action, but *used to* is more common.
- *We would play outdoors for hours. We wouldn't come inside till it was 10 pm.*

We use *used to* but **not** *would* to talk about past states.
- ✓ *She used to like ice cream when she was young.*
- ✗ *She would like ice cream when she was young.*

Used to is also more common in the negative and interrogative forms.

There is no present form of *used to*.
- ✓ *I do yoga once a week.*
- ✗ *I use to do yoga once a week.*

Used to can describe actions and states, but *would* can only describe actions.
- ✓ *They used to be crazy about Doctor Who.*
- ✗ *They would be crazy about Doctor Who.*

be / get used to + something / -ing

We use *be / get used to* to express something that we are becoming accustomed to.

Be used to is used when we are already accustomed to something:
- *I live in London so I **am used to** the rain.*
- *I work at a school, so I **am used to meeting** lots of teachers.*

Get used to is used when we are in a new situation and we are in the process of becoming accustomed to something.
- *I moved to Saudi Arabia last week, and I'm slowly **getting used to** the heat.*

We often use *can't / couldn't* with *get used to* to show that something is difficult for us to become accustomed to.

- *I've always lived in the countryside, so I **couldn't get used to** the noise of London.*
- *I love cakes so I **can't get used to** not **eating** them!*

Gerunds and infinitives (1)

Gerunds are nouns that are formed from verbs. They take the *-ing* form so are sometimes confused with the present continuous.

We use gerunds:
- as nouns as the subject or the object of a sentence:
  - ***Eating*** *lots of chocolate is bad for you.*
  - *My favourite hobby is **dancing**.*
- after certain prepositions:
  - *I'm interested **in travelling** around the world.*
  - *I'm fond **of watching** horror films.*
  - *I'm worried **about cooking** dinner tonight!*
- after certain verbs and phrases, *like / hate, don't mind, can't help, give up, stop / finish, start, spend, suggest, recommend*:
  - *I **don't like doing** homework on Saturday morning.*
  - *I **can't help eating** so much chocolate.*

We use infinitives:
- when we are describing a purpose:
  - *I went to the doctor **to get** some medication.*
- after some adjectives:
  - *It's **nice to see** you.*
  - *It's **wrong to help** that man.*
- after some verbs and phrases, *afford, agree, aim, arrange, be able, choose, decide, expect, help, hope, learn, need, offer, plan, promise, refuse, threaten, want, would like, wish*:
  - *I **would like to help** you, but I can't.*
  - *He **promised to pick** me up from the station, but he isn't here!*

UNIT 9

Gerunds and infinitives (2)

As we have seen in Unit 8, some verbs take either a gerund or an infinitive. Some verbs can take both forms, but there are some differences.

Some verbs take both forms and the meaning remains the same.
- *They liked **playing** / **to play** tennis in the afternoon.*
- *She started **to watch** / **watching** the game after breakfast.*

Some verbs take both forms but the meaning is very different. The most common verbs in this category are: *remember, forget, stop, regret, go on*.
- *I **stopped to get** coffee.* (This means I stopped another activity so that I could buy coffee.)
- *I **stopped getting** coffee.* (This means I stopped buying coffee permanently.)

Look at these other examples:
- *I **regret to tell** you but you can no longer work here.* (This is something I am doing now, I regret it now because of the future effect on you.)

Grammar Reference 125

GRAMMAR REFERENCE

- *I regretted eating* so much chocolate. (In this case, I have eaten the chocolate, there is nothing I can do about it but I'll probably feel very sick.)
- *I forgot to lock* the front door when I left the house. (I didn't do an action because it went out of my mind, the front door is open.)
- *I forgot locking* the front door. (Here I did lock the front door, but I don't recall doing it.)
- **Remember to bring** your tennis shoes, so we can go to the gym. (Here I am reminding someone to do a future action.)
- *I remembered seeing* John at the party, but he didn't speak to me. (Here I am recalling a past memory.)

Reporting verbs

Some reporting verbs follow the same pattern of *tell* and *ask*:
ask / tell + object + infinitive
- They asked him to do that.
- They told him to do that.

The verbs which follow this structure along with *tell*, *ask* are *command*, *order*, *warn*, *persuade*, *remind*:
- They reminded the students to study hard before the exam.
- They warned the students to obey the instructions.

have / get something done

When somebody else does something for us, we use the structure: *have* + something + past participle
- *My father paints the house every two years.* (He does it himself.)
- *My father **has** the house **painted** every two years.* (My father arranges for painters to paint the house.)
- *My mother made a dress last month.* (She made it herself.)
- *My mother **had** a dress **made** last month.* (A dressmaker made my mother's dress.)

The interrogative and negative have a similar form as most verbs.
- **Did** your dad **have** his house **painted** last week? Yes, he **did**. / No, he **didn't**.
- She **didn't have** her hair **cut** last week, it was yesterday.

Get is often used instead of *have* in informal English.
- My grandma **gets her nails done** every week.
- We **get our car serviced** every year.

UNIT 10

Revision of modals

We use modal verbs to modify the meaning of other verbs. We use them, for example, to express ability, obligation and prohibition and to give advice.

ABILITY

- We **can** / **can't** imagine what a nuclear blast was like.
- We **could** / **couldn't** remember what happened.
- We **will** / **won't be able to** build a safer world.
- We **were** / **weren't able to** save her.

We use *can* and *be able to* to talk about someone's ability, or non-ability, to do something.

can, can't and could, couldn't

The most common forms of *be able to* in the present and past simple are *can / can't* for the present and *could / couldn't* for the past.
Look!: We use these modals with the base form of the verb.
- 'Matt can skate very well.' 'Can he surf too?' 'No, he can't.' (ability and non-ability in the present)
- 'Although he couldn't hear well when he was older, Beethoven could still compose music.' 'Could he do this until the end of his life?' (ability and non-ability in the past)

It is also possible to use *can* when we make present decisions about the future.
- I can't help you today but I can help you **tomorrow**.

be able to

We use *be able to* to express ability and non-ability in other tenses.
Present perfect
- She's been able to design clothes since she was 14.
- We haven't been able to sew since the machine broke.
- Has he been able to design my dress?

Past perfect
- They'd been able to buy everything before we arrived.
- I hadn't been able to find a coat I liked before the shops closed.
- Had you been able to sell your old clothes before you started university?

Future
- Sophie'll be able to study design if she passes her exams.
- We won't be able to finish this project without your help.
- Will you be able to pack your bags before I come back?

Conditional
- Damian'd be able to finish his homework if you stopped talking.
- We wouldn't be able to go abroad this year if we didn't have a house in France.
- Would you be able to do it on your own, if necessary?

could v was / were able to

We use *could* in the past for general ability, but if we are talking about ability in a specific situation, we use *was / were able to*.
- Mozart **could play** the piano well when he was six. (general ability)
- We **were able to get** the cat **down** from the tree. (specific situation)

Look!: In this type of specific situation, we often use *managed to* instead of *be able to*.
- We **managed to** get the cat **down** from the tree.

OBLIGATION, NECESSITY AND PROHIBITION

have to and don't have to

We use *have to* to talk about things we are obliged to do or which we feel are necessary for us to do, and *don't have to* when there is no obligation to do something.
- Patri has to wear a helmet when she's cycling. (obligation)
- Do you have to go to sewing class on Saturdays? (obligation)
- We don't have to finish this project until after the school holidays. (no obligation)

126 Grammar Reference

GRAMMAR REFERENCE

must and have to

Must and *have to* are similar. We use *must* in the same way as *have to* to talk about what we feel it is necessary to do (i.e., for personal obligations).
- *I must clean my room – it's filthy!*

Have to is like *must*, but it's impersonal and we don't use it for our personal feelings. We use it for facts.
- *I have to wear glasses because I can't see very well.*

We never use *must* when somebody or something else obliges us to do something.
- *We have to finish our project for Monday.* (Our teacher is obliging us to do it.)

In contrast *must* is used in written rules and instructions rather than *have to*.
- *Students must bring pens and pencils to the exam.*

Must exists in the present tense. So we **always** use *have to* to express obligation in other tenses.

Past simple: *They had to study hard to pass the exam.*
I didn't have to buy the concert ticket – my uncle gave it to me.

mustn't

We use *mustn't* for prohibition.
- *Silence = You **mustn't** talk in here.*
- *No eating or drinking on the bus = You **mustn't eat or drink** on the bus.*

We also use *mustn't* when we want to say that it's necessary that you don't do something.
- *I mustn't be late for the interview or I won't get the job.*

Contrast this with *don't have to* which is an absence of obligation.
- *You don't have to use that computer, you can use mine.*

needn't

We use *needn't* when we want to say something you don't need to do.
- *I needn't get up early in the morning – it's Saturday!*

RECOMMENDATIONS, ADVICE AND REGRET

We use *should* and *ought to* to give advice. The meaning is the same, but *ought* is followed by *to*. *Should* is also much more common.
- *If you don't feel well, you should / ought to go to the doctor's.*
- *We really shouldn't drink coffee before going to bed.*
- *Should we invite Ali to the party?*

We use *should / shouldn't have* to regret a past action or say what was preferable.
- *We should have phoned the police immediately! Now the thief has escaped.*
- *He shouldn't have left the cinema so quickly, he forgot his coat.*

Modals of deduction

When we make deductions or speculations about circumstances, we can use modals: *must, can't, could, may, might* + base form of verb.
The situations can be present situations or past ones.

For deductions in the present we use different modals, depending on how sure we are of the events.

We use *must* + base form if we are sure of a deduction.
- *John must be here. Look, there's his coat on that chair.* (We are sure he is here.)

We use *could, may* or *might* + base form if we are less sure.
- *She's late, she might be lost.* (We aren't sure what has happened to her.)
- *Jane may be at a lecture. She's not answering her phone.* (We aren't sure why she isn't answering.)
- *The game hasn't finished yet. They could still be at the stadium.* (They haven't come home, this is what we are assuming, but we aren't sure.)

We use *can't* when we are sure that something is not the case.
- *That can't be John's coat. It's too big for him.* (We know this for sure.)

For deductions in the past, we use *must, could, may,* or *might* + *have* + past participle.
The same principles of certainty apply.
We use *must* + *have* + past participle when we are sure of a deduction.
- *John failed his exam. He must have been disappointed.* (We know John has high expectations so we are sure he would be upset.)

We use *could, may* or *might* + *have* + past participle when we are less sure.
- *We don't know where the criminals are. They could have left the country or they might have hidden in a secret location.* (We aren't sure of the location of the criminals.)

We can also use *could have* to suggest an alternative action, even though it is too late now.
- *You didn't have to stay at Jane's house. I could have given you a lift home.*

We use *can't have* to express an impossibility in the past.
- *You can't have seen Sarah today. She's still in France.*

Permission and obligation: can / can't, be allowed to, let, be supposed to

We use *can / can't, be allowed to* and *let* to express permission or the denial of permission.
- *My parents let me go out on Saturdays and Sundays.*
- *My parents don't let me go out during the week.*
- *You can take your bike to the park.*
- *You can't come home at 10 pm. It's too late.*
- *I am not allowed to wear my own clothes to school. I have to wear a uniform.*
- *They are allowed to go out at lunch time, because they are in the sixth form.*

We use *be supposed to* to express obligation or expectation.
- *You are supposed to stay at home.*
- *You aren't supposed to go out in the evening.*

THANKS AND ACKNOWLEDGEMENTS

The authors and publishers acknowledge the following sources of copyright material and are grateful for the permissions granted. While every effort has been made, it has not always been possible to identify the sources of all the material used, or to trace all copyright holders. If any omissions are brought to our notice, we will be happy to include the appropriate acknowledgements on reprinting and in the next update to the digital edition, as applicable.

The publishers are grateful to the following for permission to reproduce copyright photographs and material:

Key: T = Top, TL = Top Left, TR = Top Right, CL = Centre Left, CR = Centre Right, C = Centre, B = Below, BL = Below Left, BR = Below Right, L = Left, R = Right, Ex = Exercise, B/G = Background, U = Unit.

Photos
Cover Title: Lostanastacia
Cover Image: GlobalP
All photos are sourced from Getty Images.

p. 4 (TL): Marsbars/E+; p. 4 (B): Skynesher/iStock; p. 11: Sturti/E+; p. 12: Nirodesign/iStock; p. 13 (fair trade): Aquir/iStock; p. 13 (t-shirt): Petmal/iStock; p. 16: Outline205/iStock; p. 16 (BL): Peter Dazeley/Photographer'S Choice; p. 19: Monkeybusinessimages/iStock; p. 20: Mbbirdy/iStock; p. 21: Jhorrocks/iStock; pp. 24-25: Grant Faint/Photolibrary; p. 27 (Furniture): Tatianadavidova/iStock; p. 27 (pizza board): Natanaelginting/iStock; p. 27 (burger): Mammoth19/iStock; p. 28: D-Keine/iStock; pp. 34-35 (map): Iconeer/Digitalvision Vectors; p. 34 (orange): Atoss/iStock; p. 34 (banana): Boarding1Now/iStock; p. 34 (meat): Karandaev/iStock; p. 34 (tomato): Dave King/Dorlingkindersley; p. 35 (lamb): Tobias Titz/Fstop; p. 35 (cocoa beans): Andreygorulko/iStock; p. 35 (fruit market): Doug Mckinlay/Lonely Planet Images; p. 37: Asiseeit/E+; p. 38: Coldsnowstorm/E+; p. 39 (CR): J614/Digitalvision Vectors; p. 39 (CL): Dave Hogan; p. 41: Drbimages/E+; pp. 42-43: Ariel Skelley/Digitalvision; p. 45: Noah Berger; p. 46: Tooga/The Image Bank; p. 52 (TR): Robin Smith/Photolibrary; p. 53 (TL): Hulton Archive; p. 54: Mikmann/iStock; p. 56: Paul Kennedy/Lonely Planet Images; p. 57: Dglimages/iStock; p. 59: Joe Raedle; p. 60: Creativenature_Nl/iStock; p. 61 (TL): G. Sioen/De Agostini Picture Library; p. 61 (BR): Lucy Brown - Loca4Motion/iStock; p. 63: Andresr/E+; p. 70 (BL): Vovashevchuk/iStock; pp. 70-71: Shutterworx/iStock; p. 73 (photo a): Evi Oravecz/Green Evi/Picture Press; p. 73 (photo b): Lsantilli/iStock; p. 73 (photo c): Www.Stevejohnstonphoto.Com/Moment; p. 73 (photo d): Joegough/iStock; p. 73 (photo e): Glow Cuisine; p. 74: Bianka Wolf/Eyeem; p. 75 (CL): Solstock/E+; p. 75 (CR): Sturti/E+; p. 75 (BR): Peopleimages/E+; p. 76: Simonbradfield/iStock; p. 77: George Douglas/Hulton Archive; p. 81 (icons): Nettel9; p. 82: Akindo/Digitalvision Vectors; p. 83 (teenager): Estudi M6/iStock; p. 83 (snowboarders): Ascent/Pks Media Inc/The Image Bank; p. 87: Theasis/E+; p. 89 (coffee shop): Cecilie_Arcurs/E+; p. 89: Maurizio Siani/Moment; p. 89 (smoothies): A_Namenko/iStock; p. 89 (chocolate): Artisteer/iStock; p. 91: Tommaso79/iStock; p. 93: Vcandy/Digitalvision Vectors; p. 95: Katarzynabialasiewicz/iStock; p. 97: Shutterworx/E+; p. 98 (swimming): Chokkicx/Digitalvision Vectors; p. 98 (smoking): Chokkicx/Digitalvision Vectors; p. 98 (litter): Lessandro0770/iStock; p. 98 (dog): Tombaky/iStock; p. 98 (camp): Patiwit/iStock; p. 98 (football): Svetap/iStock; p. 98 (alcohol): Mizar_21984/iStock; p. 98 (BR): Paul Bradbury/Caiaimage; p. 99 (photo a): Archive Photos/Moviepix; p. 99 (photo b): Universalimagesgroup; p. 99 (photo c): Print Collector/Hulton Archive.

Illustrations by Damiano Groppi.

The publishers would like to extend a special thank you to all the teachers who helped shape the content of this book.